LEONID I. BREZHNEV

Pages From His Life

WITH A FOREWORD BY

Leonid I. Brezhnev

*Written under the auspices of
the Academy of Sciences of the USSR*

SIMON AND SCHUSTER

NEW YORK

Designed by Irving Perkins
Manufactured in the United States of America
Printed by The Book Press, Inc.
Bound by The Book Press, Inc.
1   2   3   4   5   6   7   8   9   10

Library of Congress Cataloging in Publication Data

Main Entry Under Title:

Leonid I. Brezhnev : pages from his life.

1. Brezhnev, Leonid IL'ICH, 1906-   2.   Russia—Presidents
—Biography.   3.   Heads of state—Russia
Biography.   I.   Akademiia nauk SSSR.
DK275.B7L44   947.085′092′4   [B]   77-25538

ISBN 0-671-24111-7

THE TEXT OF THIS BOOK
WAS COMPLETED AT THE
BEGINNING OF OCTOBER 1977.

Contents

5

Picture sections follow pages 96, 224 *and* 288.

To the American Reader

This book has been written at the suggestion of Simon & Schuster Publishers. I agreed to write the foreword because its publication in the United States will, it seems to me, help the American reader get a better knowledge of the life of the Soviet people and thereby promote understanding between our nations, which bear a special responsibility in the world today.

Moreover, I feel that my biography is a part of the biography of the entire Soviet people. I had not yet reached the age of eleven when a historical event of immense significance, the revolution of October 25 (November 7), 1917, occurred in Russia. I witnessed the birth of a new era in modern history—although, naturally, I realized this only as I grew older.

Today, in the year of the 60th anniversary of the Great October Revolution, as I look back over the years that have passed, I see with utmost clarity that the victory of that revolution determined the whole course of my life. It was only Soviet power that enabled me, the son of a worker, who began life as an ordinary worker, to rise to the leadership of a glorious many-millions-strong party and of history's first socialist state. Through all my life I worked hard. I worked in industry and in agriculture, in the center and in remote areas of the country. When our Motherland was invaded, I joined millions of Soviet people in the trenches to defend her and spent all four of the war years at the front. I often recall those bitter years—the war in which the peoples of the Soviet Union, the United States, and other countries fought shoulder to shoulder against fascism, the most sinister enemy of humankind, the enemy of civilization, humanity, and culture. The memory of those who did not return home, of the razed towns and villages, and of the incalculable human tragedies of those years intensifies the desire to prevent a military conflagration from ever again enveloping the globe. Having gone through the entire war, I know well what this means. For that reason I am determined to devote all my life to preventing the outbreak of another world war.

Needless to say, at various stages life posed different tasks. I met and worked together with many people in different parts of my tremendous country. Perhaps I was lucky. Life usually brought me into contact with good, strong, and interesting people. I gained experience, and my world outlook widened. I grew together with my people, country, and party and shared with them the joys and sorrows, successes and anxieties, achievements and hopes.

In our country, the Communist Party is not only the ruling party but also the recognized leader, inspirer, and organizer of all of the people's major affairs. By virtue of this, the party organizations, the Central Committee and its Political Bureau, have to deal with a wide range of questions. Party and state matters and duties occupy not only most of the working day but the *entire* day of party officials, particularly those who are in leading posts, including, of course, myself as the General Secretary of the Central Committee of the Communist Party of the Soviet Union. In fact, they occupy their entire lives. In June 1977 I was accorded great trust: I was again elected also as Chairman of the Presidium of the Supreme Soviet of the USSR.

Everybody knows that there is a considerable distinction between the Soviet Union and the United States in the social and political systems and the world outlook, in historical backgrounds and long-standing traditions, in the ways of life, and in the geographical and international political positions.

But one can easily see that there is also much in common in the character of our peoples, as indeed of many other peoples. Besides, the Soviet Union and the United States share much that is similar: the size of territory, natural wealth, the scale of production, and the development of a high level of science and technology. Our two countries can, by virtue of their positions in the world, do a great deal to avert another world war and its unprecedentedly catastrophic consequences.

Also, much depends on our two countries' abilities to carry out such complex and pressing human tasks as protecting the environment on our planet, exploring outer space, reproducing and intelligently utilizing the earth's energy and food resources, and combating the most dangerous mass diseases.

However, *the most important and the most urgent* task is that of the preservation of peace, the prevention of war. The road to this lies through ending the arms race.

Some unscrupulous politicians and economically influential circles, and the mass media associated with them, are endeavoring to intimidate Americans with the false claim that the Soviet Union is preparing to attack the United States and Western Europe.

I have said more than once that this "Soviet menace" bogey is malicious nonsense. Ever since the days of Lenin we have been emphatically and in principle against settling the historic dispute between socialism and capitalism by war. Look at the plans for the economic and social development of the Soviet Union: they are oriented toward the preservation of peace, toward the exclusion of war from the life of present and future generations. This applies fully to the plans charted by the 25th Congress of the Communist Party of the Soviet Union in 1976. The arms race, on the other hand, signifies not only the material preparation for war but also a colossal dissipation of wealth that could be used for the benefit of our two peoples, as well as for the benefit of many other peoples.

The Soviet people are a peace-loving nation. The spirit of wars of aggression, militarism, and aggrandizement is profoundly alien to them. Our country is making vigorous efforts to prevent war, to consolidate détente, to complement détente in the political field with détente in the military field. The Soviet Union has advanced many concrete and realistic proposals for the attainment of these aims. They are dealt with in the relevant sections of this book.

In short, the Soviet Union is doing its utmost to prevent war, to stop the preparations for it, to halt the manufacture of the endless succession of new types of armaments. We are holding out our hand to all who are prepared to join us in fulfilling this truly great objective.

Some years ago I had an opportunity to visit the United States. There were many meetings and talks with statesmen, civic leaders, members of Congress, businessmen, journalists, and even astronauts. Far from being always in agreement with everybody and on everything, we were able to talk quietly and frankly. As far as we know, not only my comrades and I but also the people we talked to found much evidence that the Soviet Union and the United States can and do enjoy a mutually beneficial association in vast fields. Many also found that we could and should settle peacefully the outstanding and acute problems worrying our peoples and all humankind and that there were considerable possibilities for cooperation between our countries. This is needed, above all, so that American and Soviet children can grow up beneath a peaceful sky, will not hear the whistle of bullets and the explosion of bombs, will not know the tragic calamities of war, so that their future may be not the battlefield but the sphere of peaceful creative work, so that they will never share a feeling of hostility toward each other.

I should like to remind you that our countries had a good experience of fruitful cooperation during the Second World War. In those years, despite their different social and economic systems, the Soviet Union and the United States successfully cooperated and complemented each other's efforts in the struggle against fascism. Today, when it is a matter of delivering humankind from the threat of nuclear annihilation, cooperation between our two countries acquires particularly great significance. The edifice of détente cannot be allowed to collapse under the onslaught of the protagonists of cold war and the arms race.

The establishment of a spirit of mutual understanding and confidence is one of the vital preconditions of cooperation. Cooperation is possible only when relations are founded on mutual benefit and mutual respect and on noninterference in each other's internal affairs. As everybody knows, this has become a cardinal principle of the modern world community. The more so must this become a norm of relations between two powerful states. The attempts to gain something out of inflammatory artificial propaganda campaigns and out of a feverish race to develop new means of mass annihilation can only lead to the deterioration of the international atmosphere and an aggravation of relations, and this is something in which our peoples are not at all interested.

I should like to make the point again: the Soviet people have friendly feelings for the people of the United States. The development and strengthening of our relations with the United States of America constitute one of the paramount tasks of our country's foreign policy. A good foundation has been laid and some important progress has been made in this direction in the past few years. However, much remains to be done. For our part we are prepared to do it. I profoundly believe that the further and stable improvement of relations between our countries is possible, and I intend to do everything in my power to make Soviet-American relations a factor of lasting peace and international cooperation.

L. BREZHNEV

CHAPTER I

Among Workers

On February 2, 1935, the tabloid newspaper of the Dzerzhinsky steel mill in the town of Kamenskoye, the Ukraine, ran a report that sixty-eight engineers had been graduated from the Arsenichev Metallurgical Institute. It carried the photographs of the four top graduates. The name of one of them was Leonid Brezhnev.

The author of the report wrote the following about Brezhnev: "I cannot imagine where this man gets so much energy and capacity for work. The son of a worker, he has himself worked at the factory as a stoker and a fitter. . . . From the factory he was sent to party-economic work. He had a tight and difficult schedule. This same man studied at our institute. He was our best party group organizer. . . . And he was at the top of his class, receiving the highest marks for his diploma project. . . . As he goes into industry, this young engineer has the makings for achieving much. . . . I'm certain he will achieve it. . . . I say this because he is made of tough material."

These words were spoken of Brezhnev in those distant days when he never expected that he would eventually be an outstanding political leader and statesman of the Soviet Union.

He was born of strong working-class stock. The working-class environment from which he came and with which he never lost contact powerfully influenced his views, world outlook, and character.

I. CHILDHOOD IN KAMENSKOYE

From what Leonid Brezhnev relates of his childhood we get a vivid picture of that period of his life.

The village of Kamenskoye—a typical village of tsarist Russia—with its small, one-story houses lining the streets, its decrepit buildings and unpaved lanes, stood near the gubernia capital, Yekaterinoslav, in a southern bend of the majestic Dnieper River. It would have been no different from similar villages in tsarist Russia had not an "iron heel" (as Jack London would have said) of the industrial age, a steel mill of the South Russia Dnieper Metallurgical Company, been built in those parts. It was there, in Kamenskoye, that a center of the Ukraine's metallurgical industry emerged.

Yakov Brezhnev and his family—his wife and son Ilya— were among the thousands who came to Kamenskoye from Kursk Gubernia in search of employment. As was true of many others, he found work at the steel mill. As soon as Ilya was big enough, his father took him to the mill. Ilya quickly became a member of the family of steelworkers and found his place among people of his own age. There he met a girl, Natalya, daughter of a worker at the same factory, and he married her. They soon had a daughter, and in 1906 their son Leonid was born. Subsequently Leonid went to work in the mill's steel-smelting department, representing the third generation of steelworkers in a family whose life was associated entirely with the mill. The steelworkers called the Brezhnevs a mill dynasty.

Leonid grew up in the same conditions as all the other children of working-class families in prerevolutionary times. Early in life he came to know the great hulk of the mill over-hanging the village. He usually ran to the mill gates to take his father lunch tied in a kerchief.

Young Leonid played in the dusty village streets, and on hot summer days he would race with the other boys to swim in the wide, deep Dnieper. At home he listened attentively to the talk of his elders. The talk was always about the mill, its owners, the hard work, the low wages, the daily frustrations and cares. An idea of the working conditions at the mill is given in a leaflet circulated in those days by the Bolsheviks:

"One will hardly find more unbearable conditions than at the Kamenskoye mill. Work continues all year round without any holidays. People work twelve and sometimes even eigh-teen hours running! The profit they are getting from our labor is evidently not enough for these bloodsuckers, and they use every pretext to impose fines on us. . . . Is it conceivable for one to prevent hunger at a monthly 13 to 30 rubles? . . .

"While it robs us, the management humiliates us practi-cally every minute of the day with curses and sometimes even blows from the foremen and the engineers. Our human dignity is trampled at every step.

"We work day and night and live in squalor only in order to keep the purses of the bosses full and our bellies empty. . . ."

The leaflet was read and passed from hand to hand among the outraged and indignant workers.

Like all the other lads in the village, Leonid soon learned that he belonged to the class at the lowest rung of the social ladder, to those disinherited people whose only possession was their work-hardened hands. Like all the other children, he knew that there was another class of people who did not know the meaning of work and lived off the labor of his family and the families of his friends.

In Kamenskoye these people of the other class lived as far as possible from the tiny wretched dwellings near the factory. They lived in the part known as the Upper Colony, in shining, freshly painted brick houses with orchards of apple and plum trees. Leonid learned early that workers were not welcome there. Nor were they allowed into the club, with its richly decorated hall from whose ornate ceiling hung brilliant chandeliers that cast a glitter on the glossy parquet floors. The strains of music often came from the Upper Colony, signaling that a ball was being held for the management and the technical elite of the mill. Sometimes, perching on the wall, children of steelworkers watched as the masters played tennis or croquet.

The village began to grow rapidly when the new-built tracks of a railway linked Yekaterinoslav with the nearby Krivoi Rog area, which was rich in iron ore. Polish businessmen, along with their Belgian and French partners, invested considerable capital in the South Russia Dnieper Metallurgical Company. The peasants, squeezed out of their land by developing capitalism, trooped there in search of work. People of the many nationalities that constituted Russia came to the mill. Particularly large numbers came from the Ukraine, Byelorussia, and Central Russia.

Leonid played with children whose parents spoke the different tongues of the huge country. All had a common language, however—the language of poverty.

At the turn of the century Russia abounded in deep-seated social and political contradictions. The mass of the people, denied the most elementary rights, lived in poverty, hunger, and disease. The landowners and capitalists, both local and foreign, relied on the despotic regime. They held the people ''in obedience'' by means of the police and the gendarmerie.

Custodians of the national conscience, as they were called at the time—writers like Gorky, Tolstoy, and Chekhov—wrote eloquently and passionately of the tragic condition of the people. The seething discontent, stirring deep among the masses, led to a storm, the revolution of 1905. Lenin called it the dress rehearsal of the October Revolution that came in 1917.

This was the period when the working class grew numerically and organizationally and already showed much political experience. The Communist Party, formed by Lenin at the turn of the century, was the mainspring of working-class revolutionary thought and activity.

It was in the year 1917, as a new revolution was gathering momentum, that the boy Leonid Brezhnev began to mature. His life inevitably became interwoven with the life of his contemporaries.

The Bolsheviks did not spare themselves in the struggle against tsarist despotism. They suffered penal servitude and imprisonment for the sake of the truth they were bringing the working class. Their tireless work was felt in Kamenskoye too.

Leonid always met his father at the mill gate at the end of the shift. On the way home his father would often tell him of things he was to remember all his life. He told him of the strike in December 1903, when the imperial double-headed eagle emblem was torn from the mill gate and trampled in the mud. He told him of the events of 1905 and 1906, when red flags were flown in the streets of Kamenskoye in the face of bullets. The flags challenging the autocracy were flown in every street, for there was no street where the inhabitants were not involved in the strike that lasted for days.

In 1915, when several strikes were staged at the mill, Leonid was almost nine. Like the other children, he sensed the determination of the workers and their exultation when they managed to wrest concessions from the millowners.

One such powerful action was the strike of the Kamen-skoye steelworkers in April 1916, which was the most significant working-class action in Yekaterinoslav Gubernia during the First World War. It began on April 1, after the mill-owners rejected the workers' demand for a higher wage and an eight-hour working day. The boiler operatives, 450 of them, were the first to down their tools. The management took steps against them, announcing that they were discharged. In solidarity with the boiler operatives, work was halted in the blast furnace, the new and old open-hearth furnaces, and other departments. The strike spread to the entire mill, involving more than 7,000 workers. Only two of the five blast furnaces were kept going, served by war prisoners who had the threat of being shot hanging over their heads. The steelworkers, their ranks solid, continued to press their demands, adding a new demand: the reinstatement of the boiler operatives.

Police and military reinforcements soon arrived at Kamen-skoye. The mill manager dismissed all the strikers, with all the consequences that this entailed in wartime. Scores of workers were arrested, and more than 360 steelworkers were impressed into the tsarist army and sent to the trenches. But the strikers held firm. They resumed work only when the management agreed to raise the pay in many categories.

Leonid and the other children waited with bated breath for the outcome of this grim drama of their fathers. Sharp class battles unfolded before Leonid's eyes.

Many years later Leonid Brezhnev said, "My own perception of life was shaped largely by factory life, by the thoughts and aspirations of the workingman, by his approach to life. The lessons of those years have never been forgotten."

At the age of eight the boy heard the word "war." He understood its terrible significance when he saw the frightened eyes of women and the tears of girls bidding farewell to their fiancés going to the front, when he heard the sobbing in the neighboring houses where families soon began receiving notifications of the death of their sons and husbands.

Leonid's father sent him to the local school. The boy was an industrious pupil. How else could he have approached his studies when, in a class of forty-five, he and six other working-class lads were allowed to attend as charity pupils? The seven poorly clad boys banded together and did not let the others bully them. "We all helped each other, but the going was tough because the children of the local elite got together in the afternoons and received additional tutoring from their teachers," one of Leonid's classmates, Sergei Alimov, recalls.

Then came the year 1917, and with it the February Revolution. After 1905 this was the second important stage in Russia's fundamental transformation. The February Revolution overthrew tsarism and destroyed the autocracy. Nonetheless, the major deep-seated aspirations and hopes of the working people were not fulfilled. The February Revolution did not give the people true power, and it did not abolish exploitation and oppression. That could be achieved only by the socialist revolution that came later that year, led by the Bolsheviks with Lenin at their head. Tempestuous events were taking place in and around the steel mill on the Dnieper. The Bolsheviks were calling on the working people to give decisive battle to the remnants of the autocracy. The workers of Kamenskoye deposed the tsarist authorities, disarmed the police, and elected the Kamenskoye Soviet of Workers' Deputies. In addition, they formed combat detachments, which were reorganized into a unit of the Red Guards in May and June 1917. This unit was formed of volunteers but was composed of only the most reliable, tested fighters in the ranks of the workers, the finest representatives of the working class.

Childhood impressions are usually the most lasting. Brezhnev, then eleven, never forgot how the October Revolution reached the banks of the Dnieper, how the Civil War began in his hometown, where the supporters of the Soviet power had to fight both the German invaders and the local counter-revolution. The social and political sympathies of the Brezhnevs, a poor working-class family, lay with the revolution that was asserting a new principle of life, echoed in the words of the "Internationale": "We have been naught, we shall be all."

2. SCHOOL YEARS

Soviet power won across Russia. For this victory and in defense of the gains of the revolution, thousands of courageous fighters laid down their lives.

The Soviet Republic, beating off the savage onslaught of its enemies at home as well as that of the foreign interventionists, began to build a new society and to launch economic and social changes.

This was complicated by the fact that the country lay in ruins as a result of the Civil War and the intervention and had to advance along new, unexplored roads. To use Lenin's figure of speech, when the bourgeoisie came to power, it had a "tested vehicle, a well-prepared road and previously tested appliances"; the proletariat, who won power, had "no vehicle, no road, absolutely nothing that had been tested beforehand."

The English author H. G. Wells wrote a book at the time with the title *Russia in the Shadows*. Many people in the West imagined that Russia was in the shadows and that its creative efforts were no more than a "Bolshevik experiment," senseless and doomed to failure.

These prophets did not take into account the people's inexhaustible creative energy, which had been awakened by the revolution, the mighty creative potential of the generation of the October Revolution, spurred on by unparalleled enthusiasm.

"Victory will be on the side of the exploited," Lenin wrote in December 1917, "for on their side is life, numerical strength, the strength of the mass, the strength of the inexhaustible sources of all that is selfless, dedicated and honest, all that is surging forward and awakening to the building of the new, all the vast reserves of energy and talent latent in the so-called 'common people,' the workers and peasants."

Economically the country was in an extremely difficult situation. The national economy had been laid waste. The output of pig iron, for instance, dropped to 3 percent of the prewar level. The annual per capita output of cotton fabric was less than one meter. There was a shortage of bread and of the ordinary needs of life. Then there emerged Lenin's New Economic Policy strategy, the course toward industrialization, the GOELRO Plan (the plan for the electrification of Russia), and, simultaneously, the plan for creating cooperatives in the countryside, in which the accuracy of scientific analysis was combined with profound knowledge of the peasant mentality.

Lenin's work in theory and practice in the early 1920s was of colossal significance. He worked out and put into effect a scientifically substantiated, coherent system of socialist construction.

In Kamenskoye the Soviet authorities faced innumerable problems, each more complicated than the next. The mill was standing idle—the furnaces had gone out, and the workshops were empty. In the village, which had grown to the size of a town, there were piles of broken brick and gutted houses everywhere.

Leonid Brezhnev would later recall this period: "I remember my school years, my own and those of lads of my age.

Soviet Russia had been ravaged by the World War and then by the Civil War against the landowners, capitalists, and foreign interventionists, who tried to stamp out our revolution. There was unprecedented dislocation and starvation. In those trying days, when we had to economize on practically everything, Lenin, the Communists, and the Soviet power were doing all they could to feed and clothe the children and teach them to read and write.''

In 1921 the young Soviet Republic was hit by a fearful calamity—drought and famine. The center of this catastrophe was the Volga area, but other parts of the country, including the Dnieper region, were also affected. Kamenskoye was experiencing a very bad time, compounded by the postwar dislocation. The mill continued to remain idle. Some workers left for the surrounding countryside; others made their way to their native villages far away. Ilya Brezhnev moved to Kursk with his wife and children. A new period opened in the life of Leonid, who had turned fifteen and had finished school.

Boys matured early in those years. Leonid got work as a stevedore, for he was already big and strong, but his thirst for knowledge led him to enroll at a land reclamation and surveying technical college in Kursk.

Important in itself, land organization and surveying acquired a special significance in those years. It meant not merely surveying and demarcating but also defining the most rational use of land, which had become the property of the people. The young Soviet state had nationalized the estates of the rural gentry and was turning over many millions of acres to the peasants. The land surveyor and organizer had an important role in allocating land to the peasants and in charting roads and building enterprises.

Having received training as a land surveyor, Brezhnev began to gain experience as an organizer and leader.

After graduation from the technical college he worked as a

land surveyor in Byelorussia, Kursk Gubernia, and the Urals. In the Sverdlovsk region he was elected to the Bisert District Soviet of Working People's Deputies. He headed the land department and was eventually named deputy chairman of the District Executive Committee.

Brezhnev was a good mixer and sought the company of people of his own age, especially those who were bold, energetic, and eager and considered the building of the new world something close to their hearts.

Leonid became acquainted and made friends with members of the Young Communist League (Komsomol). In those years there were relatively few Komsomols—just over 300,000 throughout the vast country. At the factories and offices and in the villages the Komsomols were usually no more than a tiny handful, but they were noted for their enthusiasm, revolutionary passion, and courage.

In 1923, at seventeen, Leonid joined the Komsomol. Later he was to say, "For me the Komsomol was a fine school. My world outlook and my attitude to the policy of our government and party lead from it."

He wanted more knowledge, and this urge coincided with the tasks the country was working on. He was also strongly influenced by the family tradition of working in the metallurgical industry. The immense economic and cultural transformations taking place in the country demanded a steadily growing number of new specialists, particularly metallurgists with a scientific training.

In 1930 Leonid Brezhnev went back to Kamenskoye, where his father had already returned, and resumed work at the factory. With him came his wife, Victoria, and their baby daughter, and they moved into a small two-room flat. Later a son would be born. That same year Leonid enrolled in the newly opened evening metallurgical institute.

The country, and Kamenskoye with it, was changing.

Everything that was being done in the country—industrialization, collectivization of agriculture, and the cultural revolution—was mirrored in the developments in the Dnieper region and, of course, in Kamenskoye. The mill, which had stopped work during the years of dislocation and famine, resumed production in 1925.

The mill, now modernized, grew quickly. Alongside it arose electric power stations and new factories—a railway car works, a coking chemical plant, and a nitrogen fertilizer plant.

Recalling this period, Leonid Brezhnev said, "In those years we had to economize on everything. But the party and the government allocated resources for promoting education, science, and culture with a generosity that even the richest capitalist nations could envy. If the world is now amazed at the Soviet Union's achievements in science and culture, the foundations of those achievements were laid in the period when the Land of Soviets began to build a dense network of schools and libraries, workers' faculties and technical colleges, and higher education and research institutions."

Kamenskoye, now Dneprodzerzhinsk, offers a vivid example of Soviet policy in education. A technical college was set up in 1920, a difficult year. Ten years later it was converted into an evening metallurgical institute. Its classes met in the evening because all its students worked in industry. There were also a technical college and a workers' faculty. Many who graduated from the latter enrolled in the institute. Today this institute, with a student body of 5,000, is an academic and scientific center with many departments, well known throughout the country. Leading scientists, statesmen, and business executives are among its graduates.

In the early 1930s the metallurgical institute at Kamenskoye offered training in a number of specialties, and its student body consisted of about 600 young men and women. Another 300 were studying at the factory's crash courses in higher engineering in specific metallurgical fields: blast-furnace operatives, steel smelters, and steel rollers. The students took a very serious attitude to their studies. They included many talented young people, a fact noted by prominent academic metallurgists who studied their graduation projects. The best of these were applied at the mill.

During the first year as a student Brezhnev continued to hold his job at the mill. At first he was a boiler stoker, then an oiler of steam-driven machines, after which he quickly learned the trade of fitter. He worked with efficiency and did his best to learn from veteran workers. His friends rejoiced when, together with other foremost people in production, he was admitted to the metallurgical institute (later renamed the Industrial Institute). Veteran workers recall that "he was a good fitter and an even better gas purification machine operative. He was respected by the other workers." Mikhail Filichkin, who was foreman in the gas shop, recalls: "Leonid Brezhnev worked on my team. Among his ingrained qualities were honesty and application in the performance of his duties, initiative, a flair for organization, and active involvement in anything that was going forward. The workers found him a fine and considerate comrade, always ready to offer businesslike and comradely assistance."

3 · WORKER AND ENGINEER

Leonid Brezhnev joined the Communist Party in 1931, having been admitted as a candidate member two years earlier. This was a natural step dictated by his youth as a worker and student. The logic of life brought Leonid into the vanguard of the builders of the new society.

From examples of Communists he knew that membership in the party gave no privileges; on the contrary, it entailed important duties.

A party meeting discussed the question of boosting labor

productivity in the gas shop. It was a stormy affair. Some argued that there could be no question of raising productivity—the equipment was old and run-down, and it had to be replaced before they could decide what to do next.

Fitter Leonid Brezhnev took the floor. The country, he said, was in need of more pig iron, steel, and rolled stock, but it could spare no money now to renew equipment. It was the duty of the workers to help their country. He spoke calmly and knowledgeably, going into the details of which parts could be made at the mill, which could be restored from written-off equipment consigned to the scrap heap, and what should be done to prevent the gas shop from being a drag on the operatives of the blast and open-hearth furnaces.

The meeting agreed with the young Communist. The shop soon reached a higher level of productivity.

Disaster struck unexpectedly. The floodwaters of the Dnieper spread to the foundation pits of a projected thermal power station. Machinery, stores, and material goods were in danger of being flooded.

It was Sunday evening, and the young people were in the park. Brezhnev ran to them. He signaled to the band to stop playing, appealed to the young people who were dancing, and persuaded them to leave the park and run to the building site, which was threatened by the Dnieper's waters.

The battle lasted for several days. In response to an appeal by the town's Emergency Flood-Control Commission, which Brezhnev headed, all the students joined to fight the rising waters. After filling sacks with earth, they erected a dike, and the building site was saved.

Brezhnev's subsequent years as a student were equally eventful. He was always among the people, in the thick of life. His comrades and fellow townspeople esteemed him for his resourcefulness, quick thinking, and abilities as an organizer.

He was elected chairman of the trade union committee and then secretary of the party organization at the institute. From 1933 through 1935 he was director of the Metallurgical Workers' Faculty. It was reorganized into a technical college under his direction in 1935. The workers' faculty is a form of education unknown in most countries. It sprang from the Soviet state's acute need of trained personnel. Those who enrolled in these faculties were mostly men and women of mature years with experience of life and work, but lacking the prerequisite education to enroll in a technical college or institute.

Brezhnev was actively involved in the work of the institute's research sector, which had been formed by the mill to solve some of its many production problems.

A good organizer is judged by his ability to inspire and lead people. Brezhnev organized a student building group, and the young people worked enthusiastically as they added two stories to the institute building, providing premises for an operating blast furnace used for training, a rolling mill, and a department for the thermal treatment of metal.

A buoyant personality, Brezhnev found the time to join in singing and dancing. He was an organizer everywhere and always among people.

This was a period when the entire country was a gigantic construction site. The First Five-Year Plan for the development of the Soviet economy was fulfilled ahead of schedule, in four years and three months.

Soviet large-scale industry was turning out more than three times as much annually as it had in tsarist Russia. The Five-Year Plan had not been easy to fulfill: the people still lacked knowledge and experience; there was a shortage of many materials. But the intensive labor effort fired by the revolutionary enthusiasm of millions did wonders and changed the face of the country.

The map makers were unable to keep up with the builders. New factories were built and new towns sprang up around them. During the five years, 1,500 industrial enterprises were put in operation thousands of miles apart in a land that comprises one-sixth of the earth's land surface. Take a few examples: the tractor factories in Chelyabinsk and Kharkov; the car and machine-tool factories in Gorky; the oil refineries in Baku and Grozny; a huge power station under construction on the Dnieper. The first blast furnaces were started at the steel mills in Magnitogorsk and Kuznetsk. Unparalleled rates of industrial development were registered during the five-year period. The Kharkov tractor plant was built in fifteen months, the Gorky car factory in seventeen.

Under the heading "New Industries," the newspaper *Izvestia* gave a list of fifteen, including aircraft, machine tools, harvester combines, synthetic rubber, and watch and clock manufacturing. By the end of the first five-year period 13 million peasant households had been united in collective farms.

In that five-year period 100,000 engineers and technicians, representing the new technological intelligentsia which had sprung from the October Revolution, went to work in industry.

One of these highly skilled professionals was the young engineer Leonid Brezhnev.

After graduating from the institute, Brezhnev took a job at the mill as chief of a shift in the shop where he had worked as a fitter.

Today he says of the life of people of his own age in those years, "Their ardent desire to study and become active builders of the new world made them real specialists, whose knowledge and labor effort had a great part to play in turning our country into an advanced and mighty socialist industrialized state." It is his own life, too, that he is describing.

With his usual energy he immersed himself in practical work. Not yet thirty, he already showed commitment to principle, firmness in upholding his convictions, efficiency, and patience. Above all, he respected his comrades.

This is his essential quality. When his colleagues recall their work with the young engineer Brezhnev, they say that a respect for people was the main trait of his character. With his inherent humanity he was a man of the new socialist system.

He frequently spoke to workers, explaining the policy of the party and the government to them and telling them what was happening abroad.

His friendly advice encouraged people. He influenced many to study and develop themselves. Many of his associates say they are indebted to him for subsequently becoming highly skilled specialists.

In November 1935 Leonid Brezhnev was drafted into the Soviet Army, where he served in a tank unit. He did his tour of duty in the Trans-Baikal Military District. He served for only one year, but an atmosphere of war was already developing in Europe, under the crawling shadow of the nazi swastika. The realization grew that the world's first socialist state would soon have to fight grimly for its right to exist. Once in uniform, Brezhnev got down to mastering military skills with the same energy he had put into learning his trade of fitter and then his profession as engineer. His unit's command repeatedly mentioned his name as a disciplined and dedicated soldier.

In the late autumn of 1936, suntanned, fit, and energetic as always, Brezhnev came back to his native Dneprodzerzhinsk.

He did not return to the mill, for he was appointed director of the Dneprodzerzhinsk Metallurgical Technical College. But his ties with the mill, where his grandfather, father, brother, sister, and he himself had worked for an aggregate period of several decades, became even stronger. The technical college trained expert operatives for the blast furnace, steel-smelting, and rolling shops, needed most at the mill. Constantly in contact with the mill's management, engineers, and foremen, he knew what to concentrate on in the study process and was able to determine where graduates would work. This made it possible to reduce to a minimum the time new men needed to get into the rhythm of the work. Brezhnev did not confine his activity to the "technical college-mill" framework. He associated with Komsomol members working on urban improvement and arranged for students to meet with the mill's veterans, who told them of conditions under the tsarist regime. He spoke frequently at meetings of the town's party activists.

With characteristic vigor he plunged into the affairs of his town in 1937 and was elected deputy chairman of the Executive Committee of the Dneprodzerzhinsk Town Soviet of Working People's Deputies.

An engineer had become deputy mayor. He became concerned with problems and needs of the townspeople, with the town's modernization. One of his first acts was to help extend the tramway to the township of Bagley, which made it easier for the workers to get to the mill. New schools, nursery schools, and day-care centers were built. A House of Engineers and Technicians appeared where dilapidated huts once stood. Many streets and squares were paved. The town became cleaner and more modern.

"Look at our Dneprodzerzhinsk," Brezhnev said joyfully at a meeting with workers of the railway car plant. "In it you will see the grandeur of our growth as in a mirror. The former village of Kamenskoye is becoming a flourishing industrial town with unparalleled speed."

The door of the deputy mayor's office was always open to the people, who went to him with the most diverse requests, big and small: to help get an electric line extended to an area set aside for the construction of individually owned cottages, to look into housing problems, to ascertain why the building of a hostel had fallen behind schedule, or to talk to individuals who had neglected the education of their children. No request was ever ignored.

In May 1938 Brezhnev, then thirty-two, was appointed to a responsible post in the Regional Party Committee. Eyewitnesses recall that he was always in the midst of the people, always in the center of events. He was soon elected a secretary of the Regional Party Committee.

His intimate knowledge of the people and the life and his purposefulness enabled him to cope with the duties of secretary of the party committee of one of the country's largest regions.

This region, almost 40,000 square kilometers in area, had a population of 2,273,000 at the time. Before the Second World War it had been making a significant contribution to the nation's economy. It accounted for 19.7 percent of the nation's output of pig iron, 16.5 percent of steel, 18.2 percent of rolled stock, 28.2 percent of pipes, 15 percent of coking coal, 33 percent of manganese ore, and 61.4 percent of iron ore. It produced a considerable portion of the country's grain. Education—secondary, specialized, and higher—was developing rapidly. The many palaces of culture, the hundreds of clubs and libraries were always crowded with people eager for knowledge and culture.

The Regional Committee's propaganda secretary never ignored any area of life, whether it was industry, agriculture, science, culture, or public health. He took an interest in everything that concerned the welfare of the people. At the factories he told the workers of the assignments of the Third Five-Year Plan. The workers would listen attentively and ponder his words. When everybody knew what the goal was, the way to it was shorter and easier.

He had frequent meetings with Communists from the countryside and listened intently to their problems. He inquired into everything, even the smallest details, including

33

how many amateur art circles there were at the palaces of culture and clubs. However busy he was, he would ask the charwoman at the Regional Committee about the health of her grandson, inquire of an official of the Regional Committee about the news from his son in the armed forces, or congratulate a girl from the typists' pool on her marriage.

He had the knack of hearing people out, and this encouraged them to tell him of their joys and worries. They saw in him a warmhearted, considerate man.

He had a keen memory and took an intense interest in people, remembering hundreds of names, facts, and figures. He gave his associates useful advice and learned from them.

Having an exceptional sense of responsibility himself, he encouraged his subordinates to adopt a similar attitude to their work. Slipshod work ran against his grain.

In the autumn of 1940 Leonid Brezhnev was agriculture secretary of the Regional Party Committee. Many collective farmers in the Dnepropetrovsk region were decorated with orders and medals for successes in work. The region was listed as a participant in the Soviet Agricultural Exhibition on the strength of its achievements.

Brezhnev traveled a great deal in the countryside, meeting with collective farmers and listening to the recommendations of agronomists. He ascertained the advantages of one crop variety over another, asked collective farmers what they thought about the work methods of collective-farm chairmen, and in general went into the smallest details.

His range of knowledge widened through his constant contact with people and his painstaking work with them. Although he was in charge of agriculture, he was also well informed on the state of affairs in industry, so much so that his colleagues in the Regional Party Committee Bureau often came to him for advice.

It was due to the tireless efforts of men like him that the

Soviet people were able to make rapid economic and social progress. The Soviet Union's achievements attracted attention everywhere. The world saw the seething energy and dedication of the Soviet people, who had turned backward Russia into an industrialized nation within only two decades.

The French writer Romain Rolland noted: "The faith reigning in the USSR is an ardent and indestructible faith in social happiness. Maxim Gorky, who was born and bred in old Russia's atmosphere of pessimism, spoke of Lenin with admiration, saying that he believed this beautiful vision of the future happiness of all men would come true. . . . Among the millions reborn by the revolution over the past 18 years this faith is so strong that it is capable of moving mountains. . . . It is impossible to withstand this tide of joy and energy generated by the heroic optimism of an advancing world. . . ."

This faith in social progress and the people's unity around the Communist Party and devotion to the revolution enabled the Soviet Union to build the material and technical basis of socialism and then to win the war against the fascist aggressors.

Aware that nazi Germany was preparing to start a war against the Soviet Union, the country took steps to increase its defense capability. In the Dnepropetrovsk region some plants were switched to the production of armaments. In this situation a plenary meeting of the Regional Party Committee elected Brezhnev secretary for the defense industry. To him now fell the burden of the preparations in the region to repulse the fascist aggressors.

CHAPTER II

In the Fire of Struggle
Against Fascism

1 . FIRST MONTHS OF THE WAR

Leonid Brezhnev recalls how the war began: Saturday night of June 21, 1941, the last peacetime night before the war, appeared no different from earlier Saturdays. Brass bands played in the gardens and parks. Festive crowds strolled along the streets of Dnepropetrovsk, enjoying the fragrance of acacia trees. The people were taking their weekend rest and planning how best to spend Sunday.

At the Regional Party Committee, however, the lights burned late that Saturday night. A very important matter, that of nominating Communists for political work in the Red Army, was being discussed by the committee's bureau. This meeting was the logical sequel to the committee's work over the preceding months, when, in line with the decision of the party's Central Committee and the Soviet government, vigorous action was being taken in every sphere to strengthen the country's defense might. For that very reason the post of secretary of the Regional Party Committee for the defense industry had been instituted in the Dnepropetrovsk region, which had a considerable industrial and economic potential. This important sector of work, as already noted, was headed by Brezhnev.

To ensure the uninterrupted operation of the plants in the event of war, it was necessary to have, above all, a good knowledge of the potentialities of each of them. It was necessary to determine the minimum time it would take to switch them to war production and to plan the retraining of skilled workers to meet the requirements of the armed forces. It was necessary to work out the mobilization plans and to decide in advance how replacements were to be secured immediately for the skilled personnel going into the armed forces and who precisely was to replace them. The construction of defense installations also required unremitting attention.

At about 2 A.M., after everyone had left the Regional Party Committee premises, Brezhnev ordered a car and drove to an airfield under construction to see for himself that work on this important project continued without stop on Sunday. By 6 A.M. he was back at the Regional Party Committee. That morning, June 22, 1941, nazi Germany treacherously attacked the Soviet Union. The fascists were already bombing Brest, Riga, Vilnius, Grodno, Bobruisk, Sevastopol, Kiev, and other cities. Heavily equipped armies, which no West European state had been able to stop, were hurled against the Soviet Union. They invaded Soviet territory, sowing death and destruction. On the peaceful Soviet soil, houses burst into flame, cities were reduced to ashes, villages and orchards were destroyed, factories collapsed under the rain of bombs, and long lines of refugees—women, children, and the aged—moved along the roads, seeking safety from the enemy. They were attacked by diving fascist aircraft, which strafed civilians, killing thousands.

The news that Hitler had attacked the Soviet Union was flashed across the world. All the newspapers carried banner headlines: "Hitler Invades Russia." In the West the Soviet Union was still called Russia. But this was no longer the old Russia—it was the Union of Soviet Socialist Republics, a country which, in addition to Russians, had more than 100 different nationalities united in a close-knit family, the Soviet people, who had built the world's first new socialist society. Hitler had attacked not merely Russia but also the land of socialism.

Later there were to be innumerable testimonies by Western statesmen and the military extolling the courage and heroism of the Soviet people and recognizing their decisive contribution to the destruction of Hitlerite fascism.

In these testimonies and admissions, however, one important fact is frequently omitted: the Soviet people not only defended their homeland but fought for their socialist homeland, for the socialist way of life. It was not a war of Russians against Germans, but a war of the Soviet people against the nazis, who were obsessed with ideas of world supremacy and even planned to cross the ocean and invade the United States of America after a victorious blitzkrieg against the Soviet Union.

Calamity had struck the family of all the nations of the Soviet Union. It had come suddenly, bringing deep pain. But it did not cause panic. On the contrary, millions rose to fight the enemy. For these men and women this was the beginning of the Great Patriotic War against the fascist invaders, the commencement of a selfless struggle to defend the cause and ideals of socialism and the freedom and independence of other peoples and countries.

Later the United States of America was to enter the war against fascism, and Soviet and American soldiers were to fight the common enemy.

As soon as the Red Army was ordered to repulse fascist aggression, bitter fighting broke out along a vast front extending from the Barents Sea to the Black Sea. No other country would have withstood such a sudden strike as was delivered by fascist Germany against the Soviet Union. But the Soviet state held firm. The Soviet people believed in the invincibility of the Soviet socialist system, in the Communist Party, in its ability to organize resistance to the aggressor and crush him. The Communist Party roused and organized the Soviet people for the Great Patriotic War. It appealed to the working class, the collective farm peasantry, and the Soviet intelligentsia with the summons "Everything for the front! Everything for victory!"

Hitler had grossly miscalculated. Like some reactionaries in the Western democracies, the fascists could not imagine that the people of a workers' and peasants' country could rise to such levels of courage, patriotism, and self-sacrifice as were demonstrated during the Great Patriotic War.

As everywhere else in the country, meetings were held in those days at the factories, offices, educational institutions, and collective and state farms of the Dnepropetrovsk region. At these meetings the people declared their resolve to wage a merciless struggle against the enemy, who had encroached on their happiness. Every person who took the floor spoke of his deep faith in victory, in the triumph of the just cause. The Soviet people carried this faith in victory through all their grim trials. It inspired the soldiers at the front, the partisans and underground fighters in occupied territory, and the Soviet people working in the rear.

Like all the other officials of the Regional Party Committee, Brezhnev donned his uniform. On the eve of the war he had been promoted to the rank of regimental commissar. During the first days of the war this young, vigorous officer was to be seen in many towns and townships of the region, at factories and defense installations, and in the city and district party committees. He gave encouragement and valuable advice.

It required a tremendous collective effort by the Communist Party, the Soviet government, management bodies, and all the working people to place the economy and, in fact, the country's whole life on a wartime footing. Industrial enterprises were successfully switched to work in two shifts and were geared to military production. New sources of primary and other materials were found for industry because the war had disrupted the old economic ties. The manpower problem became acute during the very first days of the war: people had to be found to operate machine tools in place of those who had gone to the front. Throughout the country the number of factory and office workers dropped from 31,500,000 at the beginning of 1941 to 18,500,000 at the close of the year. The Dnepropetrovsk region sent 14,000 Communists, upwards of 80,000 Komsomol members, and many thousands of nonparty people to the armed forces. Workers' trades were quickly mastered by housewives, boys too young to join the army, women who had worked in offices, and men exempted from military service because of their health. The countryside was emptied of men. Tractors and harvester combines were driven by the wives, sisters, younger brothers, and sons of those who had gone to fight for their country.

What seemed to be impossible was accomplished thanks to the patriotism of Soviet people and the vast organizational and educational work to which Brezhnev and his comrades were dedicated. The region, which had sent many thousands of working people to the front, continued to live and work under the slogan "Everything for the front! Everything for victory!" This became the motto of every person in the region and throughout the country.

The firing lines were still far from Dnepropetrovsk. Many in the region thought Hitler's armies would never reach them. But those who headed the region did not conceal the truth from the people. They explained the mortal danger hanging over the country during those critical days. In July the enemy approached Leningrad and began shelling the city—the bombardment lasted for 800 days and nights. Enemy troops were advancing in the Ukraine, in the south, and fighting their way toward Moscow. The unvarnished truth about the situation at the front, where the life and death of the Soviet state were being decided, made the people more conscious of what was taking place around them and awakened fresh strength in them.

Then, one day in July, nazi aircraft raided Dnepropetrovsk for the first time. Bombs fell on residential areas.

"The regional, town, and district committees of the Communist Party of the Ukraine did everything to ensure the evacuation of industrial enterprises, the population, and the property of the machine-and-tractor stations, the state and collective farms, and the offices in the region," Brezhnev related subsequently. "Most of the factories and enterprises in the region were evacuated, together with the industrial and office workers, engineers and technicians, and their families. The state farms were evacuated with the tractors and other property of the machine-and-tractor stations. Many collective farms were evacuated with all their property into the interior of the country. A total of 99,000 railway cars of equipment and other freight belonging to state enterprises and offices were evacuated. The railwaymen drove away all the rolling stock and the locomotives."

Behind the statistics—99,000 railway cars of equipment and other freight—lay tremendous organizational work by party and government agencies, the bitterness of parting with hearth and home, and the firm determination to return.

Brezhnev prepared the dispatch and personally saw off many trains going to the east. Many went to the east after he left.

He felt he could not remain in the rear, although there was nothing to distinguish this rear from the front. As soon as the radio brought to the Dnepropetrovsk region the terrible news of the invasion by nazi Germany, he decided to go to the front. He pressed the party to allow him to join the army in the field. During the first days of the war many ranking party officials, members and alternate members of the Central Committee, had been sent to the armed forces by the party's Central Committee. Nearly one-third of the members of the party's Central Committee and many secretaries of the Central Committees of the Communist Parties of the Union Republics and of the territorial and regional committees went on active service. Brezhnev waited for his reply. At last, in July 1941, he received the permission of the party's Central Committee. As he recalled later, he "left for the front, hardly having time to run home and say goodbye to the family." In October of the same year he was appointed deputy chief of the Political Administration of the Southern Front. But even in this post he telephoned Dnepropetrovsk regularly to ascertain how the evacuation was proceeding, how the factories were working, and how the people were taking it all.

During these days the Soviet people carried a heavy load in their hearts. The news from the front became worse and worse. Under the onslaught of numerically superior enemy forces, for whom the entire industrial apparatus of Western Europe was working, the Soviet troops, fighting selflessly for every inch of ground, were compelled to leave one city after another. The enemy suffered heavy losses, but the number of those who fell in battle, blocking the enemy advance, was also immense. Defeats and setbacks were a bitter cup to drink, but it had not been drained—the Soviet people still had much to bear and much to accomplish.

The Southern Front HQ was then in a small town on the boundary of the Donetsk region. From there Brezhnev kept the leaders of the Dnepropetrovsk region informed of the situation at the front by telephone. The staff of the Regional Party Committee knew his code name and frequently telephoned him at the front's Political Administration. But it was difficult to reach him at the office; even in peacetime he had never been an armchair executive. It was easier to find him in the army units.

Yet he found the time to visit Dnepropetrovsk. Early in the morning of August 7 he went to the Regional Party Committee with a special assignment from the Front Military Council. Konstantin Grushevoy, secretary of the Dnepropetrovsk Regional Party Committee, recalls that he found Brezhnev as energetic as always. "Tanned, looking a little thin, but vigorous as ever, constantly smoothing back his unruly black hair from his high forehead, Brezhnev smiled at meeting his old comrades, shaking hands and embracing them. Only the dark circles under his eyes and his tense look showed that behind his outward serenity there was a sense of concern and anxiety."

Indeed, there was good cause for anxiety. Brezhnev showed the secretaries of the Regional Committee a map of the combat situation with blue arrows converging on the Dnepropetrovsk region. He briefed them on what was happening, telling them of the intended lines of retreat for the troops of the Southern Front, and hurriedly left the building.

After a visit to the Dnieper, where pontoon bridges were under construction, to the Petrovsky plant, and then to Dneprodzerzhinsk, Brezhnev returned to Dnepropetrovsk—an hour's drive. He passed columns of troops heading for the front. The men were hopefully watched by people from the nearby villages who had already started leaving their homes for the east. Here and there smoke was rising from ruins, and there were burned-out trucks along the roadside.

Messerschmitts appeared in the sky; this meant that the front was getting closer and that these villages might very soon be occupied. The eyes of the thirty-four-year-old commissar acquired a sterner look. Within a few hours he was to report to the Southern Front Military Council about everything he had seen, about his meetings with people and the words of encouragement they said to the troops on their way to the front and the pain he saw in the eyes of the women as they led children into the unknown only to be out of danger. . . .

Brezhnev was back in Dnepropetrovsk on August 19, 1941, the most bitter period for the city. The Germans were already shelling the streets. Waves of fascist bombers flew over the city, dropping thousands of tons of bombs. It seemed that no living being would survive the flames and the suffocating smoke. But the city continued to live and fight. Workers of the Petrovsky plant completed their assembling of an armored train under heavy artillery fire. The train left directly from the shop floor for the battle lines.

The railwaymen repaired rolling stock on the way as they strove to get the last trains out to the east. Students, now being trained at an artillery school, were putting up a defense that was as staunch as that of regular troops. The personnel of civilian and military hospitals worked under pressure, for now they were also tending wounded men brought in from the front. Telephone and telegraph operators stayed at their posts around the clock to ensure uninterrupted communication.

The heavy fighting for Dnepropetrovsk continued for five days and nights. Soldiers of the 230th, 255th, and 275th infantry divisions, the 28th Cavalry Division, the 12th and 8th

Armored Divisions, and the 11th Infantry Brigade fought gallantly, bearing the brunt of the defense of the city. But the forces were unequally matched. At 6 A.M. on August 28 the troops were ordered to withdraw and dig in on the eastern bank of the Dnieper. Within a few hours nazi units had entered Dnepropetrovsk.

Brezhnev has never forgotten those five days and nights. He treasures the memory of the men's determination to defend the city on the Dnieper to the death. He remembers the faces of many commanders with whom he spoke at the time. Some of them were wounded and had no strength to rise from the ground, but they continued to command their troops, inspiring them with valor by their own example. He has never forgotten his pain at the thought that the city had to be abandoned despite the huge losses.

The front moved eastward under pressure from numerically superior enemy forces.

When the offensive started along the entire front, the German command announced to the world that this blitzkrieg against the Soviets would end very soon, with the seizure of Moscow. At the close of September the Germans launched a general offensive on Moscow. A huge battle, involving millions of troops on both sides, commenced. The situation was dangerous. A state of siege was declared in the capital on October 19. The Soviet people were determined not to surrender Moscow. And Moscow was not abandoned.

A meeting of the Moscow Soviet of Working People's Deputies with party and public organizations to commemorate the 24th anniversary of the Great October Socialist Revolution was held on November 6, when the enemy was at the city's approaches. The traditional military parade was held in Red Square in front of the Lenin Mausoleum on November 7. The troops marched to the front directly from the parade.

In mid-November the enemy launched another offensive

on Moscow. The fighting was more bitter than ever. This was a historic battle in which the Soviet people and their Red Army performed miracles. The fascist armies were not only stopped but defeated and driven back from the capital. The defeat of the nazi forces at Moscow was the decisive military and political development of the first year of the Patriotic War and the first major defeat of the nazis in the Second World War. The blitzkrieg plan was finally disrupted, and the myth of the invincibility of the German army was dispelled. It was shown that the nazis had miscalculated by believing that the Soviet social and state systems and the Soviet rear were unstable.

Fierce fighting for Kiev, the Donetsk Basin, and Rostov-on-Don lasted through the last months of 1941. Now and then the Soviet Army succeeded in halting the enemy and even mounting an offensive. This was the case, for instance, at Rostov, where the Soviet troops retook the city from the enemy.

"The fighting for Rostov in the autumn of 1941," Brezhnev said many years later, on May 9, 1972, the day on which a memorial to heroic artillery men was unveiled in that city, "was historic: there our Red Army went over from the defensive to the offensive. The memorial you have erected will remind coming generations of the Soviet people of the sublime heroism of their fathers and grandfathers, who responded to the call of the Leninist party, coming from all the fraternal nations of our country to defend the Motherland. Their feat of arms, which was of tremendous importance for our country and for all mankind, will never fade from the memory of the people."

In March 1942 Brezhnev was decorated with the Order of the Red Banner for his part in the fighting at Barvenkovo. Men who fought in this battle recall that he was at the front of an infantry regiment. When he was asked for the details, he confined himself to the words "It was hard."

2. IN THE NOVOROSSIISK AREA

The fascist forces, which had suffered a crushing defeat at Moscow and were unable to make any headway toward Leningrad, continued to advance toward the south. Savage fighting for the Caucasus began in the summer of 1942 simultaneously with the historic battle for Stalingrad, which had been reached by the German forces at the close of June. Having concentrated more than fifty divisions (upwards of a million men) at Stalingrad, the nazis moved twenty-six picked divisions in the direction of the Caucasus; eight were spearheaded at the Black Sea coast. They mounted their offensive in several directions, including Tuapse and Novorossiisk. To organize the defense of these areas, the Soviet command formed a special group of Black Sea troops within the Transcaucasian Front. It included the armies and units fighting in the Tuapse and Novorossiisk areas, as well as the Black Sea Fleet. Brezhnev was promoted to the rank of brigade commissar and appointed first deputy chief of the Political Administration of the Black Sea group of armies.

In September 1942 Novorossiisk was garrisoned by the 47th Army. Before leaving for the army, Mikhail Kalashnik, who had been appointed chief of its Political Department, was received by Brezhnev, who knew the situation there. This is what Kalashnik relates:

"Brezhnev took me to a modestly furnished room and got down to business at once, describing in detail the situation in the Novorossiisk area, the condition of the troops of the 47th Army, and giving me thumbnail sketches of some of the commanders and commissars.

" 'I'm not going to console you,' Brezhnev said, frowning. 'The situation there is difficult.'

"From Brezhnev I learned that since September 8 the army had been under the command of Major General Andrei Grechko. Regimental Commissar Evdokim Maltsev had been

appointed in place of Brigade Commissar Osip Abramov, a
member of the army's Military Council, who had been killed
in action. Major General Alexander Yermolayev, the Chief
of Staff, was also a new man in the army; he had taken over
only a week earlier. The units were not up to full strength,
and reinforcements were coming in slowly. Some units were
short of weapons, and there were many problems with the
supply of ammunition and food. Signs that the troops were
fatigued multiplied.

" 'That's the situation in a nutshell, Kharitonych,' Brezhnev said, calling me by my patronymic, 'There's a lot that
will have to be done. The principal task is to have the men
show more staunchness, to repulse the enemy, to grind down
his strength in the mountains and prevent him from gaining
the Transcaucasus.'

"Brezhnev gave me a smile of encouragement and put his
hand on my shoulder.

" 'I know what you are thinking. You think it will be hard.
Am I right? There'll be difficulties enough, there is no doubt
about that, but I expect that in the end everything will turn
out right. The men of the 47th are good fighters, well tried in
battle. They are men who can be depended upon; they will
move mountains if the need arises. One can only envy their
courage, endurance, and staunchness. The marines have
been fighting especially well. They're heroes, every one of
them.'

"He told me about the fighting in the area of Glebovka,
Moldavanskoye, and the Volchyi Vorota pass. For twenty-
four hours, with the support of an artillery battery commanded by Senior Lieutenant Pyotr Lavrentyev, the 83rd
Marine Infantry Brigade and the 16th Marine Battalion had
held back an enemy force that was several times superior in
strength.

"The men and officers of the 103rd Infantry Brigade did

yeoman service in the fighting for the village of Verkhne-Bakanskaya. They were surrounded by the enemy, but they fought for three days, diverting large enemy forces and enabling the other units to withdraw in good time to the inner defense lines of Novorossiisk.

"The brigade then broke through the enemy ring and took up new positions in good order in the vicinity of Mount Dolgaya.

" 'Every man must be made to realize,' Brezhnev said, 'that further retreat is impossible. He must realize with his mind and heart that this is a matter of the life and death of the Soviet state, of the life and death of the people of our country. It is time we put a stop to the empty talk about the enemy's being exhausted and ceasing the offensive. The nazi troops must be stopped *now,* before it is too late. It is equally important to put the men in the mood to advance, to prepare them for a decisive offensive, to drive the nazi scum from our land. The time for this will eventually come in the Caucasus, as it has come at Moscow.'

"Brezhnev paced the room.

" 'That, I think, is about all. There's a lot of work to do. And now it is time for you to go. When you get there, call me after you have been briefed on the situation and have got to know the men.' "

The situation was deteriorating not just in the Novorossiisk area. The nazis attempted to break through to another Black Sea port—Tuapse. They planned to capture Tuapse, cut off the entire group of Soviet forces at Novorossiisk, eliminate the bases of the Black Sea Fleet, and reach the Transcaucasus through Tuapse, Sochi, and Sukhumi. As Hitler planned it, this would have enabled Germany to link up with Turkey and carry out the further strategic aim of seizing the Middle East and then marching on to India.

This prospect worried British Prime Minister Winston

Churchill. That was why he asked Joseph Stalin if the Russians would hold firm in the North Caucasus. Stalin replied that the Germans would not cross the Caucasus.

There was heavy fighting in the Tuapse area. To break the resistance of the Soviet troops, the nazis threw into this area huge numbers of forces specially trained for mountain fighting. That was when Brigade Commissar Brezhnev threw in all his energy.

In order to stop the nazi onslaught on Tuapse, it was necessary not only to concentrate the entire system of party-political work on raising the morale of the troops defending the area but also to organize special units consisting of Communists who would stand fast at the approaches to Tuapse. Several such assault units were formed under Brezhnev's direction. Each consisted of 500 Communists and Komsomol members, and they occupied the key hills along the main lines of the enemy offensive.

In addition to carrying out this task, Brezhnev, with his customary energy, worked on another important assignment among the troops, often appearing in the front line of the Tuapse defenses.

Alexei Kopenkin, the commissar of a mortar battalion of the 107th Infantry Brigade, recalls that at the time when the brigade was bitterly resisting the enemy's main thrust, cutting the railway and highway to Tuapse, when the Pshish River was becoming red with the blood of those who were fighting on its banks, Brigade Commissar Brezhnev spent two days in the forward lines of this brigade, setting a personal example of courage and military duty.

A fierce battle, time and again developing into savage hand-to-hand fighting, raged at Tuapse. However, all of the enemy's three desperate attempts to break through to the city failed. All three "decisive," to quote the nazis, offensives were repulsed.

Meanwhile, after six months' fighting the Red Army crushed the nazi hordes at Stalingrad in early February 1943. This was one of the major military and political events of the Second World War. It marked the beginning of a fundamental turn in the course of the Great Patriotic War and World War II.

The defeat of the nazi forces at Stalingrad was the starting point for the subsequent crushing blows dealt the enemy and laid the foundation for the Red Army's powerful offensive of the winter of 1942–43 along almost the entire length of the front. The mass expulsion of the enemy from Soviet territory was started. This was the time when preparations for the decisive battles for Novorossiisk were also under way.

A naval task force under Major Caesar Kunikov landed in the vicinity of Myskhako, near Novorossiisk, in February 1943. The operation was successful, and the task force was soon reinforced by a marine infantry brigade and other infantry units, making up two corps. This section with an area of some thirty square kilometers was called the Little Land. The enemy was held at bay for 225 days with incredible doggedness. This battle has gone down as a heroic chapter in the history of the Great Patriotic War.

The landing operations and the entire course of the fighting in the Novorossiisk area were directed by the 18th Assault Army under General Konstantin Leselidze. Leonid Brezhnev was appointed chief of that army's Political Department in April 1943. On his frequent visits to the troops at Novorossiisk, while he was still deputy chief of the Political Administration of the Black Sea group of armies, he came to understand the crucial significance of the fighting in that sector of the front. After he was appointed chief of the 18th Assault Army's Political Department, he devoted himself entirely to training the troops for the decisive battles for Novorossiisk.

Few people in the West know what the job of a Soviet Army political instructor is. He is the deputy of the combat officer and is responsible for the fulfillment of the orders received by the troops. He has innumerable duties: he is responsible for the continuous political education and combat training of the troops and must make sure that the soldiers are informed of developments and understand what is taking place in political, economic, and military affairs at home and abroad. He has to set the troops an example of military discipline, courage, high morale, and organization. The political instructor has to be an example for the Communists in the armed forces, who are always in the front ranks, do the impossible, volunteer for the most difficult assignments, are the first to respond to the requirements of their comrades in arms, encourage the wounded, and think first not of themselves but of their comrades.

The situation was extremely difficult on the Little Land, as it was throughout the Taman peninsula. In a leaflet written on Brezhnev's initiative, this was mentioned:

"Having suffered a heavy defeat at Stalingrad and in the North Caucasus and having been hurled back to the Taman peninsula, the enemy is now staking his all as a losing gambler. He is attempting to slow down the advance of the Red Army. At the cost of huge losses the nazi gang of murderers and plunderers is trying to cling to Novorossiisk. The heroic landing on Myskhako has created a real threat to this strongpoint on the scrap of Kuban land still in the hands of the enemy.

"The Little Land is a deadly knife sticking in the back of the foul enemy!"

The Military Council called on the troops to stand firm along their lines, to destroy the enemy and his equipment, and to counterattack.

The document had a powerful mobilizing effect. It was read at meetings in all the units.

This was a grim period for the Little Land. Storms had made communication difficult with the mainland. This communication was maintained by small motorboats and fishing vessels.

At this critical time Brezhnev was a frequent visitor on the Little Land. Marshal Georgi Zhukov, who came to the Novorossiisk area with a special assignment from the Supreme Commander in Chief, Stalin, regretted that he had missed seeing Brezhnev at the Army Field Administration. In his book *Reminiscences and Reflections,* he writes: "Indeed, this was a bridgehead with a total area of no more than thirty square kilometers. All of us at the time were concerned with one question: Would the Soviet soldiers withstand the trials that fell to their lot in the unequal struggle with the enemy, who was bombing and shelling the defenders of this small bridgehead day and night?

"That was what we wanted to discuss with L. I. Brezhnev, chief of the Political Department of the 18th Army, who had been there repeatedly and had a good knowledge of the situation, but on that occasion he was on the Little Land, where extremely heavy fighting was going on."

Brezhnev's comrades made special note of his ability to mix with people, to establish friendly contact quickly. Ivan Zhurukhin, a political instructor of the 255th Marine Infantry Brigade, recalls Brezhnev's visits to units of that brigade: "I was amazed at his ability to get along with people. He would enter a dugout, ask everyone to move up closer, and begin talking right away as if he had known everyone for a month." Indeed, he knew many of the soldiers, noncoms, and officers, knew what each could do, and guided their combat activities accordingly. When he was on a visit to the Little Land in April of that year, he learned that in one of the sectors the Germans had driven a wedge into the Soviet lines. He at once telephoned the units in the adjoining sectors and with his usual tact gave no orders, only asking,

"How is Mamayev making out? They need his submachine gunners badly there. I'm sure they would chop off the enemy wedge." Alexander Mamayev had just been decorated with the Order of Lenin. When these words were passed on to him, he and his submachine gunners closed the breach.

It was during those days of intense fighting in April 1943 that a winged phrase uttered by Brezhnev passed from mouth to mouth on the Little Land: "You can kill a Soviet man, but you cannot defeat him!"

It was at that time, when he was visiting a unit consisting of Kazakhs, Azerbaijanians, Ukrainians, and Russians, that he said, "It would be no mistake to say that men of all the nationalities of our country are fighting on the Little Land. This land will be a memorial to friendship among peoples, as indeed the whole war we are now fighting will be."

To go to the Little Land was a journey of extreme peril, and Brezhnev made such journeys frequently. The Germans kept torpedoing the tiny craft carrying Soviet troops, laying mines in their way, and strafing and shelling them. One day as Brezhnev was inspecting the landing places, which were constantly shelled by the enemy, he noted how fearlessly the sailors were keeping them going and said to the soldiers, "The sailors merit your respect, for without these heroes you would not have held the bridgehead." And he added with a smile, "True, they give us infantrymen a bath now and then, but that is not their fault."

These "baths of infantrymen" are described by Ivan Solovyov, who was an apprentice seaman at the time: "On one of these trips we sailed out of Gelendzhik while it was still dark, passed Kabardinka, moving in the shelter of the high coast to keep out of sight of aircraft, and cut across the Bay of Tsemess in the direction of the open sea. We were followed by two or three motorboats.

"The weather was foul. There was a cold rain, visibility

was poor, but the Germans did not harass us—that was the most important thing. When we had covered half the way across the bay, we saw the silhouette of a fishing boat directly ahead. Ivan Dotsenko said, 'It must have left earlier than we today.'

"We were about six hundred meters away from the fishing boat when a pillar of water rose directly in front of its bow. The sailors cried, 'It's hit a mine!' Dotsenko ordered full speed ahead, using everything our motor had.

"When we approached the fishing boat, it was still afloat but had a list to starboard. Several men were swimming in the water. We picked up three; the others were picked up by the fishing boat. Just then we were joined by the other motorboats, and together we reached the shore.

"A steep cliff gave shelter from the German shells, and a half-sunken barge served as a pier. When all the men picked up from the damaged fishing boat had stepped onto the barge, Dotsenko looked at one of the officers and exclaimed, 'Why, it's our commissar!'

"I had never seen the man before and learned only then that he was Colonel Leonid Brezhnev, chief of the Political Department of the 18th Assault Army. They said that he had been thrown overboard by the blast and that it was a miracle he was not killed. He looked cheerful, but it was obvious that he was feeling very cold after his dip in the icy water. Meanwhile, an inferno raged on the shore: artillery and machine guns were firing away, submachine guns were rattling, and shells were bursting. One sailor said to me, 'Young fellow, we're having a steam bath today. The Germans are making it hot. They want to get us out of here. See, even the chief of the Political Department is here with us!'

"Everybody went ashore together with Brezhnev. Then Dotsenko ran back and said to me, 'Get my emergency rations. We must put some warmth into the commissar. The men need him badly just now!' I ran to the motorboat, got the flask of alcohol, and took it to the cellar of what used to be a wine distillery. The officers, soldiers, and sailors had gathered around Brezhnev. He was given the flask, and Dotsenko said, 'Take a swig of this sailor's milk. The weather's bad, and it's cold for a swim.' Brezhnev laughed, pulled at the flask, and thanked Dotsenko, but reproached him for having sent a boy to fetch the alcohol. Just then German mortars opened fire, and Brezhnev and the other officers went to the firing lines along a ravine.

"A naval officer ran up and shouted to the men in the motorboats, 'The men are getting hell. They are being attacked by the Germans and must be helped.' We grabbed our submachine guns and hand grenades and rushed forward. Three German attacks were repulsed.

"At nightfall, when we returned to the motorboats to take away the wounded, I saw Brezhnev again among the soldiers. Somebody said, 'It would be fine, comrade commissar, to celebrate May Day in Berlin.' Brezhnev smiled, saying, 'That's what we'll eventually do, but for Hitler there'll soon be nothing to celebrate. He personally issued the orders to throw you into the sea, but nothing has come of it. You fought like lions. You and I will yet reach Berlin!'

"On the way back I heard some wounded men say, 'The commissar's a brave man, but his is an intelligent bravery. He will not let the men take unnecessary risks. He inquired into everything, inspected all the trenches, saw everything for himself, and got the feel of everything. You feel confident when you are with a man like him.'

"One felt that this was said with sincerity and respect. Brezhnev had visited the Little Land time and again. Everybody there knew and esteemed him and always gave him some token of soldierly concern."

Thirty years later, when he visited the Little Land and gazed at the green-clad hills surrounding this tiny patch of

land, Brezhnev said, "These hills were held by the fascists.
. . . We took the risk of landing a force. What with? All we
had were some fishing boats.

"Caesar L. Kunikov, a man following a humanitarian
profession, was appointed commander of the task force. . . .
Prior to the war he was editor of a newspaper. The task force
landed. And for two hundred and twenty-five days and nights
everything was red-hot there. . . . Later, after we had built
up our strength, we struck at Novorossiisk from three directions. . . . And very soon we reached Taman.

"When I was in Cuba, Fidel Castro asked me where the
fighting had been heaviest. I said that throughout all the four
years I did not remember heavier fighting than on the Little
Land. We had only thirty square kilometers of land and a
huge density of troops.

"Of course, our soldiers were very resourceful. To prevent our aircraft from bombing them in view of that density,
they took off their underwear and laid it out along the dugouts. . . . This helped."

Brezhnev looked at the faces of those who had been on the
Little Land with him. "We could not abandon that land.
With it we would have given away the Black Sea and much
else. When we liberated the Caucasus, we laid the beginning
for the liberation of the whole of the Ukraine."

"I congratulate you on the fact that Novorossiisk has been
entered on the list of hero cities," Brezhnev told the people
of Novorossiisk. "Moscow, Leningrad, Stalingrad, Novorossiisk, and the other hero cities are the pride of our people.
For a long time I wondered if I could go through that experience again. . . . I knew that you cherished the memory of
the heroism shown by the defenders of Novorossiisk. The
North Caucasian Front, the Black Sea, the Little Land—
these were one of the main sectors of the war fought by our
people. Together with Stalingrad we were tackling one and
the same task."

Brezhnev's assistant Victor Golikov handed him a photograph.

"This was the machine-gun emplacement on the extreme left flank of the front," Brezhnev said. "Our machine gunners challenged the machine gunners at the extremity of the right flank to a competition."

A monument stands today in Novorossiisk near the sun-kissed vineyards. It is made of 2,750 pounds of smelted splinters, mines, shells, and bombs.

This was the amount fired in terms of each soldier fighting on the Little Land. Throughout the Little Land there were only four wells. In the Valley of Death there was one. Many men perished at this well. There were days when all who went to fetch water were killed.

Operation Novorossiisk

The operation for the liberation of Novorossiisk, conducted on September 10–16, 1943, was one of the outstanding actions of the Great Patriotic War. It involved ground, air, and naval forces.

The assault was mounted from two directions—from the vicinity of the cement factories and from the Little Land—while a powerful task force of more than 6,000 men in only the first echelon landed directly in the center of the city and its port.

A key role in planning and conducting this operation was played by Brezhnev. He was one of the army's talented leaders who urged a direct strike at Novorossiisk in order finally to breach the enemy's strongly fortified Blue Line* and complete his rout in the North Caucasus.

* This was a line of fortifications built by the enemy at the approaches to the Taman peninsula. Its right flank extended to the Sea of Azov, and its left flank stretched to Novorossiisk and the Black Sea.

Long before this operation commenced, after the battle for one of the hills north of Novorossiisk, Brezhnev, his former deputy Sergei Pakhomov relates, said to his staff at the Political Department, "We're hanging about here in one place and taking hill after hill with immense difficulty, with heavy losses, and we're getting practically nowhere. Would it not be better to concentrate all our efforts and strike directly at Novorossiisk? This would speed up the total defeat of the enemy in the Kuban area and on the Taman peninsula and deliver us from unjustified and unnecessary losses."

That is how events turned out. Novorossiisk was the key to the entire Blue Line. The successful advance of the other armies of the North Caucasian Front began only when the city was taken by the 18th Army.

Novorossiisk was liberated on September 16, and on the next day the Soviet forces slipped through the Volchyi Vorota pass, which was practically the only outlet from the Novorossiisk Valley. On September 21 they liberated the town of Anapa, and on October 3 the town of Taman. By October 9 the 56th Army, under Lieutenant General Grechko, had destroyed the Germans on Chushka Spit and cleared the enemy out of the entire Taman peninsula.

The idea of directing the main strike at Novorossiisk, which Brezhnev had shared and urged, had been maturing for a long time in the minds and hearts of the troops and was discussed in the Army Military Council. When the order for the offensive was given in accordance with instructions from GHQ, it was enthusiastically welcomed by the troops.

In the course of a year of fighting for the city every soldier, sailor, noncom, and officer had looked forward to the enemy's total defeat at Novorossiisk. This was an inspiring and major political factor and played a large role in the success of the operation.

Brezhnev took a direct part in planning this military operation and did much to help deploy and train personnel.

He thoughtfully gave assignments to the staff of the army's Political Department. For instance, he sent the older and more experienced party workers, such as Major Anushavan Arzumanyan (who was later to become an academician and member of the Presidium of the Soviet Academy of Sciences), Major Ivan Shcherbak (who later became a Candidate of Historical Sciences), and others, to the 318th Division, which was advancing from the vicinity of the cement factories, and the younger men, like Gurii Yurkin and Dmitri Matyushenko, to a company of marine submachine gunners that was to land in the port and seize the railway station or to other task units.

Brezhnev personally supervised the training of the assault groups and instructed the personnel of his own department on how to conduct political work among the soldiers and sailors with whom they would storm the city on land or from the sea. Brezhnev gave much of his attention to ensuring these troops had equipment, making sure that each had everything he needed.

He also visited the units that were to assault the port and city of Novorossiisk.

Moreover, he showed his abilities as the coordinator of the joint operations of the 18th Army and units of the Black Sea Fleet.

It must be noted that in the sector held by the 18th Army the nazis had concentrated large forces and created dense firepower. The battle would obviously be hard-fought and bloody.

On August 30, 1943, General Leselidze, commander of the 18th Army, called a conference at which General Nikolai Pavlovsky, the Chief of Staff, reported on the alignment of strength and the plan for the operation.

At this conference Brezhnev spoke of the political consciousness and morale of the troops. He stressed the fact that all the soldiers, sailors, and officers were eager to start that offensive, that they were burning with the desire to give battle and crush the enemy at Novorossiisk and on the Taman peninsula.

At 0230 hours on September 10, 1943, Soviet night bombers struck at the enemy's control center in the vicinity of Kirillovka. The fires illuminated the port installations, serving as the beacon for the approaching task force.

At 0245 hours the 18th Army's artillery commander ordered his guns to open fire. In the course of fifteen minutes more than 800 pieces of artillery fired 35,000 shells and mines.

Meanwhile, Soviet aircraft attacked incessantly. Fires broke out in the city, and the smoke formed a heavy curtain over the port, screening the ships and, at the same time, hindering observation and giving the landing craft difficulty in getting their bearings.

By 0250 hours the assault group had destroyed the submarine nets and units of submachine gunners landed on the eastern and western piers. The second task force—the 393rd Separate Marine Battalion under Lieutenant Captain Vasili Botylev—landed first. In the course of twenty minutes, under heavy enemy fire, 800 men reached the shore, bringing with them nineteen heavy machine guns, ten mortars, and forty antitank guns.

The third task force—the 1339th Infantry Regiment under Lieutenant Colonel Sergei Kadanchik—landed somewhat later. More than 1,000 troops gained a foothold at the import wharf and in the vicinity of the electric power station within thirty minutes. Simultaneously, the first task force—the 255th Marine Infantry Brigade under Colonel Alexei Potapov—landed on Cape Lyubov.

Troops advancing from the Little Land and the Main Land joined in the action as the task forces were landing.

Assault on the City

Thus began the famous assault on Novorossiisk, which the enemy had strongly fortified and believed was an impregnable fortress. The population had been forcibly expelled from the city, and there was not a single living soul in it. The streets and houses were mined.

After Novorossiisk was liberated, Soviet sappers deactivated and removed more than 100,000 mines. All the houses along the shore and on the main lines of advance had been turned into permanent reinforced concrete pillboxes.

Nonetheless, after they had seized a bridgehead, the task forces joined battle. They attacked the enemy, driving him out of his trenches and dugouts and from the buildings in the port. There was continuous fighting up to September 16.

In its address to the liberators of Novorossiisk, the 18th Army's Military Council wrote: "Comrades in arms, by a swift advance and a crushing strike jointly with sailors of the Black Sea Fleet you have breached the enemy's defenses. . . . The Army Military Council warmly congratulates you on these first successes of the task forces and calls on you to press inexorably forward, only forward, until the total liberation of the Taman peninsula, where we are awaited by our children, wives, mothers, and fathers who have suffered under nazi tyranny.

"Sailors of the Red Fleet, men of the Red Army, officers, and political instructors! Without respite or stop, follow on the heels of the enemy, surround and destroy him. One more strike at the enemy, comrades in arms, and Novorossiisk will be cleared entirely of the fascist scum."

The last of the fascists were driven out of the city and port at daybreak on September 16, 1943. There were only individual pockets of resistance. The Irkutsk Division joined in the battle. Lieutenant Captain Alexander Raikunov's company of submachine gunners, who had taken three towers of the

Novorossiisk grain elevator and controlled the railway station captured earlier, strove to prevent the nazis from leaving the city with impunity. Gurii Yurkin was the 18th Army's Political Department representative in Raikunov's company. When the battle ended, they buried their dead near the railway station.

But as they were about to fire a salute in honor of the fallen soldiers, they saw a group of high-ranking officers on the road. This was unexpected because until then there had been only reconnaissance men from other units in these places.

One of the officers—he was Brezhnev—recognized Yurkin, embraced him, and said, "They thought you were killed. Go back, and I wish you luck." Raikunov reported to Colonel General Ivan Petrov, the front commander, that his company had carried out its assignment. Petrov at once ordered all the men to be decorated with battle orders.

The 18th Task Army fought its way to the Kerch Strait, liberated Taman, and accomplished yet another feat: landing a strong task force in the Crimea. In this operation, too, a major contribution was made by Brezhnev. It was necessary to coordinate all the commandos for a bold and decisive step—to cross the wide Kerch Strait in small boats in stormy weather, seize a small bridgehead at the village of Eltigen, south of Kerch, and begin the battle for the Crimea.

As at Novorossiisk, Brezhnev sent his instructors to the task force assigned to capture Eltigen, and they honorably carried out their extremely difficult battle assignment. Completely surrounded for more than forty days, the task force showed unparalleled heroism in the fighting on this flaming land and then drove deep into the rear of the enemy, seized Mount Mitridat, destroyed the enemy's artillery positions, descended to the town and port of Kerch, and broke through the enemy ring.

All the members of the task force were awarded high government decorations, and fifty-six of them were created Heroes of the Soviet Union.

The epic of the 18th Army's participation in the battles in the North Caucasus ended with the Eltigen operation. In November 1943 the army's administration and some of its units, including marine infantry brigades, were transferred to the vicinity of Kiev and incorporated in the First Ukrainian Front. This marked the beginning of a new stage of the 18th Army's battle history.

Thirty years after the victory, on September 7, 1974, Leonid Brezhnev pinned the Order of Lenin and the Gold Star medal on the banner of the hero city on behalf of the Presidium of the Supreme Soviet of the USSR. This was a solemn and moving moment.

Speaking to his comrades—veterans who had taken part in the defeat of the fascist forces at Novorossiisk—Brezhnev had full grounds for saying, "If a person has had the opportunity to be a direct participant in any outstanding event of his time, an event that marked an important period in world history, it is remembered by him for the rest of his life. For the older generation of our party these events were the Great October Socialist Revolution and the Civil War. For you and me, for my generation, it was the Great Patriotic War. Superhuman effort and complete dedication—they were the hallmark of all of us who took part in this greatest war in history. This was so because we fought for and defended what was dearest to us, our Soviet socialist homeland, and we are happy that we won a great victory over the enemy, that we contributed our bit to that victory."

These words of a soldier who became the General Secretary of the Central Committee of the Communist Party of the Soviet Union were addressed to the minds and hearts of the Soviet people. In them are grief over the irretrievable losses borne in the war by the Soviet people and pride for those people, who displayed unbounded self-sacrifice and mass heroism in that terrible war. And how natural was his repetition of the words of the oath taken thirty years ago by the heroic defenders of Novorossiisk: "As we go into battle, we give our oath to the Motherland that we shall act with speed and boldness, that we shall not spare our lives for the sake of victory over the enemy. We shall give our will, our life, and our blood, drop by drop, for the happiness of our people, for you, the Motherland we love so passionately. . . . Our law is and shall be: only forward and forward." Remembering these men, Brezhnev said, "The heroes were true to their oath. They went forward and forward, crushing the enemy and scorning death!" And he had gone forward and forward with them, had been in the thick of the fighting, and had scorned death.

The qualities of a national leader—a soldier who subsequently became an outstanding fighter for peace, for the eradication of wars—took shape in the crucible of war.

3 . LIBERATION OF THE UKRAINE

In 1943, when the Soviet Army was expelling the nazi invaders from Soviet soil, the party began recalling its functionaries from active service. Leonid Brezhnev, too, was told that he would have to return to his former job as secretary of a Regional Party Committee, but he requested permission to remain with his unit until the end of the war.

On a cold day in November 1943 Brezhnev arrived in Kiev with his unit. He was familiar with the capital of the Ukraine, which he had often visited before the war. He had attended the 14th and 15th congresses of the Communist Party of the Ukraine and plenary meetings of its Central Committee, and he had spoken at various conferences. Now he saw the city scarred after fierce fighting and the German occupation, but free from the nazi thugs.

Late in November 1943 the military situation west of Kiev deteriorated seriously. The Germans had recaptured Zhitomir and driven a wedge of almost fifty kilometers into the Soviet battle lines. The Soviet High Command was aware of the German intention to make new strong thrusts there.

Battle fatigue plagued the Soviet troops who had forced the Dnieper and liberated Kiev and Zhitomir on the eve of these events. The nazis had brought in fresh divisions from France, Greece, and other occupied European countries and now sought to throw the Soviet troops back across the Dnieper and recapture Kiev and the entire bridgehead on the river's right bank. The First Ukrainian Front under General Nikolai Vatutin was assigned to thwart these plans.

The Supreme Commander in Chief ordered the 18th Army to be moved to the main sector—the Kiev–Zhitomir highway. The army had earned a splendid record in the Caucasus by liberating Novorossiisk and the Taman peninsula.

On December 2 the first of the 18th Army's battalions of infantry and marines moved to this sector advanced rapidly to the firing lines over the snowbound fields and the deserted Zhitomir highway west of Kiev.

The 18th Army in cooperation with other armies of the front was to engage the enemy near the village of Stavishche and turn the tide of the battle for the Ukrainian capital.

In his book *The South-Western Thrust* Marshal of the Soviet Union Kirill Moskalenko recalls the strong impression he carried away from a meeting with Brezhnev in that trying period. He first met Brezhnev during the handover of part of the sector of the planned offensive to the 18th Army, which had moved in from the North Caucasus. "Brezhnev arrived with a group of representatives of his army, and we took them to inspect the divisions of the 52nd Infantry Corps of which they were to assume command. For their part they informed us of the battle worthiness of the 74th Infantry Corps, which was to be transferred to our army.

"In the course of a general conversation and then in a narrow circle of commanding officers Brezhnev expressed his satisfaction over the fact that 18th Army units had joined those of the First Ukrainian Front operating in this major strategic area.

"We also learned that he had taken part in all of that army's defensive and offensive operations in the North Caucasus. I liked his simple manner and firmness of judgment and action. In short, we realized that Brezhnev was an excellent organizer of party-political, ideological, and educational work, who also had a broad outlook on the art of warfare. Moreover, he turned out to be a good comrade and an interesting man to talk to."

The situation in this sector of the front became particularly grave in the early hours of December 12. Captain Ivan Kravchuk, former aide-de-camp to the chief of the Army's Political Department, describes the exploit Brezhnev performed on that night.

"From the front line came a telephone call saying that the nazis were trying to break through our lines near the village of Stavishche. All of us took our weapons and rushed out. Colonel Brezhnev got into his jeep. I followed him.

"Each of us had a pistol, and the driver had a submachine gun and four hand grenades in his kit. Another submachine gunner joined us. Roughly a mile away from the front line we abandoned the jeep because of intensive German shellfire and heard the rattle of machine guns ahead.

"Brezhnev shouted to the soldiers around us, 'Comrades, there is no way of retreat! Kiev is behind us! The enemy shall not pass. Our duty is to stand to the last!'

"He had no time to say anything else: German machine

guns lashed out and enemy infantry attacked. We had only one active heavy machine gun, but that fell silent after a few moments. Brezhnev ran down the trench toward it.

"I ran after him. We jumped over a few still bodies. Brezhnev looked back. 'Ivan, take a look, some may yet be alive. See if anyone needs help!' I fell back and hastily touched two or three bodies. They were all dead. I covered their faces with their caps and followed Brezhnev. Just then I heard our only machine gun come alive, rattling away in staccato bursts of fire.

"When I got there, I saw the machine gunner lying in a heap in a pool of blood, with Brezhnev firing away. I pulled the dead man away and moved the cartridge box closer to Brezhnev. There were few rounds left. Meanwhile, the nazis were driving on, heedless of the fire, with no more than thirty to forty meters between them and our trench. They were hurling hand grenades and shouting in drunken voices, '*Rus kaput!* Surrender!' Brezhnev replied with short bursts of fire, making each round tell. German flares went up into the sky one by one, and as they burned, Brezhnev carried on his well-aimed fire. Outwardly he retained his usual self-control, but he had flung off his fur cap and gloves, and on three occasions he pushed me away when I tried to pull him down to the ground to save him from the hail of bullets and shell splinters. Loading the last cartridge belt, he said, 'Run along the trench, get everyone together, tell them to save their hand grenades for the last minute, and prepare for hand-to-hand fighting!'

"Through the rattle of fire and the drunken shouts of the nazi infantrymen we heard the dull roar of the German tanks. They had taken up their attack positions and were apparently poised for a swift push across to the Zhitomir highway. In our trench I found no more than a dozen men still alive.

"But as happened time and again in the war, we were rescued in the nick of time: from the rear our heavy artillery struck out at the enemy, and salvos of Katyusha rockets ripped the air. The guns knocked out the German tanks, and the Katyusha rockets cut down the German infantry. Within minutes a sergeant carrying an antitank rifle ran into our trench, followed by a platoon moving in file and then by a whole company.

"I returned to Brezhnev. Two men had already taken up their positions by the machine gun, while he was sitting on the ground, leaning against the wall. The front of his white sheepskin coat was smeared with blood. I rushed to him, but he smiled at me, safe and sound, and said, 'Ivan, let's have a cigarette.' I rolled a cigarette with my fingers, which wouldn't bend, put it to his lips, and passed my hand over his chest. The blood had dried up; it was the blood of the dead machine gunner. I sat down beside Brezhnev and also had a smoke. . . . All the rest of that day we paced the trenches of the front line."

In the small hours of December 25, 1943, to be precise, Soviet troops launched their offensive on Zhitomir and Berdichev. Troops of the 18th Army were once again fighting along the main direction.

A few days before the offensive began, Brezhnev issued a directive to all the heads of subordinate political departments which was typical of his constant care for the men in the ranks. He wrote: "Save the strength and health of the fighting men. The hard-and-fast rule is that they must be kept supplied with food and hot water. We must ensure the strictest control so that the men get everything the state allocates for them. Those who are neglectful or idle in this respect must be severely punished. Unflagging attention must be given to the operation of the medical services. The political departments of units must appoint men responsible for the evacuation of the wounded from the field of battle and for emergency medical aid."

The fighting for Korysteshev, Zhitomir, and Berdichev

was especially fierce. Soviet troops advanced rapidly across a roadless terrain turned into a sea of mud by a sudden thaw after a hard frost.

Brezhnev, who displayed constant concern for the officers and men, for all his subordinates, often forgot to take care of himself.

In the fighting for Berdichev he had another narrow escape when, submachine gun in hand, he took part in storming the barracks where the Germans had barricaded themselves, thereby cutting off a group of Soviet troops from the main battle lines.

Many years later, at a meeting with war veterans of his unit, Major General Timofei Volkovich recalled that on January 3, 1944, a memorable day for him, then a colonel, he had broken through with a storming party to the barracks held by the Germans there to discover a handful of Soviet troops who had made their way close to the German machine gunners.

The men were led by an officer with a submachine gun. Volkovich saw the officer quickly swing his submachine gun and give a long burst of fire that killed two nazi soldiers who appeared on the roof. A moment later a German rifleman looked out a window and fired at the Soviet officer, who was saved by a soldier; the man pulled the officer to the ground just as the German was about to fire, while another took care of the nazi. When the officer got up from the ground, Volkovich recognized Colonel Brezhnev. Volkovich was unable to contain himself and said, "Colonel, you have no right to be here. What are you doing?"

"The same as you, Colonel!"

"Please go away. This is no place for you."

"My place is where the situation requires the earliest fulfillment of the combat task. Are you aware that our forward units fighting in the city are encircled? We have to break through to them. Don't get excited, Colonel. Let's smoke these nazis out of these damned barracks together.''

Immediately after Berdichev was liberated, Brezhnev, in addition to his many military duties, took a most active part in restoring normal life. He did much to help the city with food supplies and transport facilities. He ordered twenty captured trucks and eight passenger cars to be assigned to meet the needs of the city. These came in handy for transporting food supplies from the rear. Besides, the 18th Army's Political Department secured for Berdichev some of the grain stocks from military warehouses. This was also done on Brezhnev's initiative.

In the summer of 1944 the nazis, who had suffered a major defeat in the Ukraine west of the Dnieper, entrenched themselves in the Carpathians, which blocked the way to the area beyond. This was a natural fortress, 270 kilometers wide and 100 kilometers deep, which the enemy reinforced with a ramified and deeply echeloned network of strongpoints, trenches, barbed-wire fences, minefields, and various engineering installations.

It became quite obvious to the Army Command and indeed to all officers and men that there would be intense fighting on rugged mountainous terrain. The army's Field HQ was in the area of Snyatyn, Kolomyya, and Gvozdets. The army was reinforced with the 11th and 17th Guards Infantry Corps and somewhat later with the 95th Infantry Corps. These were battle-tested units, but none had special training, experience, or equipment for mountain fighting, much less for fighting in a range like the Carpathians. There was a need to study the experience gained in the early fighting for the Caucasus and make it available to the troops as soon as possible.

In this connection, Marshal of the Soviet Union Andrei Grechko says in his book *Across the Carpathians* that the political instructors of the 18th Army, whose Political Department was headed by Colonel Brezhnev, were actively preparing the troops for the offensive.

"While preparing the East Carpathian operation, the 18th Army's Political Department set its sights on having every party and Komsomol political instructor ready to work with the rank and file during the operations on mountainous terrain," Marshal Grechko wrote. "Ten army seminars were held in the units and at the army's Political Department to train 430 men within a matter of two or three days. Apart from general political reports, these seminars discussed the various aspects of fighting on wooded mountainous terrain and the tasks of political and military education in the new combat situation."

All the work of the political instructors was being carried on while heavy fighting was going on east of the Carpathians. Officers and men set many examples of gallantry, showing a growing capability for fighting with courage, determination, and initiative in the new conditions.

Fighting in the Mountains

The closer Soviet troops got to the Carpathians, the less they saw of the familiar lowland landscape. In the 18th Army only a few units had been trained to fight on forested mountainous terrain. It was necessary to train all the officers and men to fight in the new conditions, to provide mountaineering equipment, lighter weapons, and pack animals.

It was also necessary to get the units up to full strength, to fortify the decimated ranks of the party organizations, to raise the morale of the troops fatigued by the constant fighting.

In that difficult situation the chief of the army's Political Department had men he could rely on. He had rallied together a group of principled, courageous, and resourceful men with considerable political and combat experience. An atmosphere of vigor and initiative prevailed. The Political Department functioned efficiently. Brezhnev's subordinates respected and liked him, never had to be told twice what to do, and accomplished the possible and the impossible to ensure the fulfillment of combat orders.

The dugouts and other places where the chief of the Political Department worked were always open to visitors.

Brezhnev had a friendly word for everybody, always made a point of asking how all were coping with their duties, listened to their requests and suggestions, gave them advice and instructions.

Ivan Shcherbak, who was a lecturer of the army's Political Department, recalls in his reminiscences Brezhnev's inexhaustible resourcefulness, high exactingness, kindness, sincerity, unassuming manner, and modesty.

Brezhnev never had to insist on his subordinates' always being with the troops. He set them a personal example.

The 18th Army became used to seeing Brezhnev where the main strike was to be delivered. He commanded the deepest respect of the men for this. He was well informed on the actual state of affairs in the units and responded quickly to overcome any shortcomings and meet the needs of the troops.

Nikita Dyomin, former chief of the Political Department of the 17th Guards Infantry Corps, testifies: "In any situation, however hard the going was, Brezhnev was always with his men, building up their faith in victory, carrying conviction to them, which in effect made him the heart and soul of the officers and men of our army."

Anton Gastilovich, who was in command of the 17th Guards Corps, recalls: "Brezhnev came to visit us on several occasions, spending days on end in the front-line units. He generously shared his rich experience in mountain fighting, which he had acquired in the battles at Tuapse, at the

Goitkh Pass, at Novorossiisk, and on the Taman peninsula. Brezhnev never failed to support all our requests with army HQ to strengthen the combat potential of our corps and joined the Military Council in making arrangements to provide such assistance. This did a great deal to help us in our work and added to our confidence in our own strength.''

Indeed, Leonid Brezhnev generously shared with all his experience acquired during military operations in the mountains of the North Caucasus, and the conferences he attended often developed into something like tactical exercises. He advised officers to refrain from storming the enemy in the mountains head-on, unless there was an urgent need. It was better to bypass and surround the enemy, to set up small assault groups to operate independently. He cited examples of bold initiatives taken by a soldier or group of soldiers to carry out tasks which otherwise would have taken a whole unit to perform.

"What is most important," Brezhnev said, addressing the commanders and political instructors of the 317th Division, "is to teach the small units to act on their own; reconnoiter the roads, gorges, passes; seize and hold commanding heights, roads, and narrow defiles; boldly bypass the enemy; and take him by surprise."

He was very cautious when it came to risking the lives of the men, and they appreciated this care, respecting him all the more for avoiding unnecessary risks.

Key to Battle Success

As chief of the Political Department Brezhnev explained that success in battle depended on the concerted and coordinated cooperation of commanders and political instructors. At a conference on the eve of the Carpathian-Uzhgorod operation he said:

"The commander and the political instructor have an especially important, honorable, and responsible duty to perform in battle. The commander is the man who organizes the battle, and his orders are law to all his subordinates. The political instructor is the commander's right hand and must always be where the success of the battle is being decided, where the fighting is heaviest, where there is need for personal example to inspire the soldiers to carry out their combat assignment. The commander and the political instructor are a single whole, and they must be the regiment's heart and soul."

Staying constantly with the corps, divisions, regiments, battalions, and companies, Brezhnev required commanders and political instructors personally to see to it that every officer and man had a clear understanding of their tasks in the fighting, knew how to use their weapons to the best effect, displayed initiative and resourcefulness, and were physically fit. He urged them to train their men in the finest combat traditions of the Russian soldier and the Red Army.

As a political officer Brezhnev made use of every conceivable instrument to build up morale, to raise the enthusiasm of his men; he knew the Soviet soldiers' pride in their country's history, and he dug into it for educative purposes.

On his initiative the men were reminded of the heroic exploits of Suvorov's men in the Alps and of the Russian soldiers in the Carpathians in 1916 and were told of the experience of the recent fighting in the Caucasus and at Novorossiisk.

One day, while on a visit to the 17th Guards Infantry Corps, Brezhnev inspected the regiments and the battalions of the corps' 8th Division. He spoke to many officers and political instructors and then climbed to a commanding height to see the battlefield for himself.

"Over there is the Yablonovsky Range! Beyond it are our

brothers in the Transcarpathian Ukraine! It's only a stone's throw away," he said. "And beyond that lies the valley of the Tisza, and then Hungary and Czechoslovakia. Over there the people are impatiently waiting for us. It's not a very long way to go!"

Nodding at an elderly soldier, he continued: "This man is also eager to get beyond the Carpathians. He must surely be over fifty!"

The man realized that they were talking about him and came up. "Machine Gunner Parshin," he said.

"Fyodor Parshin fought in these parts in the First World War," the battalion commander reported.

"Is that so?" Brezhnev said.

"Yes, Comrade Colonel. I did fight in these parts. Our regiment captured and defended this very height."

Parshin led them to an old overgrown trench.

"Our platoon was entrenched right here." He pointed to a hillock and added, "That was the dugout of the company commander. We made it hot for the Germans over here, and I'm sure we'll smash them this time."

Brezhnev heartily shook hands with the old machine gunner and thanked him. He saw to it that the 18th Army took the experience of the veterans into account, especially in training reinforcements.

However hard the fighting, raw troops were not, as a rule, sent into battle at once. They underwent combat training and toughening near the line of fire, outside the range of enemy artillery, learning the fighting traditions of their unit and getting advice from experienced men.

This well-organized educational work helped accustom the new recruits to the battle conditions in a much shorter period, so that they displayed skill and staunchness in subsequent fighting.

An important aspect of the political instructor's duties was that the truth should reach enemy troops.

Under the impact of the Red Army's successes, especially of the 4th Ukrainian Front, which included the 18th Army from August 1944 onward, antiwar sentiments began to spread in the Hungarian 1st Army. These sentiments were encouraged by the efforts of a special unit of the 18th Army's Political Department. This work, too, Brezhnev personally organized and guided. "In the offensive started by our troops, many Hungarians and Germans have been taken prisoner," he wrote in a directive to the chiefs of the subordinate political departments. "The testimony of war prisoners shows that enemy morale is low, and this gives us the opportunity to influence them more effectively by our propaganda."

The fact is that the efforts to shake morale among enemy troops had a substantial effect in the battle for the Carpathians. In that period something like 3,000 broadcasts were organized, 2,500,000 leaflets were published, and about 800 prisoners of war and defectors were infiltrated into the enemy rear. As a result, nearly 10,000 officers and men went over voluntarily to the Soviet side. Colonel General Miklos Bela, commander of the Hungarian 1st Army, and several of his officers surrendered voluntarily on October 18 in the sector of the 351st Infantry Division.

The disintegration of the Hungarian 1st Army assumed major proportions. However, the Germans managed to slow it down by savage reprisals. They swiftly moved several German units into the area, brought German units into the battle lines held by the Hungarians, and threatened to execute anyone trying to get out of the war begun by German fascism and hated by the Hungarian people.

The great diversity of tasks and problems and the quest for the needed forms and methods of work made up the day-to-day uninterrupted effort, which Brezhnev directed tirelessly.

On October 8 the 18th Army liberated Lavochne, the last populated locality held by the nazis in the Soviet Ukraine.

This marked the complete liberation of the Soviet Ukraine from the German invaders.

In Transcarpathia

In an order of the day issued on October 18 the Supreme Commander in Chief congratulated the troops of the 4th Ukrainian Front for successfully crossing the main Carpathian range and for taking its passes. A twenty-salvo salute was fired by 224 guns in Moscow in their honor.

In summing up the results of the 18th Army's combat operations, Brezhnev reported to the Military Council of the 4th Ukrainian Front: "In a relatively short time (the latter half of September and October) our troops successfully overcame all obstacles, drove the enemy out of his fortified defense lines, inflicted tremendous losses on him, and, contrary to the assertions of military experts about the Carpathians' being impregnable, broke into the Hungarian Plain with decisive support from troops of the 2nd Ukrainian Front.

"From September 19 to November 1 alone, 22,075 enemy officers and men were killed or wounded, and 21,269 taken prisoner. We captured 206 guns, 300 mortars, 1,054 machine guns, 12,535 rifles and submachine guns, and other weapons. . . .

"The Carpathian operation was a grueling test for all the men of the 18th Army, from private to general. This test has been successfully passed."

The people of Transcarpathia welcomed their liberators like brothers, with open arms and sincere joy. White-haired old men, children, and men, women, boys, and girls in national dress went out to welcome the Soviet troops. They offered them the traditional "bread-and-salt" greeting and bunches of flowers, invited them to their homes, regaled them with fruit and wine, and gave them whatever help they could. They acted as guides and sappers, scouts and medical orderlies, aided soldiers in rebuilding roads and bridges, cleared away roadblocks, and helped to capture fascists hiding in the mountains. For their part, Soviet troops assisted the local people—their brothers and sisters—with food, medicines, and services, helped them understand the international political situation and so decide their own future.

On October 28 Brezhnev arrived with a group of generals and officers in Uzhgorod, which was still under enemy shellfire. They were met by a delegation of the municipal council. On behalf of the city population, Pyotr Sova, a municipal councillor, wholeheartedly thanked the Soviet command for the liberation of Uzhgorod and expressed the long-standing desire of the people of Transcarpathia to reunite with the Soviet Ukraine.

The speech in reply, Councillor Sova recalls, was delivered by a slim young colonel, who bore himself with dignity. He had a manly, good-natured face with expressive features, and a smile twinkled in his eyes.

Brezhnev spoke of the sacred mission of the Soviet Army: to rout the enemy and help the peoples of Europe regain their freedom and independence.

He stressed that the Soviet troops had entered Transcarpathia as liberators. In reply to the Transcarpathian people's ardent desire to reunite with the Soviet Ukraine, expressed by the municipal councillor, Brezhnev said, "We have no intention of interfering in your affairs. That is your own business, and it is up to your people to decide. We will never act against the will of the people."

The fact was that the people of the Transcarpathian Ukraine had lived under the yoke of foreign states for centuries. Progressives of the Transcarpathian Ukraine regarded the coming of Soviet troops as an opportunity to establish their own people's government and to reunite with their motherland.

Meetings were held spontaneously in towns and villages,

and people's committees were elected. All sections of the population, including the clergy—both Orthodox and Roman Catholic—took part in the election.

It was a momentous period in the history of Transcarpathia. The masses of Transcarpathia, who for the first time had the opportunity to shape their destiny, expressed their will on November 26, 1944. On that day the first Congress of the People's Committees of Transcarpathia was held at Mukachevo and adopted the historic Manifesto on the Reunification of the Transcarpathian Ukraine with the Soviet Ukraine. In June 1945 the governments of the Soviet Union and Czechoslovakia signed a treaty under which the Transcarpathian Ukraine was reunited with the Soviet Ukraine.

As soon as Transcarpathia was liberated, the people felt the fraternal assistance of Soviet troops. The 18th Army's Political Department and its chief did much to help them build a new life. Brezhnev as usual worked around the clock. On November 2, 1944, he was promoted to the rank of Major General.

Major General Brezhnev was directly involved in the work to open schools, shops, and medical institutions and to rebuild factories and plants. On his initiative, 9 million pounds of grain from army stores were handed over to the needy population. He spoke at meetings and rallies about the liberative mission of the Soviet Army, the Soviet people's massive labor effort in the rear, and the international situation. In the meantime, he continued to guide party and political work in the 18th Army, which was still engaged in active military operations.

The people of Transcarpathia repaid Brezhnev with affection for his constant concern for them. Many of them remember his good deeds and tell their children and grandchildren about them. He won their affection by his frankness, sincerity, and respect for others. Pyotr Sova, the municipal councillor, says, "Brezhnev showed that he was a skilled diplomat and statesman. He was the most popular representative of the Soviet Command, and local people cherish their memory of him."

The young general was warmly received in every home he visited. He spent the few leisure hours he had with Sergei Stasev, chairman of the People's Committee of Uzhgorod, with artist Andrei Kotsko, chief of the people's militia, and with the civic leaders Pyotr Sova and Nikolai Katerinyuk.

Today Kotsko, who holds the title of Merited Art Worker, lives in a home on one of Uzhgorod's quiet treelined streets. On holidays and on festive occasions, when he entertains his friends, he invariably recalls the memorable days of late 1944.

Time and again he points to the place where the weary young General Brezhnev used to sit after a harrying day, to the paintings Brezhnev liked, and leafs through the general's favorite books. He comes up to a shelf and carefully shows his guests the books Brezhnev presented to him and recalls their frequent heart-to-heart talks. . . . They used to discuss the battle successes of the Soviet Army, the postwar order in Europe, pore over maps, and reckon the distance still to go to Berlin. The way ahead, every mile of it, was hard toil, but at the end of it lay the cherished goal of peace.

Brezhnev always had respect for individuality. To him the people were never a gray, faceless mass, as some in the West speak of Communist leaders. On the contrary, Brezhnev always noted and valued individual traits in every person.

"What do you intend to paint after the war?" Brezhnev asked his host. The artist was unable to reply at once. Indeed, what would he tell the people in the idiom of his art? Of the horrors of war? Of the triumph of peace?

They would then get to talking about the goals of art for

the people. They discussed at length the trends in the Western European art and literature then in vogue, and each time Kotsko was amazed by the general's erudition in the history of literature and the arts.

There were indeed many meetings and conversations, and people in Transcarpathia still remember them.

One night Brezhnev was returning in a car from the front lines to the city. Passing through a village, he caught sight of two figures in the glare of the car's headlights. He ordered the driver to stop. A man and a woman asked him for a lift, and both were invited to get in. The car drove on. The strangers introduced themselves as Noemi and Nikolai Katerinyuk.

That was the beginning of their acquaintance. The general left an indelible impression on Noemi. He was the first Soviet citizen she had met; she found that he was quite unlike what she had imagined Communists to be.

Noemi had been born and educated in Budapest, and at school she had been constantly told that Communists were little less than savages: they held nothing sacred; their ideology was inhuman; their deeds were even worse. When the 18th Army entered Uzhgorod, Noemi closed all the shutters and stayed in the house. She was sure that Soviet soldiers would revenge themselves on the Hungarians for fighting in the war against the Soviet Union.

As millions discovered about the same time and later, nothing of the kind happened. The twenty-year-old Noemi was even more confused. Today she is a correspondent of the regional newspaper *Karpathi igaz so* and recalls, with a smile, her doubts and worries. To this day she is grateful for meeting Brezhnev, who helped her see the world in a new light and answered the questions that troubled her. He explained that the Soviet Army was fighting no particular nation but the fascists. What is more, it never terrorized the civilian population.

The general had a reciprocal sympathy and respect for the young couple. He called at their house frequently. He grew fond of their two-year-old daughter, often playing a game with her or telling her a fairy tale. Now and then he grew pensive, thinking of his own son and daughter. How were they getting on?

He told them about his mother, his wife, sister, and brother and how much he wanted to see them all.

The times, however, were still strained and troubled. In Western Europe the people still languished under the nazi yoke.

4. ONWARD WEST

In January 1945 the 18th Army advanced into Czechoslovakia.

Ludvik Svoboda, who was President of Czechoslovakia for many years, reminisced about that period: "In January 1945 I went to see the commander of the Soviet 18th Army in my capacity as commander of the Czechoslovak Corps. The 18th Army HQ was in a village north of Košice. I drove there by car and met the commander of the 18th Army, General Gastilovich. We agreed on how we would cooperate and mapped out the lines of the forthcoming offensive.

"General Gastilovich and I established good businesslike relations. Until the end of the war the Czechoslovak Corps fought as part of the 18th Army. The 18th Army won its first major success on our soil when it liberated the city of Košice, where the government of the Czechoslovak Republic soon arrived and the well-known Košice Program was proclaimed as the basis for the state system of the new free republic and its policy of unbreakable friendship with the Soviet Union."

In the fighting to liberate Czechoslovakia, Poland, and Hungary, General Brezhnev organized the work of the 18th

Army's political instructors in such a way that the command could always rely on the high morale of Soviet troops, says Colonel General Anton Gastilovich, now a professor and Doctor of Military Science.

"What was especially well organized was the highlighting of the heroic exploits of Soviet officers and men. Thus, for instance, from January to April 1945 seventy-six leaflets entitled *Glory to Our Heroes!* were issued in the 650th Infantry Regiment of the 138th Division alone. The morale of the Soviet troops kept growing, and with every passing day our men struck harder and harder at the enemy."

A total of 140,000 Soviet officers and men gave their lives for the liberation of Czechoslovakia. Countless thousands were wounded or crippled.

Many years later the General Secretary of the Central Committee of the Communist Party of the Soviet Union, Leonid Brezhnev, said, "The war is a thing of the past. But our feelings have not changed. The sense of profound community that unites the peoples of our countries has struck deep root in the hearts of the Soviet people and the Czechs and Slovaks."

Wherever Brezhnev went he established warm relations with the local people, the Czechs and the Slovaks. Dr. Mikulas Stanislav, a clergyman, recalls:

"In February 1945 battles were being fought around our village. There was firing every day. And we were sitting it out in a cellar. A Russian general—tall, black-browed, youthful, and very friendly—was quartered in our house.

"One day he invited me to have dinner with him, his aide-de-camp, and three other officers. I asked him his name, and he said it was Brezhnev. I mustered my courage and asked, 'What kind of government are we going to have?' Brezhnev replied, 'You yourselves will establish your own government. This government will apparently be a popular one.

Czechoslovakia will be a free republic.' Unfortunately our conversation was cut off because the Germans started shelling the village and the windowpanes in our house were shattered. General Brezhnev did not move an eyelid, but I went down to the cellar and stayed there with my family until the fighting ended. When we came upstairs, General Brezhnev had already gone. . . .

"In the past few years I have often felt like writing Brezhnev a letter to remind him of his stay in our locality, to express to him my affection, despite the fact that he is a Communist and I am a clergyman, and to thank him for the assistance given to our people in their most difficult years."

It was explained to the public at large that the local people could safely rely on the assistance of Soviet soldiers in establishing a new antifascist power. This attitude on the part of the Soviet Command, the work of the political instructors, and the conduct of Soviet officers and men were met with great satisfaction. The population, which had been intimidated by fascist propaganda, now began to trust Soviet servicemen and regard them with affection as their liberators. Good relations were established between the population and Soviet troops. Local people helped the troops more and more often.

The events in Brezhnev's life connected with the liberation of Czechoslovakia left a deep imprint on his memory. This is why at the ceremony at which Czechoslovak decorations were conferred upon him in November 1976 he again recalled the war roads of 1945 that Soviet officers and men had traversed together with the Czechoslovak Corps, the flames of the popular uprising in Slovakia, the uprising in Prague, and the joyful days of the liberation of Czechoslovakia from the nazi invaders.

The people of Poland welcomed the Red Army with jubilation. The 18th Army was assigned to liberate part of south-eastern Poland in the area of the High Tatras. During a heavy snowfall in the dead of night the 17th Guards Infantry Corps broke through the German defenses north of the range, in the Czarny Dunajec area near Poronino in Poland.

Besides Poronino, the 18th Army liberated Nowy Targ, Gorny Dunajec, and many other population centers in that part of Poland. Poronino and Nowy Targ are associated with Lenin's life. He lived in Poronino for some time. There the Bolsheviks held a meeting under Lenin's guidance. He was detained by the Austrian authorities and kept in the Nowy Targ prison.

As the troops moved closer to these towns, Brezhnev told all the commanders and political instructors to see to it that everything associated with Lenin's name was preserved.

The Czechoslovak Corps and the Soviet 18th Army saw the end of the war at the Svitavy River. This, however, did not happen on May 9, 1945, but a few days later, on May 12. Many people in the world do not know of the following events in the history of the Second World War.

Even after all the other troops of the Third Reich had surrendered, a group of German divisions under General Field Marshal Ferdinand Schoerner, which operated in the central part of Czechoslovakia, refused to lay down their arms and attempted to fight their way to the West.

The former commander of the 18th Army, Colonel General Gastilovich, recalls: "In the early hours of May 9, I received an order from the front HQ to send our envoys to all the four German divisions entrenched in front of our army to give them the terms of surrender. But at 0900 hours all the four officers came back. They had been rudely driven away from three divisions and told that there would be no surrender. The commander of the fourth division sent me a short polite letter, saying that he had received no orders to surrender, so he would continue to fight.

"Attempts on the part of Soviet troops to advance were

met with heavy, well-organized fire. It turned out later that General Field Marshal Schoerner, commander of the German Army Group Center, consisting of more than fifty-seven divisions on May 9, had ordered his troops to continue fighting and retreat to the West."

The Schoerner group had 1 million men, 10,000 pieces of artillery, 1,000 aircraft, and 2,000 tanks. Early in May, when Hitler was already dead, the Schoerner group remained the only battle-worthy part of the Wehrmacht, on which Hitler's henchmen relied as their last stake.

The scheme of the nazis was frustrated by the successful operations of Soviet troops, in particular the 18th Army and the Czechoslovak Corps. This, however, took much effort and a large toll of lives. In those days Brezhnev displayed great energy to stimulate the entire political apparatus to maintain high morale among the troops. This was not easy to do, because everyone realized that although the war was over, more lives had to be lost.

On the night of May 10 Major General Brezhnev wrote his last battle report to the command in which he said, "The enemy, who has refused to lay down his arms, spent much of his ammunition in firing at our front lines and began a hasty retreat. During the whole of May 9 and 10 our troops pursued the retreating enemy and engaged him in various sectors. Now our troops are in pursuit of the Germans."

That was many years ago, but the veterans of the 18th Army vividly remember those trying days in May 1945 and commemorate them by meeting exactly on May 12 every year. Such meetings in Moscow are often attended by Brezhnev as former chief of the Political Department of the 18th Army.

As chief of the 18th Army's Political Department and later of the Political Administration of the 4th Ukrainian Front Brezhnev skillfully coped with the tasks facing Soviet troops abroad.

When a Victory Parade in Moscow's Red Square was planned, Brezhnev was appointed commissar of the composite regiment of the 4th Ukrainian Front.

The Victory Parade in Moscow was a spectacular national holiday. It crowned the epoch-making victory of the Soviet people in the Great Patriotic War and the victory of other nations of the anti-Hitlerite coalition.

Brezhnev's appointment as commissar of one of the composite regiments was a sign of recognition of his great services to his country.

The former commander of the 18th Army, Gastilovich, who also took part in the Victory Parade, writes: "I was glad that Brezhnev was appointed commissar of the composite regiment to represent the 4th Ukrainian Front, and I had the honor to march with him, my comrade in arms, in the ranks of the victors over the sacred stones of Red Square.

"Captured German banners collected from all the units were to be hurled down at the foot of the Lenin Mausoleum during the parade.

"The Victory Parade was held on June 24, 1945. It was a striking and majestic spectacle. It has been filmed in a documentary, and everybody has had the opportunity to see it."

For his meritorious conduct in the Great Patriotic War, for his courage and heroism in the performance of combat assignments, Brezhnev was decorated with the Order of Lenin, two orders of the Red Banner, the Order of the Patriotic War Grade I and II, the Order of the Red Star, the Order of Alexander Nevsky, and other orders and medals.

On the 20th anniversary of Victory Day he was awarded the title of Hero of the Soviet Union in recognition of his great services to the country and the party in the Great Patriotic War.

The Soviet writer Konstantin Simonov has called one of his books about the Great Patriotic War *No One Is Born a*

Soldier. Like the millions of Soviet people who took up arms in defense of their country, Brezhnev was not born a soldier. He left his civilian job and joined the armed forces.

But he lived the life of his people, and when the people had to go to war, he became a soldier, too.

Like the other Soviet people, he faced death in defensive battles, rose to attack, was cold and hungry, grieved over the loss of his comrades, and rejoiced in Soviet war successes. He was to be seen in the trenches more often than at headquarters. He was always in the midst of the rank and file, sharing their dangers and risks, their short rations and scarce ammunition.

It was not simple to withstand all the hardships of war. "Soviet generals, officers, and men experienced many trials on the roads of war. The nerve-racking retreat and continuous fierce fighting. Days, months, and years spent in the face of death. Long and fatiguing marches in winter frosts and in summer heat, in lashing autumn rains and over roadless terrain in spring." This is what Brezhnev said on May 8, 1975, of the Soviet people's great exploit. "When now, three decades later, one recalls what fell to the lot of the rank and file, commanders, and political instructors of our armed forces, it is hard to believe that all this actually happened and was actually endured. . . . But we did endure all this. We withstood all trials and won victory, defeating the nazi aggressors."

A man of a cheerful nature and excellent abilities as an organizer, Brezhnev generated around himself an atmosphere of hope and a high awareness of each man's duty to the socialist country, which sprang not from any mystic sense or fear but from the realization that the war was fought to save mankind and, indeed, civilization as a whole from the nazi threat.

Having passed through the flames of the most terrible war,

facing death, suffering, and bloodshed, seeing razed cities and burned crops, he came to love life and people still more.

Indeed, the war taught him to display even greater concern for people and to safeguard them against the scourge of war.

That is why, Brezhnev said, "we believe it to be our sacred duty to do our utmost so that not only we but our children, grandchildren, and great-grandchildren never taste war, and all the peoples live in peace and have good relations with each other."

This is the key to understanding Brezhnev's selfless dedication to the cause of peace. Nobody can defend peace better than those who have been scarred by the flames of war.

CHAPTER III

Tackling the Tremendous
Job of Building
a New Society

I. HOME TO THE DNIEPER VALLEY

The Dnieper Valley with its vast green fields and thriving industrial cities—a land Brezhnev loved dearly—lay in ruins when he returned home after the war.

"What had been the blast furnaces of the Zaporozhstal plant, the aluminum and ferroalloy factories, the Lenin Hydropower Station on the Dnieper, the Communard plant, the engine works, and other plants and factories was now a scene of wreckage," Leonid Brezhnev recalls. "The damage caused to the economy and population of the region by the German invasion was estimated at almost nineteen billion rubles."

The Soviet people were returning to their jobs to handle the tasks of civilian construction, of building a society which would meet all of man's material and intellectual wants. Brezhnev wrote and spoke about this, and we know what was in his heart and mind when he, like all other Soviet men and women, surveyed the present and contemplated the future at the end of the war.

The experience of fighting in the front lines strengthened Brezhnev's character and gave him qualities few contemporary statesmen have attained. He was already a skillful organizer with a profound knowledge of psychology. His war experience gave him still greater insight into the thoughts and aspirations of his people, with whom he had shared the bitterness of retreat and the joy of victory.

Pain gripped his heart when he discovered that many of the men he had worked with to transform this region into a flourishing industrial land would never come back and work with him again. Hundreds he had known personally were buried far away from their native places. The finest sons and daughters had laid down their lives to defend their homes, the people they loved, and their country. These were heroes, and Brezhnev thought of them as he looked at the chaos before him, and, as he told his contemporaries, he vowed to dedicate his life to preventing war from ever occurring again.

"The losses and devastation this war caused are beyond comparison," Brezhnev said. "The grief it brought people still pains the hearts of mothers, widows, and orphans." The war had invaded every family, taken from almost each a son, a father, or a brother. Brezhnev had spoken with many of the kin of the dead and had brought them whatever solace was possible since he knew all too well the infinite woe of the survivors at the loss of their loved ones. "There is no heavier loss for a person than the death of his near ones, his comrades and friends. There is no sight more depressing than that of destroyed fruits of his labor, into which he had put his energy, his talent, and devotion to his native land."

These were some of the feelings he voiced as he strode through the ruins of Dnepropetrovsk and Zaporozhye. As he said later, "There is no smell more acrid than that of homes burned to ashes. Disfigured by fire and metal, lying in ruins, was my native land, now liberated from the nazi barbarians." He examined the grim statistics of how many Soviet men and women had died in this area and the numbers of those shipped to concentration and slave labor camps in Germany.

Brezhnev walked through the wreckage of Zaporozhye, which had once been a major industrial center and was now a scene of mounds of twisted metal and rubble. The Zaporozhstal plant, pride of prewar Soviet heavy industry, lay in ruins before him like a toppled giant. Blast and open-hearth furnaces and all the machinery were destroyed completely. One forlorn building stood intact on the ground pockmarked by shells: the pumping station. The magnificent hydropower station built by heroic efforts during the First Five-Year Plan, which had proudly towered over the Dnieper, was one vast ruin. The total damage inflicted to the economy of the Zaporozhye and Dnepropetrovsk regions was estimated at 48.7 billion rubles. The scene was the same wherever the flames of war had scorched the land.

No nation in history had to pay so high a price for victory. In the war 20 million sons and daughters of the Soviet people had lost their lives. The invaders had destroyed 1,710 large and small towns and burned down more than 70,000 villages. Tens of millions had been made homeless. In their flight the vindictive nazis had wrecked nearly 32,000 factories and plants, totally or partly, and had ripped up 40,000 miles of railroad tracks.

The countryside suffered equally; 98,000 collective farms and about 5,000 state farms and machine-and-tractor stations lay in ruins. Great quantities of machinery had been shipped to the Third Reich, as had mountains of raw materials and foodstuffs. Cultural monuments had been wantonly destroyed in an effort to rob the Soviet people of their national history and reduce them to slavery.

"No statistics can give a true picture of the real scale of the losses the Soviet people suffered in the war years," Brezhnev said. "How can one count up and express in figures the great work, the wealth of thoughts and talent that many generations of our people had invested in creating the enormous material and cultural values destroyed by the nazis?" Never in human history had a state sustained such devastation.

On August 30, 1946, the Communists of Zaporozhye, on a recommendation of the Central Committee of the Communist Party of the Soviet Union, elected Leonid Brezhnev first secretary of the Zaporozhye Regional Party Committee. A year later, in November 1947, he was elected first secretary of the Dnepropetrovsk Regional Party Committee.

The tasks facing the Soviet Union were truly formidable. It was necessary to rehabilitate the economy and regear it to civilian work within an incredibly short period.

Nothing could be put off until some later time; everything had to be done immediately. Rehabilitation work had to be carried out without requisite building materials, the land plowed up when tractors were unavailable, children taught in half-ruined schools, and sick people treated in looted hospitals.

Formidable Problems of Economic Recovery

The tasks that arose before Brezhnev on a regional scale demanded immediate solution. He changed into civilian clothes on the third day after demobilization and joined in the peaceful battle for metal and bread.

The Supreme Soviet of the USSR outlined the central economic and political task of the country for the five years ahead as follows: "To rehabilitate the war-ravaged areas of the country, to bring up industry and agriculture to their prewar levels, and then to surpass them considerably."

The Fourth Five-Year Plan adopted in 1946 envisaged the rebuilding of the Zaporozhstal plant, work on which had been started back in 1944, as soon as the nazi forces had been expelled from the city. The reconstruction of the plant, however, had been slow.

Brezhnev was clearly aware of Zaporozhstal's immense importance for the national economy. The plant was the Soviet Union's sole producer of thin sheet steel, badly needed by the car, tractor, and consumer goods industries, as well as for housing construction. As secretary of the Regional Party Committee he clearly saw the difficulties that would have to be overcome. As a metallurgical engineer he knew that it would not be an easy technological job. However, he had complete faith in his people. The deeds of the dead inspired the living. Brezhnev went to the building site to discuss matters with the workers. He made them no unrealistic promises, but he left them confident that their needs would be met. His keen interest in everything the workers said led to a frank conversation in which the party leader formed a clear picture of the situation on the building site.

Meetings with workers were a high priority for Brezhnev. He visited them constantly on the huge building site, talking with groups and individual workers. He inquired about their housing conditions, about the quality of their food, about what they read, even about their children's grades at school.

As secretary of the Regional Party Committee he explained to them that the Communist Party and the government were doing everything possible to improve the condition of the people and that their living standard would be steadily raised as industry and agriculture developed.

Brezhnev consulted party executives and considered measures to improve the living conditions of the workers, engineers, and technicians. In Dnepropetrovsk he made a detailed study of the situation on the spot and stayed at the plant until he had formed a full picture of the progress of the rehabilitation work and the improvement in the housing and living conditions of the workers.

In Zaporozhye and Dnepropetrovsk Brezhnev gave close attention to the selection and placement of trained workers. He was thoroughly familiar with the staffs of the regional, city, and district party committees. He knew the secretaries of many primary organizations, as well as local government officials and economic executives. He was well aware of their professional and political qualifications and knew who could be entrusted with what kind of work.

Brezhnev carried out painstaking work among the secretaries of the primary party organizations on whom the process of economic rehabilitation largely depended. He often met with the secretaries of the party committees of Zaporozhstal. He took close to heart the large and small concerns of these enterprises, regularly addressed party meetings and meetings of economic executives, and gave them assistance in organizational work and mass political education.

Conferring with other leading executives of the region, he was never afraid to recommend demobilized servicemen, talented young men and women who had shown their mettle, for responsible jobs.

Speaking at a meeting at Zaporozhstal, he advised that a strike force should be set up to ensure plan fulfillment by the concentration of manpower and supplies to cope with priority tasks.

He set an example of how to go about one's work and direct construction efficiently. In a crucial period of construction he transferred his office and communications to the site and even stayed there overnight. The most characteristic

A view of Kamenskoye, the village where Leonid Brezhnev was born

The hillside part of Kamenskoye

Workers of the wire-making and repair shop. Brezhnev's father is second from left in the fourth row. The photograph dates from the end of the twenties

The Brezhnevs in 1930

This is where Leonid Brezhnev lived in Dneprodzerzhinsk

Graduates of the metallurgical institute in Dneprodzerzhinsk, 1935, with Brezhnev in front row

1935, L. I. Brezhnev playing chess with N. P. Dubynin

Chatting with men going into action, 1942

Admitting new members to the Communist Party during the fighting for Tuapse, 1942

With Soviet writer Alexander Korneichuk (extreme left) in the battle lines

Next to Brezhnev is his comrade-in-arms Avksenty Tikhostoop, during a break in the fighting in the Novorossiisk area, 1943

With machine gunners in the Novorossiisk area

With Captain Ivan Kravchuk in the Novorossiisk area, 1943

In the summer of 1943

Military Council of 18th Army, April 1945

At the Victory Parade in Moscow, June 24, 1945

At the Victory Parade in Moscow, June 24, 1945

Major General Brezhnev, 1945

Meeting fellow war veterans of the fighting for Novorossiisk, 1974

Brezhnev, first secretary of the Communist Party's Dnepropetrovsk Regional Committee, in his office, 1946

Addressing Zaporozhstal steelworkers in Zaporozhye, 1947

Inspecting the Zaporozhstal steel works, 1947

In the rolling mill, 1947

Inspecting a construction site

Brezhnev, First Secretary of the Communist Party of Kazakhstan Central Committee, 1956

Inspecting the dam of the Lenin Hydropower Station on the Volga, 1958

At this meeting the Zaporozhye region receives the Order of Lenin, Zaporozhye, 1958

Brezhnev, Chairman of the Presidium of the Supreme Soviet of the USSR, in his Kremlin office, 1962

A meeting of the Presidium of the Supreme Soviet of the USSR, 1963

With Yuri Gagarin, the first space traveler in history, 1961

trait of the man was the effort to gear everything to the common goal. His example was followed by regional and city party committee workers who assumed leadership of the primary organizations on the building site.

Brezhnev's working day would start on the construction site; then it would continue at the regional, city, and district party committees, on other building sites, and on collective farms. Late at night he would return to the Zaporozhstal plant to review what had been done during the day and make plans for the next day. There he received local party, government, and economic executives who had urgent business.

Calm and Confidence

Brezhnev's office at the Zaporozhstal plant became the headquarters of the construction project. His move directly to the site had created a good working atmosphere devoid of tensions despite difficult times.

"The first secretary of the Regional Party Committee created an atmosphere of exceptional, genuinely Communist goodwill around the Zaporozhstal project and its personnel. It was noted that whenever the difficulties were greatest, whenever we were plagued by setback, whenever nerves were especially tense, the voice of the first secretary would be calmest and most confident," Veniamin Dymshyts, manager of the Zaporozhstroi building organization, recalled.

Brezhnev was invariably in the vanguard. On his initiative the first-ever single schedule for an entire project was drawn up at the Zaporozhstal plant. It coordinated the work of nearly forty technical groups and hundreds of sections and work teams—in short, the project's entire personnel. He felt that such a schedule would provide a picture of the situation in every section, making it possible to control the work, to pull up lagging sections, and to encourage those who worked

97

best. "The schedule," he said, "is a pivot, an instrument for creating a climate of all-out effort."

Brezhnev personally checked on compliance with the schedule. Whenever the slightest delay occurred, he hastened to help the men at the head of the construction project and the plant. One hundred and twenty factories run by different ministries and located in ten different cities supplied equipment and materials. Machine tools came from Moscow, metal structures from Dnepropetrovsk, rails from Kuznetsk, industrial equipment from Kramatorsk, lumber from Byelorussia, railroad ties from Archangel, electric motors from Yaroslavl, bitumen from Transcaucasia, pumps from Melitopol, cable from Leningrad, trucks from Gorky. . . . If one enterprise delayed supplies, the entire schedule would fall behind. Brezhnev would immediately get in touch with the concerned ministers, Regional Party Committee secretaries, and plant managers to plead, explain, persuade. . . . He came to be widely known as the man who got things done. It was hard to say no to him.

The difficulties of reconstruction were compounded by the fact that the work force was far less skilled than that of prewar times. Many skilled workers and engineers had been killed. The war-ravaged enterprises had to be raised from ruins by unskilled workers, by women, by teenagers. Training the personnel required time and additional outlays. But funds were found. Innumerable schools and courses were opened in the region to enable ex-servicemen, young people, and women to acquire industrial skills. The training was done on the job. The schedule was met, but only by the most strenuous efforts.

In response to an appeal from the Regional Party Committee, village Communists, Komsomols, and collective farmers joined the work force at the Zaporozhstal, Dneprostroi, Communard, and other projects. All had to be accommodated and fed; there were more than enough problems.

Zaporozhstal was the number one project. This giant of the country's southern steel industry, like other enterprises, could not operate without electricity. Therefore, rebuilding the Lenin Hydropower Station on the Dnieper was a high-priority task. Its commissioning, however, was delayed. Here, too, there was a shortage of workers, engineers, and technicians, housing, and equipment. Nor were these the only headaches for the secretary of the Regional Party Committee. Brezhnev kept close watch on the quality of the reconstruction work and stressed again and again that this first among the Soviet hydropower giants had to remain one of the most impressive monumental works of architecture in the country.

He found the time to contribute regularly to the newspapers *Bolshevik Zaporozhya, Dneprovskaya Pravda, Zarya,* and *Chervone Zaporozhya* to inform the public about the situation in the country, in the republic, and in the region. In his articles "Rebuild Zaporozhstal Quickly," "Three Years of Creative Work to Revive Zaporozhye Region," "Dnepropetrovsk Region on the Eve of the Soviet Ukraine's 30th Anniversary," "We Must Not Rest on Our Laurels," and others, the first secretary of the Regional Party Committee analyzed achievements, laid bare shortcomings, pointed out ways of overcoming them, and formulated the tasks for the future.

Life Triumphs

The work carried out by the Zaporozhye and Dnepropetrovsk Regional Party Committees under Brezhnev's leadership began to bear fruit. The war-ravaged factories and plants were placed in operation one after another. In the period 1948–49 a number of enterprises actually produced more than in the prewar year 1940. Many people living in ruined houses moved into new homes. The collective farmers received thousands of tractors, hundreds of harvester combines, seeders, and trucks. The fraternal Soviet republics supplied them with thousands of head of cattle and horses.

Factory after factory was resuming production. The resurrection of each was a thrilling event. More than 10,000 people gathered one day in July 1947 in front of blast furnace No. 3.

The secretary of the Regional Committee remembered all the stages of its reconstruction.

He had personally checked how the experts from the Teplostroi building organization handled the masonry work, and he remembered their complaints about the poor quality of the refractories.

He looked about him at the happy faces of the people who had come to see the results of their effort. There—the furnace was breathing and rumbling! Its rumble was drowned by the cheers of men and women congratulating one another, hugging, kissing, and weeping for joy. He, too, shared their happiness. He, too, had put all his heart into this work.

A few months earlier the country had welcomed the heroes of the Lenin Hydropower Station when its first generator unit began producing commercial power. This was good news for everyone in the country. Once again there had risen the "Sun of the Ukraine," as the power giant on the Dnieper used to be called. The project was dear to everyone not only because of its economic importance and superb technical design but also because of the memories it evoked—memories of enthusiastic and self-sacrificing work in the thirties. The power project was memorable not just for the Soviet people. American experts had also been employed on the project. They appreciated its epic significance. In fact, six of them had been decorated with Soviet orders. Hugh Cooper, who had headed a group of consultants, had spoken at a meeting in 1932 to mark the commissioning of the power plant. He had said that the Dnieper project looked boldly at the whole world as if demonstrating its readiness to do its part in industrializing the country. He had said it was the answer to all who had earlier questioned the Soviet government's wisdom in undertaking a gigantic project without precedent in the world.

Meetings to celebrate the triumphs of labor were being held at one construction project after another. Enterprises in Dnepropetrovsk and Krivoi Rog, Dneprodzerzhinsk and Melitopol, Nikopol and Marganets reported that they were back in production. Reports of the rebirth of war-ravaged enterprises mingled with reports of the construction of new factories and ore mines, power plants, railroads, and highways.

For the successful restoration of the Zaporozhstal plant almost 2,000 building workers, assemblymen, steel smelters, and those who helped them were decorated with government orders and medals. Leonid Brezhnev was decorated with the Order of Lenin.

But industry is not the only bounty enjoyed by the Dnepropetrovsk region. It has vast and fertile collective farm fields. But to make them really fruitful, one had to put his soul in the land and skillfully organize the work force.

The land along the Dnieper is one of the country's granaries. It contributes significantly to the harvest of the Soviet Union as a whole. To restore its agriculture as quickly as possible, the government supplied seed and machinery on a very substantial scale by the standards of that time.

To find ways of helping the region restore its former agricultural reputation, the secretary of the Regional Party Committee stepped up his extensive tours of districts and collective farms, consulting agronomists, farm chairmen, and rank-and-file farmers. He asked a multitude of questions, inquired into details, studied the situation. His questions reflected his profound concern, and his advice showed his profound knowledge.

He devoted much attention to the repair of farm machinery and to supplying fuel, fertilizers, and seeds to the collective farms.

The Dnepropetrovsk region overcame the difficult situation.

In 1948 and 1949 it was among the first to fulfill the plan for the delivery of grain and other farm produce to the state. In 1948 the grain harvest on the collective farms averaged more than 24 bushels per acre. Animal husbandry also did well.

To visualize the scale, complexity, and acuteness of the problems faced by agriculture, it must be recalled that following the ravages of war and the dire effects of drought, the country was unable to end food rationing until 1947. With the termination of rationing it was necessary not merely to provide essentials to the population but also to lay a firm foundation for a future state of plenty.

An important feature of the Dnepropetrovsk region was the broad spectrum of its farm production. Wheat was undoubtedly the main crop. Animal husbandry, orchards, vineyards, and fishing were other important food sources.

All of them required close scrutiny. One must remember that far from all types of farm work were mechanized in those days. Power transmission lines had not yet been extended to all villages. At a meeting with collective-farm chairmen in May 1950, Brezhnev spoke of the many tasks facing the countryside. He urged the farmers, thinking of today's grain, to look ahead to the bountiful harvests of the future. At that meeting his audience was led to conclude that management required knowledge, skill, and a constant striving to accomplish still more.

In 1950 the region, together with the entire country, completed the Fourth Five-Year Plan ahead of schedule. The prewar industrial level had been surpassed, and grain harvests were bigger than in the best prewar years. The network of educational institutions, hospitals, health and holiday homes, and nursery schools and day-care centers had been rebuilt and enlarged. It was a miracle of reconstruction. Many people in the West were astounded. They did not believe it could be done without extensive foreign aid. Once again they underestimated the limitless potentialities, capabilities, and enthusiasm of the builders of socialism. The boastful forecast of the nazi General Joachim Stulpnagel, who was guilty of the immense damage caused to the Dnieper area and who had written in a wartime report to Berlin, "It would take Russia 25 years to restore what we have destroyed," did not come true.

The Ukrainians highly appreciated Brezhnev's great contribution to the restoration of the national economy and his outstanding abilities as an organizer. In January 1949 a congress of the Communist Party of the Ukraine elected Brezhnev to its Central Committee. This further extended the range of his duties and enhanced his responsibility to the party and people.

In January 1950 at a general meeting of workers of the Petrovsky steel plant in Dnepropetrovsk, Brezhnev was nominated for election to the Supreme Soviet of the USSR. This nomination was supported by workers of other factories of the region. Brezhnev was elected to the Soviet parliament.

In July 1950 he took leave of the Dnepropetrovsk region—there was new work waiting for him, this time in Moldavia. All his preceding activities had prepared him for leadership of a republic. Naturally, he felt attached to the Ukraine, where he had been born, had grown up, had been educated, and had passed through the school of life. "I worked in the Ukraine for many years," Brezhnev recalled later. "I fought on its soil in the war, and like many other Russian people, I am familiar with the Ukrainian people's fine qualities and have a sincere affection for them." His work in the Ukraine had broadened his horizons and outlook on life. It was there that he developed the qualities of an outstanding statesman.

2 . IN MOLDAVIA

It is hot in Moldavia in the summertime, and the air is redolent with the fragrance of grass and flowers. The landscape is a bright canvas of orchards, fields, and meadows; the voices of people, the songs of birds, and the hum of machines ring loud and clear. Summer was in full riot when Brezhnev came to Moldavia. On June 15, 1950, Soviet newspapers ran a report on a plenary meeting of the Central Committee of the Moldavian Communist Party, which elected Leonid Brezhnev to the post of First Secretary of the Central Committee.

In photographs of those years we see a sturdy, stocky man with a youthful (he was forty-three at the time), energetic, smiling face, crowned by a shock of curly hair. His comrades and fellow workers said that his great optimism and joy of life made a deep impression on all.

The Moldavian Soviet Socialist Republic of the early fifties confronted Leonid Brezhnev with a tangle of social, political, and economic problems.

Situated in the southwesternmost part of the Soviet Union, this region with a small area and a high population density, which had proclaimed Soviet power after the October Revolution, had been divided from 1918 to 1940 against the will of its people. The Dniester River had separated one part of Moldavia from the other. The region on the left bank of the Dniester had been Soviet, while the region on the right bank had been occupied by the fascist Rumanian gentry.

In 1940 the people's aspirations and historical justice triumphed. The two parts of Moldavia were reunited within the framework of the Moldavian Soviet Socialist Republic. Then came the year 1941, bringing with it the dark night of the fascist occupation, not as lengthy as in previous years but equally bitter and humiliating.

When units of the 5th Strike Force under General Nikolai Berzarin (who became the first commandant of Berlin in 1945) liberated Kishinev, the Moldavian capital, in the last days of August 1944, they encountered devastation that staggered even hardened soldiers. The center of the city was a solid mass of ruins; it looked more like a lifeless lunar landscape than a city. As they were driven out by Soviet forces, the invaders took away with them everything they could carry. Before retreating, they had looted Kishinev so wantonly that they had even ripped out window frames and unscrewed door handles. Not a single factory in Moldavia had escaped destruction.

As the saying goes, misfortunes never come alone. In addition to the destruction wrought by the invaders and the grief of the widows and orphans, crop failures struck. Drought devoured the farm fields and meadows of Moldavia for two years in a row in 1945 and 1946.

Characteristically, in that period the Moldavian economy, industry first and foremost, was not merely restored but actually built from scratch.

Before the war nearly 70 percent of Moldavia's population was completely illiterate. There were whole villages without a single literate inhabitant. The newspaper *Sovetskaya Moldavia* wrote on October 15, 1950, that since the end of the war about half a million people had been taught to read and write. Nevertheless, there were still about 40,000 illiterates and 100,000 semiliterates in Moldavia. Thick scholarly monographs devoted to that period and eyewitness accounts testify that the early fifties were an important turning point in Moldavia's history.

What the republic needed was leadership which could infuse the people with energy and buoyancy, give them confidence in their powers, and lay the groundwork for Moldavia's rapid advance on a new socialist basis.

Any passerby on Sadovaya Street in Kishinev will show you a one-story building separated from the roadway by a lawn. Leonid Brezhnev and his family moved into this house in 1950 and lived there for two years.

The Central Committee of the Moldavian Communist Party had its headquarters at 115 Kiev Street in a two-story building faced with white and red brick. In January 1918, when Soviet power was first established in Moldavia, the Executive Committee of the Soviets of the Rumanian Front, the Black Sea Fleet, and the Odessa Region had its offices in this building.

The office of the First Secretary was on the second floor in the left wing of the building. This was the headquarters and brain center of Moldavia. The strings of the management of industry, agriculture, and culture converged in it.

Every morning, punctually at eight, the First Secretary walked briskly to the entrance. Leonty Sheetov, a member of the Central Committee staff in those years, recalls:

"On the way to his office Leonid Brezhnev would step into nearly every room to say hello, tell a joke, inquire about people's health and mood and the latest news.

"All this took ten to fifteen minutes—Brezhnev treasured time and taught us to value it, too. Yet in those few minutes he set a vibrant tone for the entire Central Committee staff. Not only did he infuse us with fresh energy, but he knew how to draw energy for himself from the people around him. . . . This quality is a distinguishing feature of a born leader, a man who is always among the people and not on top of them, who lives together with them, for them, and thanks to them.

"When Brezhnev returned from trips to Moscow, he would gather the entire Central Committee staff and tell them what had transpired and how affairs were progressing in various regions and republics of the Soviet Union.

"He emphasized our place in the Soviet family of nations and pointed out our prospects. We were impressed by his ability to link minor and major problems into a single whole, to link the city and the country, the destiny of an individual and the destiny of the nation."

There is an old aphorism that you can judge a man by his style of work. Brezhnev's style of work reflects his essence, his nature as a man and a leader.

Lukeria Repida, now a Doctor of Science and a prominent scholar of Moldavia, who was a minister of the republic in the fifties, recalls the years of work together with Brezhnev.

"We already saw that he was a born leader, astute and broad-visioned," she says. "Even in the most difficult circumstances he was able to keep the situation under control and to carry people along with him not only by his tireless energy but also by presenting the problem in a new way. He was a very highly organized person, with a daily program worked out to the minute. A man of extensive practical experience, he posed and solved problems on a solid theoretical foundation. He worked a great deal, day and night, and he always worked methodically."

Everybody who worked with Brezhnev in Moldavia noted the constant attention he paid to people. In the photographs of the fifties on display in the Museum of History of the Moldavian Communist Party, Brezhnev is always seen with a group of people, never by himself.

In a photograph taken in a farm field together with collective farmers of the Tarakliya district in the summer of 1950 he stands beside a harrow, listening attentively to the farmers. In another picture, taken at an agricultural exhibition in Kamenka in 1951, he stands beside Hero of Socialist Labor Maria Kardonskaya. Neither in dress nor in manner does Brezhnev stand out among the others. But even if you have never seen him, your attention is instantly drawn to him because he is in the center of a group of people listening and looking at him.

In a recently published book entitled *Reminiscences of Communists,* Faina Medeokritskaya, a former secretary of the Kishinev City Party Committee, writes: "As a Communist I should like to tell about the impression people here formed of Brezhnev while he worked in our republic. First of all, we remember him as a splendid orator who could inspire his audience. We listened with rapt attention, although sometimes he spoke for as long as three hours.

"Brezhnev's reports and speeches were politically sharp, backed up with instances from life, and illustrated with passages from works of fiction. He always set himself very high standards when preparing for a speech and demanded that all party functionaries do the same."

His exactingness combined with his concern for people. Medeokritskaya recalls further: "He is a very understanding and considerate person. I remember the following episode. When he learned that Lidia Teplyakova, the managing director of the Styaua Roshie knit-goods mill, had fallen ill, he rang her up in the hospital, spoke encouraging words to her, and then contacted the doctors and told them to do everything they could for her. Unfortunately, at the City Party Committee we learned about Teplyakova's illness only later. When we visited her, she told us about Brezhnev's call. We could see that it had given her morale a great boost and multiplied her strength to fight a grave illness. . . ."

On his arrival in Moldavia in 1950 Brezhnev quickly ac-

quainted himself with the situation and the people, discerned
the needs of the times, and acted capably in conformity with
the tasks required by the social and economic development
of Moldavia and the country as a whole.

Timofei Troyan, curator of the Museum of History of the
Moldavian Communist Party, recalls:

"Brezhnev was remarkable for his inexhaustible and dynamic energy and efficiency. He would summon an official to
his office, have a long talk with him, and compare opinions
(but never try to overawe the latter with his authority). Then
he and the visitor would climb into a car and drive to a project, to a near or distant district, for two or three days, sometimes for a week.

"He was democratic and very accessible both to colleagues and to the public, to workers and peasants. Sometimes, after a long and intensive conference, he would say,
'Now let's knock it off and take a stroll around town.' "

Troyan also speaks about the master plan for the reconstruction of Kishinev and other Moldavian cities, which
was drafted with Brezhnev's active participation.

On Brezhnev's initiative the Central Recreation Park was
laid out, and Lake Komsomolskoye was dug. Work on this
project began in 1951 in a marshy waste full of crags. Local
people, especially Komsomols, took an active part in the
work.

In October 1950, soon after Brezhnev was elected to the
leading post in the Moldavian Communist Party, the sixth
plenary meeting of its Central Committee was held. At the
meeting Brezhnev put forward proposals for further measures to strengthen the republic's collective farms politically,
organizationally, and economically.

An interesting table in one of the displays in the Museum
of History of the Moldavian Communist Party contains the
following figures:

	1949	1950	1951
Number of collective farms	925	1,770	1,355
Number of collective farmers	375,000	917,000	3,388,000

It is clear from the table that in the course of a single year, from 1950 to 1951, the number of collective farms decreased because of amalgamation, while the number of members more than trebled. The Moldavian countryside took a big stride along the road of socialist reorganization.

When Brezhnev took over the direction of the republic's economy, he set Moldavia's working people the task of advancing the standards of crop farming, so that high yields could be stable and independent of weather conditions.

The Soviet government handed over the former landlords' estates, orchards, vineyards, and more than 20,000 head of livestock to Moldavian peasants. A total of 130,000 poor farmsteads were exempted from taxes. Industry developed at a fast pace in the republic, and unemployment was completely eradicated.

In a characteristic gesture of the socialist system, the fraternal peoples of other socialist republics gave a helping hand to industrially backward Moldavia. This is the way of life in the Soviet Union; each republic helps the other whenever help is needed. Moscow and Leningrad, the Ukraine and the Urals, the Caucasus and Siberia all helped.

Machine tools and machinery, locomotives and trucks, tractors and harvester combines, metal and coal, oil and other goods necessary to restore and develop industry and transportation, farming and cultural life arrived in Moldavia in an endless stream.

The enormous assistance from the Soviet government and the Central Committee of the Communist Party of the Soviet Union enabled Moldavia not only to reconstruct the enterprises that had been destroyed and looted but also to build many new factories and plants equipped with up-to-date machinery. More than 40,000 acres of new orchards and vine-yards were laid out after the war.

In the Central Committee's Report to the 3rd Congress of the Communist Party of Moldavia, in March 1951, Brezhnev described how the republic's towns and villages were changing beyond recognition: "In the Chadyr-Lunga district, for example, before 1940 there was one secondary and eight primary schools, which were staffed with 20 teachers and had 300 pupils. Illiteracy among the population was as high as 85 percent. Now there are seventeen schools with 275 teachers in the Chadyr-Lunga district. The schools have 5,000 pupils. Illiteracy has been wiped out. There are fifteen village clubs, a district House of Culture, a Young Pioneers' House, a cinema theater, and fifty-four libraries. Three radio rebroadcasting studios operate in the district."

Moldavia, predominantly rural then, made remarkable progress agriculturally. Brezhnev reported that 94 percent of the peasant households in the republic had formed collective farms. The young collective farms of Moldavia provided a striking illustration of the revolutionizing role of machinery. Machine-and-tractor stations with a fleet of thousands of tractors, harvester combines, and other farm machines were set up in the republic. Mechanization increased the productivity of the collective farms and raised the standards of farming and crop yields. In the first five-year period following the war, the yield of grain crops in the republic increased 150 percent.

The fulfillment of the three-year state plan for advancing livestock breeding increased the collective-farm herds of cattle sevenfold, the flocks of sheep and goats fivefold, and the number of hogs 730 percent. Whereas in 1949 the farmers had been paid 110 million rubles in cash and kind for their work on the collective farms, in 1951 their earnings reached 567 million rubles.

The achievements of agriculture in the republic vividly

demonstrated the vitality of the collective-farm system and the advantages of large-scale socialist agriculture, which made the use of machinery and intensive diversified farming possible.

Industry also developed rapidly in the republic. In 1951 industrial production rose by 41 percent over the previous year. The major part in this increase came from the food industry, which boosted production by nearly 50 percent.

Work was in progress on the construction of the Dubossary Hydropower Station, a silk complex, new sugar refineries, canneries, and wine distilleries. The foundation was being laid for mechanical engineering, electrical engineering, and instrument making—industries new to the republic.

Rapid progress was in evidence in the field of education, too. By October 1952 forty-six higher and secondary specialized educational institutions were functioning in the republic. They had a student body of 17,500. A state university and twenty-six research institutes were opened, and fifty-six newspapers and magazines were published.

The Moldavian people had been denied the benefits of culture for centuries. Under the Soviet system they displayed a tremendous thirst for enlightenment, learning, and science. They were able to share in the cultural achievements of the peoples of the other Soviet republics.

The year 1952, the last year of Brezhnev's work in Moldavia, was just as busy as the two previous years. On Brezhnev's initiative the republic submitted to the Council of Ministers of the Soviet Union thoroughly substantiated proposals for the continued development of Moldavia's agriculture and food industry. The Soviet government made decisions which outlined further measures to promote agriculture and the food industry in the Moldavian republic. In March Brezhnev delivered a report at a meeting of leading party functionaries of the republic on how these decisions could be carried into effect and what measures should be taken to advance the economy to a still higher level in Moldavia. Observing that the food industry was accounting for 70 percent of the republic's gross industrial output and had made important progress, he pointed out at the same time that local primary material resources were still largely unused.

Although Brezhnev did not work in Moldavia long, he accomplished much of importance. Not only had he laid the basis for a breakthrough in Moldavia's development, but he had also outlined the main directions of its future progress.

Today Moldavia exports tractors, foundry machines, deepwater pumps, and electrical precision instruments to more than sixty countries; with an area amounting to only 0.2 percent of the total area of the Soviet Union, Moldavia accounts for more than 2 percent of the country's gross farm output, including more than 10 percent of the fruit, 26 percent of the grapes, and 42 percent of the tobacco. The sources and roots of this economic prosperity go back to the early fifties, when Brezhnev worked hand in hand with the people of Moldavia.

He has never forgotten Moldavia and revisits it from time to time. During the celebration of the republic's 50th anniversary in October 1974 he was the one who pinned the Order of the October Revolution on Moldavia's flag.

The republic gave an enthusiastic welcome to this man, under whose leadership, a quarter of a century before, it had laid the foundation of today's and tomorrow's successes.

Speaking in October 1974 at a meeting to commemorate the 50th anniversary of the Moldavian Soviet Socialist Republic and the founding of the Communist Party of Moldavia in Kishinev, Brezhnev recalled those times:

"It seems just recently that we met in the conference hall of the Central Committee of the Communist Party of Moldavia, nearby on Kiev Street, to discuss the organizational, political, and economic consolidation of the young collective and state farms. We selected Communists who moved to the villages to remake life in them along socialist lines. That was a difficult, strenuous time. However, one cannot but speak well of it since it was then that the foundations of the present successes were laid.''

Brezhnev's businesslike grasp of matters and his talents as an organizer were widely recognized in party circles. On September 23, 1952, the Communists of Moldavia delegated him to attend the 19th Congress of the Communist Party of the Soviet Union. At the Congress in October he was elected to the Central Committee of the Communist Party of the Soviet Union and a plenary meeting of the Central Committee elected him an alternate member of the Presidium and Secretary of the Central Committee of the Communist Party of the Soviet Union.

3 · IN THE VIRGIN LAND AREAS

In 1953, 31,100,000 tons of grain were procured in the Soviet Union, while the amount consumed for food and the country's other requirements was 32,400,000 tons. The shortage of grain was offset from the state reserves. Effective steps were therefore needed to help provide the country with more grain in a brief time.

In the spring of 1954 the Central Committee of the Communist Party of the Soviet Union adopted the decision ''On Further Increases in Grain Production in the Country and on Developing Virgin and Long-Fallow Lands.'' Millions of acres of fertile land were to be brought under the plow beyond the Urals and farther east, in the Asian part of the Soviet Union, mainly in the Kazakh Soviet Socialist Republic. The land was to be used to raise wheat and other crops.

Brezhnev was assigned by the Central Committee of the Communist Party of the Soviet Union to assume the political leadership of this enormous project outlined by the party and to organize the development of virgin lands in Kazakhstan. The Communists of Kazakhstan elected him Second Secretary of the Central Committee of the Communist Party of Kazakhstan in February 1954 and First Secretary in August 1955.

The republic was faced with the tremendous task of plowing 15 million acres of land in two years—that is, nearly half of all the unused lands in the Soviet Union that were to be made fertile. This was a formidable task not only because of its magnitude but also because of the record time in which it was to be carried out, unusual even in the Soviet Union, which has more than once astounded the world by its spectacular accomplishments.

This project was without precedent in the history of agriculture. The Communist Party and the government allocated large financial resources for it. The republic was provided with enormous quantities of machinery—tractors, harvester combines, seeders, trucks, and farming implements. But machinery alone was not enough. Manpower was also needed.

In response to an appeal from the party and government scores of thousands of enthusiasts volunteered to join in the work. Thousands of farm-machine operatives and other skilled workers—members of the Komsomol and young people from all over the country, including its remotest parts —came to the virgin land areas. Nearly 1 million volunteers arrived there in the early years of the project.

Within two years the machine-and-tractor stations and the state farms received more than 122,000 tractors, 26,000 harvester combines, more than 22,000 trucks, and large quantities of other machinery and equipment.

Experienced leadership and organizing talent were needed to cope with the project. It was necessary to set up scores of new state farms (90 were established in 1954 and about 250 in 1955)—that is, to build new villages and settlements in the areas to be reclaimed. The scale of the work increased month after month.

In 1955 the budget of the Kazakh Republic was almost double that of the year before. The problems that arose concerned not only the organization of work and the timely acceptance and transfer of the large number of machines from one area to another but also the provision of accommodations and food for thousands of people and the satisfying of their household and cultural needs.

Work teams to be employed on the project were made up of new arrivals from different parts of the country, from different republics. In most cases they were strangers to each other. They had to live and work under quite difficult conditions. In view of this, the Central Committee of the Communist Party of Kazakhstan had to take urgent steps to enable the newly formed teams to work with maximum efficiency.

Brezhnev was in the lead of this drive. People who worked on the gigantic development project warmly recall their meetings with him. Here is an account of the battle for grain by one of them, Fyodor Morgun, now the first secretary of the Poltava Regional Party Committee:

"In 1954–55 we often saw a single-engine AN-2 plane in the air, and we knew that it carried Brezhnev, Secretary of the Central Committee of the Communist Party of Kazakhstan. He toured many of the farms and knew most of their managers quite well. His visits helped us a great deal. After seeing the situation and the difficulties of the settlers with his own eyes, he was able to make the necessary decisions and thereby help all the new farms, even those he was unable to visit, because in most cases they had common problems."

Spirit of Confidence

Brezhnev still recalls those difficult but exciting days:

"There were jubilant crowds welcoming new arrivals, and new songs, born of the throbbing pace of life. There was the romance of performing exploits and a genuine spirit of adventure inherent in pioneering work.

"There was the splendid feeling of confidence that arises when difficulties are overcome and made to retreat. Many such difficulties had to be dealt with. Within a few months it was necessary to receive several hundred thousand settlers, provide them with accommodations, satisfy their everyday needs, begin the construction of state farms, grain elevators, roads, and bridges.

"Many things went wrong at first, hitches and misunderstandings would arise, and mistakes, too, were made. People were arriving in uninhabited areas; they were unfamiliar with local conditions and the specific climate and sometimes knew little about farming in general. However, they were inspired by an idea of great national importance and by the wish to get to grips with nature and to remake it."

Brezhnev would search for an answer to the many problems posed by the project. He called upon the experience of old-timers. He demanded that the republic's ministers, party executives, and economic managers concern themselves more with the specific problems and needs of the new settlers and take a day-to-day interest in the work of the state and collective farms.

"I recall this episode from my latest tour of the regions," Brezhnev told a conference of Communists of Kazakhstan. "We were flying from the Zhdanov state farm in the Bulayevo district. The secretary of the District Party Committee was on the plane with me. I told him that somewhere in the vicinity there was a state farm named after the Taman division. The secretary confirmed that this was indeed so; this recently organized state farm was about forty miles away. We found the farm, located a suitable place to land, and landed.

"The people were living in vans. The builders had pitched their tents nearby. The farm had just begun acquiring machinery and was given an assignment to sow 7,500 to 10,000 acres of land plowed up in spring and another 40,000 acres of land plowed up the previous year—50,000 acres in all. And this at a time when the farm was only just getting on its feet and was short of both manpower and machinery. They had actually sown only 7,500 acres by that time. You can imagine the quality of the work done—nearly all of it was unacceptable.

"I asked if anyone had visited them. They replied that the District Party Committee secretary had, three days before. Now this was a good secretary, a member of the Supreme Soviet of the republic. But evidently he still thought that helping a state farm was a matter of concern only to the Ministry of State Farms and noticed nothing and gave no help.

"The people on that state farm were feeling pretty low. There were no roads, bread and other foods were supplied to the local store irregularly, and other goods were also scarce, even though the wholesale supply depot, as I learned, was well stocked. The District Party Committee secretary realized he was at fault at once when he saw this. A bakery was brought to the farm overnight, as were food supplies and two truckloads of consumer goods. In short, everything went well."

From the first steps of his work in Kazakhstan Brezhnev sought ways of boosting the yields of wheat, sunflower, and other crops in the republic as a whole, and he encouraged livestock farming. He urged the farmers to study the experience of other republics. In his speeches he stressed the importance of friendship between the peoples of the Soviet Union which enabled them to benefit from their mutual assistance and fraternal support.

The results of such teamwork by people of different nationalities were strikingly evident in Kazakhstan, where agricultural experts from the Russian Federation, the Ukraine, Byelorussia, and other republics of the Soviet Union joined efforts in their work on the virgin land development project.

This project was a school of internationalist education, a school of intellectual and physical training, a school of vocational training in the true sense of the word. In a speech on the occasion of the 20th anniversary of the virgin and long-fallow lands project, Brezhnev said, "This project set many on the right course in life. Scores and hundreds of tractor drivers, harvester combine operatives, and builders have become managers of state farms, leading experts, party and government executives. When we say that the virgin land development project advanced people to a higher level, we mean not only their record of promotions. There is another kind of advancement just as significant and noble in terms of human achievement. I have in mind their intellectual advancement, the improvement of their skills, and their attainment of moral maturity."

Despite the difficulties, more land was plowed up than had been planned. In Kazakhstan 45 million acres of virgin land had been reclaimed by the end of 1955. As a result, the crop area in the republic reached 67,500,000 acres—that is, nearly three times the 1953 figure. In 1954 alone the republic supplied the country with 1,600,000 tons of grain above the year before.

This was reported by Brezhnev in January 1956 to the 8th Congress of the Communist Party of Kazakhstan and later to the 20th Congress of the Communist Party of the Soviet Union. Kazakhstan's success was an achievement of the whole country—it meant that the task of providing the country with adequate quantities of grain set by the party and government was being successfully accomplished.

History recorded a spectacular human achievement when the Soviet people won the victory in their battle to plow up the virgin lands. Hundreds of state farms, modern industrial enterprises, and research centers have sprung up on this formerly barren land.

Brezhnev contributed greatly to Kazakhstan's industrial development. In August 1955 he made a detailed report to a plenary meeting of the Central Committee of the republic's Communist Party which discussed the problems of improving the management of industry and advancing technology, as well as the application of scientific and technological achievements to production, specialization, and cooperation.

As a result, in the latter half of the fifties, Kazakhstan accounted for more than half the national output of copper, lead, and zinc. Electric power output increased several times, compared with what it had been in tsarist times. The industrial centers, such as Karaganda, Balkhash, Temir-Tau, Ust-Kamenogorsk, and others, developed rapidly.

Not only has a new large grain-growing area been developed in the east of the country, but the economy and the entire image of a vast region have been transformed.

"Kazakhstan today is one of the Soviet Union's main granaries and the biggest livestock-breeding area," Brezhnev stated with full justification in 1976. "Kazakhstan today has hundreds of up-to-date industrial plants, which are contributing greatly to the country's economic progress. Kazakhstan has thousands of scientists and cultural workers, whose art has earned the well-deserved recognition of all the Soviet people."

Great credit is due Brezhnev for the rapid advancement of this virgin land area, which a little more than two decades ago was mostly a land of endless expanses untouched by the human hand.

4. WORKING IN THE LEADING BODIES OF THE COUNTRY

At the 20th Party Congress in February 1956 Brezhnev was reelected to the Central Committee of the Communist Party of the Soviet Union. A plenary meeting of the Central Committee elected him an alternate member of the Presidium and a Secretary of the Central Committee. At the same time, beginning in 1958, he was Deputy Chairman of the Central Committee Bureau for the Russian Soviet Federative Socialist Republic. Since June 1957 he has been a member of the Presidium of the Central Committee, the highest party body in the periods between the plenary meetings of the Central Committee (later, in 1966, the Central Committee Presidium was renamed the Politburo of the Central Committee, as it was called when Lenin was alive).

Holding these posts, Brezhnev traveled all over the country, touring factories and collective farms. He remained the same Brezhnev: modest and straightforward, considerate and untiring. At a factory in Omsk, in distant Siberia, for example, he talked to shop managers and workers directly on the shop floor, inquiring into their living conditions.

Visiting a state stock-raising farm, he looked over its facilities and spoke to the specialists, the milkmaids, and the women who tended the calves, asking about their needs and wishes. At the Chapayev collective farm near Omsk he met the chairman and members of the farm board and visited the farm's library and club. He was most attentive to the opinion of the people concerning one or another decision of the party and in turn expounded the party's policies and furnished help on the spot. He was thoroughly acquainted with the life, thoughts, and aspirations of the workers, peasants, and the working intelligentsia.

The Central Committee entrusted Brezhnev to work on problems connected with the development of heavy industry and capital construction, the equipment of the armed forces with the latest weapons, and the promotion of space exploration. He directly supervised and controlled the preparations for the first manned flight in outer space. After the successful mission of the world's first cosmonaut, Yuri Gagarin, in the Vostok spaceship, Brezhnev was made a Hero of Socialist Labor for his outstanding contribution to the development of rocketry and for ensuring the success of the spaceflight performed by a Soviet citizen.

Referring to space exploration, Brezhnev emphasizes that it is not only paving the way for humanity's future gigantic achievements, whose fruits will be used by coming generations, but is also directly benefiting the whole world, the Soviet people, and the building of communism. He frequently repeats that the development of outer space should serve the cause of progress, peace, and the happiness of all the peoples of the world and not become a means of destruction and war.

As before, he devoted a great deal of attention to the virgin land development project. "I clearly remember Comrade Brezhnev's visit to the Tolbukhin state farm in August 1957, when he was already a Secretary of the Central Committee of the Communist Party of the Soviet Union," recalled Fyodor Morgun, an old-timer of the virgin land development project. "It had rained heavily for a whole week, and there were puddles on the roads. The district authorities expected his plane to land at the district center and asked the state farm to send its two cars there. I myself settled down to wait at the farm office.

"At about nine in the morning I heard the drone of an approaching aircraft. I walked out on the porch and saw that it was coming in for a landing. It circled once and smoothly landed next to a cowshed we were building. It made a turn and taxied up almost to the office building.

"The door opened, and Leonid Brezhnev and the leaders of Kazakhstan stepped out of the plane.

"Almost all the state farm workers rushed to meet the guests, and right there by the side of the aircraft a lively conversation ensued about the affairs at the farm and our life. Brezhnev said that he would like to see the ripening grainfields.

" 'We'll have to wait for a while,' I said. 'Our cars are at the district center. They'll be back soon.'

" 'We can take this truck; the cars can join us later,' he replied, waving his hand in the direction of a machine-repair truck which had just driven up. The crew of this vehicle, consisting of a driver and mechanics, repaired farm machinery directly in the field. I urged Brezhnev, who began to walk toward it, and the other guests to wait for the cars because the truck was packed with tools and spare parts.

"Fortunately, just then several jeeps appeared from behind a bend in the road, their wheels throwing up fountains of mud. We climbed in and headed for the fields.

"The standing crops were straight and clean, but they were somewhat stunted, and the ears were not too heavy. That year we had a poor harvest. The drought hit our farm, too. We visited almost all the field teams and inspected most of the crop area.

"The grain where team number two worked was better than the rest. Looking over one of the fields, Brezhnev asked, 'Do you intend to employ swath harvesting or straight-combine harvesting here?'

" 'We haven't decided yet,' I replied. 'The crops are

shortish and not bushy at all and, therefore, stand far apart. The sheafs will be thin and may fall to the ground between the stubble. But we are also ready for swath harvesting.'

" 'Do whatever you think best. The main thing is to prevent losses,' Brezhnev replied.

"He returned to his car, and we drove on, stopping at two millet fields of the third team under Ivan Surkov. The millet was pretty good that year, and it was already being machine-harvested. The sheaves of millet lay in even rows. Brezhnev walked up to them, took a heavy ear, looked at it carefully, rubbed it between his fingers, and said, 'This crop deserves serious attention here in the virgin lands. Its cropping capacity is not lower than that of wheat. In this drought year the millet looks much better than the other grain crops. What yield do you expect on these fields?'

" 'From fifteen to twenty centners per hectare, while the wheat yield will hardly be eight.'

" 'You did the right thing by sowing millet, and you should sow more of it in the future,' said the Secretary of the Central Committee. 'Without millet we cannot solve the country's cereals problem.'

"Back on the central estate the guests looked over the houses that were being built and talked again with those who had moved into new homes. I invited the guests to my house for dinner. While we had been inspecting the fields, my wife, Alexandra, had made borshch and cutlets. The guests ate with appetite. After dinner Brezhnev took a few books from the shelf, thumbed through them, carefully looked over my modest library, and said a few words to his assistant Victor Golikov. After that he warmly bade goodbye to my wife and walked out. A few pigeons were fluttering about near the door.

" 'Whose birds are these?'

"I pointed to my nine-year-old son, Vladimir.

" 'I used to keep pigeons when I was a boy, too,' Brezhnev said with a smile. 'I also have a pigeon fancier—my son. But he's a bit older than yours. Whenever I get a new assignment and have to move to another place, we take the pigeons along. Our Moldavian pigeons have been in Alma-Ata, and now they are in Moscow.'

"As we drove back to the aircraft, Brezhnev recounted some amusing episodes connected with his son's pigeons. Stopping at the side of the aircraft, the guests wished all of us who had gathered to see them off every success in work and good health, said warm words of parting, and flew to Kokchetav.

"A couple of weeks later I received a large parcel of interesting new books from the dispatch office of the Central Committee of the Communist Party of the Soviet Union. It was a gift to our family from Leonid Brezhnev."

In the four years of his work as a Secretary of the Central Committee of the Communist Party of the Soviet Union Leonid Brezhnev became widely known throughout the country. His study was a headquarters where key problems connected with the development of the Soviet economy, including heavy industry and capital construction, were solved. His name was indissolubly linked with concrete accomplishments in the economy and with unprecedented achievements in space exploration. Many prominent foreign personalities and statesmen, with whom he had had personal meetings either when they visited the Soviet Union or during his trips abroad, came to know him well.

In the summer of 1959 Leonid Brezhnev and other Soviet leaders visited an American exhibition in Moscow which gave an idea of some aspects of life in the United States and its achievements.

In May 1960 the Supreme Soviet of the USSR elected Leonid Brezhnev Chairman of its Presidium, one of the most distinguished and responsible posts in the country.

The Supreme Soviet is the highest organ of state power.

Its Presidium is accountable to the Supreme Soviet for all its activities and performs a wide range of important state functions. Among other things, it issues ordinances, interprets the laws of the Soviet Union, revokes decisions and orders of the Council of Ministers of the Soviet Union and of the Councils of Ministers of the Union Republics when they do not conform to the law, exercises the right of pardon, appoints and removes the High Command of the Soviet armed forces. In the recesses of the Supreme Soviet of the USSR the Presidium has the authority to declare war or to order a general or partial mobilization. It ratifies international agreements signed by the Soviet Union, appoints and recalls Soviet ambassadors, receives letters of credence, and so forth.

Leonid Brezhnev held the post of Chairman of the Presidium of the Supreme Soviet for four years. In this period the Supreme Soviet examined and adopted legislation submitted by the government designed to improve the management of industry and construction, increase state pensions, abolish some taxes levied on the salaries of industrial and office workers, and complete the transfer of all industrial and office workers to a seven- and six-hour working day. It also passed other legislation in the interests of the Soviet working people, including a law on raising the wages of workers in public education, health, the housing and utility services, trade, public catering, and other branches of the service industry.

Holding the high post of Chairman of the Presidium of the Supreme Soviet of the USSR, Leonid Brezhnev carried on extensive work to enhance socialist democracy, ensure the rule of law, and perfect the state apparatus.

He always paid a great deal of attention to improving the work of the Soviets of Working People's Deputies, stressing that it was important for them to report regularly back to the electors, thus making their work more public, and to involve the masses of working people in the direct administration of public affairs, to criticize shortcomings and combat red tape.

The October 1964 plenary meeting of the Central Committee of the Communist Party of the Soviet Union relieved N. S. Khrushchev of his duties and elected L. I. Brezhnev as First Secretary of the Central Committee.

5. WITH THE PARTY AND AT ITS HEAD

Leonid Brezhnev's election to the post of First Secretary of the Central Committee of the Communist Party of the Soviet Union followed naturally from the very content of socialist democracy and the Soviet Union's political and social development, which create conditions for promoting from the midst of the people outstanding organizers with extensive and diverse experience in political, economic, and state administration to leading party posts.

The year 1964 marked the beginning of a drastically new stage in Brezhnev's life. In the past he had had to deal with important matters, surmount formidable difficulties, and carry a heavy burden of responsibility. But the problems, difficulties, and responsibilities now became even greater since he had to make decisions of national and international significance.

In order to give the reader a clear idea of the range of problems with which Leonid Brezhnev is now concerned, it is necessary to see the Communist Party's place in the life of the people. He notes with good reason that the nature of his activities as General Secretary is, above all, defined by the role which the Communist Party plays in the country.

The party is the leading and guiding force for the continued improvement of the developed socialist society in the Soviet Union and the building of communism.

The Communist Party of the Soviet Union is a mighty and dynamic organism. It formulates its policy on the basis of a scientific approach to and a searching examination of the needs of the people. It unites all sections of society and all nationalities, and it cultivates in the people the will, preparedness, and ability to fight for the Communist ideals.

"As far as I know, many people in the West do not have a clear idea about our political system," Leonid Brezhnev said. "Erroneous views are expressed. It is asserted, for instance, that the party substitutes for other organizations, both state and social. This, of course, is incorrect."

The competence of Soviet state bodies—the Supreme Soviet of the USSR, the Council of Ministers of the USSR, republican and local organizations of power—is clearly defined in the Constitution, Brezhnev explains. They frame laws and supervise their observance, ensure the functioning of the economic organism, and promote science, culture, public education, health protection, etc. Social organizations have their own fields of activity: the trade unions are above all concerned with protecting the interests of the working people and organizing their work and leisure; the Komsomol's duty is to educate the younger generation along socialist lines. But, Leonid Brezhnev stresses, it is the party which is the inspirer and political organizer of all the achievements of the Soviet people.

Guiding the development of society as a whole, the party does not substitute for state and social organizations. On the contrary, it encourages them to work with the maximum efficiency and to bear full responsibility for their jobs. The party does not command but uses means of persuasion, relying on its enormous prestige and experience and the support of the broad masses. Brezhnev points out that the party strives to promote the all-around development of the activities of the state organizations and stimulates their initiative in every way.

In postwar years the membership of the Communist Party

of the Soviet Union has increased almost threefold and today numbers more than 16 million. But this does not mean that applicants are admitted indiscriminately. It is a great honor to be a member of the party, one that has to be earned. Only those who constitute the most advanced sections of the working class, the collective farmers, and the intelligentsia are admitted to its ranks.

As regards its composition, the Communist Party of the Soviet Union above all is a party of workers, who, as stated at its 25th Congress, constitute 41.6 percent of its members. The percentage of representatives of other sections of the population is as follows: collective farmers 13.9; technical intelligentsia nearly 20; scientists, literary and art workers, and people working in public education, health protection, the administrative apparatus, and the military more than 24.

The Communist Party is a well-organized, smoothly functioning organization. There is a total of more than 390,000 primary party organizations in the 15 republics and 154 territories and regions, and 4,243 organizations in the cities and districts.

The party's entire activity is guided by its Central Committee, the Secretariat, the Politburo, and the General Secretary. The regular plenary meetings of the Central Committee (there were eleven such meetings in the period from 1971 to the beginning of 1976, *i.e.,* between the 24th and the 25th Party Congresses) examine the most important and urgent questions of the all-around development of the Soviet society and state, as well as questions of domestic and foreign policy. The Central Committee elects a Politburo to guide the work of the party between its plenary meetings and a Secretariat to guide current affairs.

An immense responsibility rests with the General Secretary of the Central Committee, who directs the implementation of all the collectively made decisions and coordinates the activities of the party apparatus. He plays a key role in the Central Committee and the Politburo.

"The range of questions dealt with by the Politburo and myself as General Secretary is considerably wider than those dealt with by Western leaders," said Leonid Brezhnev. "We keep in our field of vision practically all the spheres of human activity, everything that takes place in our vast country. This includes the ideological activities of the party and society, the economy and social problems, and the development of socialist democracy. It is impossible to list everything. International affairs also take a great deal of effort."

One can judge the truly immense range of questions which lie within the sphere of activity of the General Secretary by what is written into the 1977 Constitution about the role of the Communist Party of the Soviet Union.

Addressing the Extraordinary Session of the Supreme Soviet of the USSR on October 4, 1977, when it met to discuss the draft Constitution, Leonid Brezhnev said:

"The majority of bourgeois analysts have also criticized the provisions defining the role of the Communist Party of the Soviet Union in the life of Soviet society. They have made much of the alleged 'proclamation of the dictatorship of the Communist Party,' 'the primacy of the party over the state,' 'a dangerous integration of the party and government institutions,' 'the obliteration of the boundaries between the party and the state.'

"How is one to regard this? The motives for this attack are clear enough. The Communist Party is the vanguard of the Soviet people, their most conscious and progressive section, inseparably united with the people as a whole. The party has no other interests at heart but the interests of the people. To try to counterpose the party to the people by talking about the 'dictatorship of the party' is tantamount to trying to separate, say, the heart from the whole of the body.

". . . As the Soviet people tackle the increasingly complex and responsible tasks of building communism, the Communist Party will have a growing role to play," Brezhnev said. "This leads not to restriction but to the increasingly profound development of socialist democracy in full conformity with our party's program."

A New Stage in the Development of Soviet Society

As we have already noted, Leonid Brezhnev in his capacity of General Secretary has always considered his prime duty to be the promotion of the development of socialist democracy. He said in his report at the 25th Congress of the Communist Party of the Soviet Union:

"Socialism is a dynamically developing society. . . . And the time has come to sum up all that has been accomplished." The words "sum up all that has been accomplished" meant that it was necessary further to develop socialist democracy and extend the people's rights. That was why when referring to the new Constitution of the Soviet Union, which was already being drafted, he observed that one of its basic features would be "the further consolidation and development of socialist democracy."

Leonid Brezhnev became the head of the Constitution Commission which worked scrupulously and thoughtfully, looking closely into each arising problem. Finally, by May 1977, the draft of the new Constitution was completed. It was the result of many years of intensive work by a large group of people. The Constitution Commission, set up by the Supreme Soviet of the USSR, included experienced party and government workers and representatives of the working class, the collective farmers, the people's intelligentsia, and the country's numerous peoples. Eminent scientists, specialists, and men and women working in state bodies and public and social organizations were involved in the preparation of the draft. It was examined at a plenary meeting of the Central Committee of the Communist Party of the Soviet Union and then at a session of the Supreme Soviet of the USSR. It was then published in the press, and a nationwide discussion of the draft began.

The discussion of the draft Constitution took place over a period of nearly four months and was nationwide in the true sense of the word. Altogether it involved more than 140 million men and women—that is, over 80 percent of the adult population of the country. Never before had our country known active participation by the public on such a scale.

The draft was discussed at some 1,500,000 meetings of working people at enterprises and collective farms, in military units and in residential areas. The draft was considered by all the Soviets, from the rural Soviets to the Supreme Soviets of the Union Republics—that is, by more than 2 million deputies, representing the whole people. Each of these forums approved the draft Constitution.

An unending flow of letters was received from the Soviet people. Their writers, like those who took part in the discussion at meetings, are men and women from all walks of life and different age-groups, representing all our nations and nationalities, party members and not, and all of them, like the masters of the country which they are, thoroughly examined the draft Constitution, making proposals for improving the text and expressing other considerations bearing on various aspects of the life of the country and society.

"We can say with confidence and pride," Leonid Brezhnev noted, "that it is the whole Soviet people who have in fact become the true creators of the fundamental law of their state," adding, "the nationwide discussion has made it possible to improve the draft Constitution significantly and to write into it a number of useful additions, clarifications, and amendments."

The true extent of socialist democracy is seen from the fact that altogether some 400,000 proposals for amendments to individual articles have been made for the purpose of clarifying, improving, and supplementing the wording of the draft.

In early October 1977, at the Extraordinary Session of the Supreme Soviet of the USSR, which was addressed by Leonid Brezhnev, the new Constitution was adopted. Compared to the draft which had been published a few months before, it incorporated amendments to 110 articles and an additional article, as proposed by the Constitution Commission, as well as amendments and additions proposed by the deputies in the course of deliberations at the session of the Supreme Soviet of the USSR.

Speaking about the importance of the new Constitution, Leonid Brezhnev emphasized that it, one might say, epitomizes the whole sixty years' development of the Soviet state.

Why was it necessary to adopt a new Constitution? "During the past four decades deep-going changes have taken place in our country and in the whole of our society," Brezhnev said. "When the 1936 Constitution was adopted, we had essentially just completed laying the foundations of socialism. What we now have in the Soviet Union is an advanced, mature socialist society."

Developed socialism, Brezhnev said, is "that stage of maturity of the new society at which the restructuring of the entire system of social relations on the collectivist principles intrinsic to socialism is being completed. Hence, the full scope for the operation of the laws of socialism, for bringing to the fore its advantages in all spheres of the life of society. Hence, the organic integrity and dynamic force of the social system, its political stability, its indestructible inner unity. Hence, the closer drawing together of all the classes and social groups, all the nations and nationalities, and the formation of a historically new social and international community, the Soviet people. Hence, the emergence of a new, socialist culture, the establishment of a new, socialist way of life. Of course, only that socialist society can be described as developed which is based on powerful, advanced industry, on large-scale, highly mechanized agriculture, which in practice permits an increasingly complete satisfaction of the varied requirements of citizens to become the central and direct goal of social development.''

As a result of the complete triumph of the socialist social relations, the Soviet state, which arose as a dictatorship of the proletariat, has developed into a state of the whole people.

Describing these changes and referring to what today distinguishes our society, Leonid Brezhnev said, ''New harmonious relations, relations of friendship and cooperation, have taken shape between classes and social groups, nations and nationalities, during the years of socialist construction, in joint labor, in the struggle for socialism, and in the battles fought in its defense. All the nations of the Soviet Union demonstrate this monolithic unity by their labor and by their approval of the policy of the Communist Party of the Soviet Union.'' He then underscored one of the most important features of Soviet society. ''A new historical community, the Soviet people, has taken shape in our country,'' he said. ''It rests on the inviolable alliance of the working class, the peasantry, and the intelligentsia, with the working class playing the leading role, and on the friendship of all nations and nationalities of the country.''

By ''a new historical community, the Soviet people'' is not meant that national distinctions have disappeared or are ignored in the Soviet Union, let alone that there has been a merging of nations. ''The Soviet people's social and political unity,'' Leonid Brezhnev explained, ''does not at all imply the disappearance of national distinctions. Thanks to the consistent pursuance of the Leninist nationalities policy we have, simultaneously with the construction of socialism, successfully solved the nationalities question, for the first time in history. The friendship of the Soviet peoples is indissoluble, and in the process of building communism they are steadily drawing ever closer together and are being mutually enriched in their spiritual life. But we would be taking a dangerous path if we were artificially to step up this objective process of national integration." The more than 100 nations and nationalities inhabiting the Soviet Union have retained their distinctions, their national features, their languages, and their finest traditions. They have every opportunity for attaining a still greater development of their national cultures. At present, for example, more than seventy languages of the peoples of the Soviet Union are written, literary languages, whereas prior to the revolution, literature developed in only thirteen languages, and even so, the possibilities for their progress were extremely limited.

At the same time another aspect typical of Soviet people should be borne in mind. The Soviet people are not simply an aggregate of nations living side by side in one state. Whatever their nationality, the Soviet people have many common features which unite them as an entity. These features are a common ideology, a common historical destiny and joint work, similar social and economic conditions, basic interests and aims, and a developing unity of Soviet socialist culture which absorbs all the real values inherent in each of the national cultures.

"All the nations and nationalities of our country, and, above all, the great Russian people, have played their part in the formation, consolidation, and development of the mighty union of equal nations that have taken the road of socialism," noted Leonid Brezhnev. "The revolutionary en-

ergy, utter selflessness, industriousness, and profound internationalism of the Russian people have justly won them the
sincere respect of all the other peoples of our socialist homeland."

The Soviet people have built a developed socialist society,
a socialist state of the whole people, in which, as mentioned
above, the leading role is played by the working class.

Once a worker himself, Brezhnev has never broken his
ties with his class. He has always shown and continues to
show concern for the working people, and their work is accorded honor and respect.

"Our working class today constitutes two-thirds of the
country's population," said Brezhnev. "It includes tens of
millions of educated, technically proficient, and politically
mature men and women. Their labor is increasingly approaching that of engineering and technical personnel. The
workers' public activity and their participation in administer-
ing the affairs of the state have considerably increased. By
its direct participation, the working class not only multiplies
the material wealth of the country but also builds up its own
intellectual potential." The working class has been and remains the main productive force in society. It enhances its
leading role as its general culture, its level of education, and
its political activity increase. The last two population cen-
suses convincingly attest to the growth of the culture of the
working class. In 1971 more than 550 out of every 1,000
workers had a higher and secondary education, compared
with 386 in 1959.

Socialist Democracy Is Genuine Democracy

Few statesmen have had the experience of working in
elective offices that Brezhnev has. This is a very important
and significant fact. He has served at almost all levels of rep-

resentative democracy, from deputy of the district and city Soviet to Chairman of the Presidium of the Supreme Soviet of the USSR—that is, the President of the country.

In his capacity as top party and state leader Brezhnev devotes much attention to the development of socialist democracy. "Now we know not only from theory but from years of practice that just as real democracy is impossible without socialism, so is socialism impossible without the constant development of democracy," Brezhnev said. "We understand the improvement of our socialist democracy, above all, as the continuously increasing involvement of the working people in managing all the affairs of society, as the further development of the democratic foundation of our statehood, as the creation of conditions for the all-around development of the individual."

The base of the socialist state and the fullest embodiment of its democratic nature are the organs of people's rule, the Soviets of People's Deputies: the town and village Soviets, the district and area Soviets, the Soviets of People's Deputies of the autonomous regions, the Supreme Soviets of the autonomous republics, the territorial and regional Soviets of People's Deputies, the Supreme Soviets of the Union Republics, and, finally, the Supreme Soviet of the USSR. All told, there are more than 2 million deputies of the Soviets who administer the affairs of state of the whole people at all levels. In addition, almost 30 million Soviet citizens are activists of the Soviets, voluntarily and without remuneration involved in performing the enormous and complicated task of state administration.

A Law on the Status of the Deputy has been adopted in the Soviet Union. It clearly defines the rights and duties of deputies, as well as the duties of state and social bodies with respect to deputies. The Soviet state guarantees each deputy the necessary conditions for the unhampered and effective exercise of his rights and duties. Persons who prevent a deputy from exercising his powers or encroach on his honor and dignity as a representative of state authority are responsible before the law. Deputies of the Supreme Soviets have the right to initiate legislation. At present many important issues are raised and resolved on the initiative of the deputies of the Soviets. "The proposals being put forward by the deputies on the basis of mandates from their electors," Brezhnev told the 25th Congress of the Communist Party of the Soviet Union, "reflect the requirements and needs of our people as a whole."

"These mandates are an expression of the most diverse requirements of the population, reflecting the concrete interests of individual groups of working people and of society as a whole. That is why fulfillment of these mandates is an important part of the work of the Soviets and of their deputies," stated Leonid Brezhnev in his report to the Extraordinary Session of the Supreme Soviet of the USSR on October 4, 1977. "Suffice it to say that in the past two years alone more than 700,000 electors' mandates have been fulfilled. That is one of the real expressions of socialist democracy. It is important that not only deputies but also the heads of enterprises, collective farms, construction projects and offices should give due attention to the carrying out of mandates."

In response to the suggestions made in the course of the discussion the new Constitution contains the article which says, "Electors give mandates to their deputies. The appropriate Soviets of People's Deputies shall examine electors' mandates, take them into account in drafting economic and social development plans and in drawing up the budget, organize implementation of the mandates, and inform citizens about it."

This gives a very good idea of Soviet reality. A deputy is

duty-bound to heed the voice of his constituents. In the past five years more than 1,800,000 mandates of the electors concerning various aspects of economic and cultural development, public education and health protection, trade and food catering, the municipal services, and the service industry have been translated into reality with the deputies' direct participation. The Supreme Soviet of the USSR and the Supreme Soviets of the Union Republics have intensified their supervision over the work of the ministries and departments, over the main areas of economic and cultural development. Deputies are taking a deep interest in the work of the executive bodies and are active in framing legislation. The new Constitution provides for greater accountability of the executive bodies to the Soviets at all levels.

More effective legislation designed to improve health protection, strengthen family ties, further improve labor protection and the environment, and ensure rational use of natural resources, as well as other social measures, has been adopted in recent years. The new Constitution is an important incentive for enhancing the activities of deputies.

Elections to the local Soviets strikingly demonstrate the real nature of socialist democracy. Take the elections of June 19, 1977. They attest to a high degree of political involvement by the electorate. At present there are 166,200,000 voters in the Soviet Union. And as many as 166,170,000 of them, or 99.98 percent, went to the polls. The fact that 99.8 percent of them cast their ballots for the candidates of the bloc of Communists and nonparty people speaks for the unity of the Soviet people.

Workers account for 42.3 percent of the elected deputies, collective farm peasants 26.1 percent, and representatives of the people's intelligentsia 31.6 percent. Among the deputies there are 49 percent women, 43.2 percent Communists, and 56.8 percent nonparty people.

Such is the general picture of the state of the whole people.

Referring to the nature of the new Constitution, Leonid Brezhnev noted that the main purpose of everything new it contains is designed to broaden and deepen socialist democracy. What does this mean? In the first place, the further development of the democratic principles of the formation and activity of the Soviets and their increased role in the solution of vital questions of the life of society.

Now that the Soviet Union has completed the construction of a developed socialist society, we are in a position to improve substantially the clauses of the Constitution dealing with the rights of Soviet citizens. The famous lines from the *Manifesto of the Communist Party*—"The free development of each person is the condition for the free development of all"—have, in fact, become the fundamental principle of the Soviet state. This has been inserted in the Constitution, which has a special clause proclaiming the general principle of equality of all Soviet citizens irrespective of nationality or race. With the utmost clarity the Constitution consolidates socialism's gains in such an important matter as ensuring equal rights to women and men.

Leonid Brezhnev noted that the 1936 Constitution also guaranteed a broad range of socioeconomic rights bearing directly on the very foundations of life. But now their content has been deepened and enriched, and the material guarantees made are even more clearly defined. This is reflected in the new Constitution. If, for example, it was said that the people had the right to work, now this is supplemented with the right to choose a trade or profession, the type of job and work in accordance with the vocation, ability, training, and education of the citizen and, what is no less important, with due account taken of the needs of society.

Here is another principle. The 1936 Constitution guaranteed the right to social maintenance in the event of illness or disability. The new Constitution treats the question more widely by guaranteeing Soviet citizens the right to health protection. While the right to education was referred to in general terms, now the reference is to universal, compulsory secondary education and to broad development of vocational, specialized secondary, and higher education.

A new principle has been introduced, one which is not to be found in any constitution in the world—namely, the right to housing. This right is ensured to an ever-increasing extent through the implementation of the program of housing construction and through state assistance in building cooperative housing and individual dwellings. Brezhnev pointed out that our new Constitution will be one of the first in the world to proclaim this vital human right.

The Constitution more fully and concretely defines the political rights and freedoms of Soviet citizens, including the right of every Soviet citizen to take part in the management and administration of state and public affairs, and lists the concrete forms of such participation.

The freedoms of speech, press, assembly, meetings, and street processions and demonstrations inscribed in the old Constitution are fully confirmed in the new Constitution. The former constitutional guarantees of individual rights have been largely supplemented by the right of citizens to submit proposals to state bodies and public organizations, to criticize shortcomings in their work, and to appeal against the actions of officials in a court and by the right of citizens to protection by the courts against encroachments on their honor and reputation, life, and health, personal freedom, and property. The Constitution states that persecution for criticism is prohibited. Persons guilty of such persecution shall be called to account.

Naturally, the Constitution proceeds from the assumption

that enjoyment by citizens of their rights and freedoms must not be to the detriment of the interests of society or the state or infringe the rights of other citizens. Citizens' exercise of their rights and freedoms is inseparable from the performance of their duties and obligations.

"Our 'critics' pretend to be unaware of the fact that the clauses in the Constitution causing their dissatisfaction fully conform to fundamental international documents," Leonid Brezhnev said. "Let us remind them of this fact: the UN Universal Declaration of Human Rights says unequivocally that 'everyone has duties to the community in which alone the free and full development of his personality is possible' and that the exercise of rights and freedoms by citizens requires 'due recognition and respect for the rights and freedoms of others and of meeting the just requirements of morality, public order and the general welfare in a democratic society.' "

The broadening and deepening of human rights in the new Constitution upset the fabrications of those Western propagandists who misinterpret this issue and turn it inside out. In Brezhnev's opinion such "operations" and campaigns are attempts to weaken the socialist community and undermine the socialist system. "Our enemies would like nothing better than to find forces of any kind that oppose socialism in our countries," Brezhnev said. "And since such forces do not exist, for there are no oppressed, exploited classes and no oppressed, exploited nationalities in a socialist society, they invent a substitute and by means of specious advertising create the semblance of an 'internal opposition' in the socialist countries. Hence, the noise about the so-called 'dissidents' and the outcries about alleged violations of human rights in the socialist countries.

"What is there to say on this score?" he went on. "It is not forbidden in our society to 'dissent' with the majority and to be critical of some aspect of social life. We regard comrades whose well-grounded criticism is designed to be of help as honest critics and are grateful to them. And we regard those who criticize groundlessly as mistaken.

"It is another matter if a handful of people who have broken away from our society actively come out against the socialist system and embark on anti-Soviet activities, violate laws, and, lacking support inside the country, seek help from abroad, from subversive imperialist propaganda and intelligence centers. . . . Quite naturally we take and shall continue to take those measures against them which are in keeping with our law."

A distinctive feature of the new Constitution is that it includes for the first time a section on the foreign policy of the Soviet Union.

It says that the Soviet state steadfastly pursues a Leninist policy of peace and stands for strengthening of the security of nations and broad international cooperation. The foreign policy of the Soviet Union is aimed at ensuring international conditions favorable for building communism in the Soviet Union, safeguarding the state interests of the Soviet Union, consolidating the positions of world socialism, supporting the struggle of peoples for national liberation and social progress, preventing wars of aggression, achieving universal and complete disarmament, and consistently implementing the principle of the peaceful coexistence of states with different social systems. In the Soviet Union war propaganda is banned.

The Soviet Union is the first state which has included in its Constitution the ten principles governing relations between states which constitute the core of the Final Act of the conference on Security and Cooperation in Europe.

"Our new Constitution," said Leonid Brezhnev, "shows most convincingly that the first state of victorious socialism has for all time inscribed on its banner the word 'peace' as the highest principle of its foreign policy, meeting the interests of its own people and all the other peoples of our planet.''

Trade Unions in the Life of Soviet Society

The new Constitution broadly reflects the important role played by the trade unions, the Komsomol, and other public organizations in the life of the country. It includes a clause concerning the role of work collectives. Brezhnev noted that this was consistent with the fundamental course of the party and the significance it attaches to the development of democratic principles in production management.

Not everybody abroad has a clear idea of the role played by the trade unions in the life of the Soviet people and in Communist construction. Their status differs greatly from that of the trade unions in capitalist countries, and they, as Brezhnev observed, ''are given an important place in the life of our society.''

The trade unions are the biggest mass social organization of Soviet people. It has a membership of nearly 114 million; *i.e.,* it embraces almost the entire working class, the intelligentsia, and the large contingent of the agricultural population.

The General Secretary of the Central Committee defined the role of the trade unions in the following words: ''The trade unions have the task, above all, of protecting the rights and interests of the working people and actively dealing with everyday social questions. But they would be unable to do much in this sphere if production did not develop and if labor discipline and labor productivity did not rise. It is precisely because our trade unions are dedicated to the workingman's interests that their duty is to show concern for boosting production.''

Soviet trade unions operate in a socialist society, and that determines their character.

One of their main and distinctive features is that they directly and actively participate in the development of the whole of society and in the management of the economy.

Being a key link in the general system of socialist democracy, they draw the working people into the administration of the state. They take part in working out solutions to many problems of the development of the national economy, ranging from the elaboration of state plans to the management of each enterprise.

They play an important role in the production and social activities of the personnel at industrial enterprises, construction sites, and offices, and they participate in their administration through permanently functioning production conferences. "It is necessary to encourage heads of production associations and enterprises, as well as leading ministerial officials, regularly to report directly to the workers on the work done," said Brezhnev.

In addition to wage issues and incentives, social insurance comes within the competence of the trade unions. The unions have considerable funds and resources at their disposal for organizing leisure and recreation facilities, treatment at sanatoriums and health resorts, tourism, physical training, and sports. Furthermore, they are concerned with improving all the aspects of the living conditions of the working people and food catering.

Addressing the 16th Congress of the Trade Unions in 1977, Leonid Brezhnev said, "The trade unions have a rich arsenal of forms and means to exercise their rights—workers' meetings, permanently functioning production conferences, and collective agreements. They have the right of legislative initiative. In a word, the trade unions have many rights and opportunities." He made the point that they should be used more fully and effectively.

The Soviet Youth

As mentioned earlier, the new Constitution speaks of the place occupied by the youth organization—the Komsomol—in our society. This is done with good reason. Young men and women under twenty-six constitute half the population of the Soviet Union. It is indeed a "youth country."

The Central Committee and Brezhnev personally pay much attention to youth problems. "It may be said without exaggeration," he emphasized, "that no major matter is decided without the participation of the youth, whether it concerns the affairs of the Soviet Union, a region, a district, or the personnel of an enterprise."

The rising generation occupies a worthy place in all the key areas of building the new life. A fifth of the deputies of the Supreme Soviet of the USSR are under thirty, while the proportion of young people in the local Soviets is even higher—nearly one-third.

The growing thirst of young people for fruitful creative work and their wish to turn it into a vital prime necessity are a progressive trend in the development of the Soviet society.

Brezhnev takes all these features of the younger generation into account in all his activities. "It has always been in the Communist tradition to trust the young people," he said, "to rely on their inherent enthusiasm and noble desire to work for the common weal, and at the same time to help them correctly orientate themselves in life and to arm them with the knowledge and experience of the older generations."

The Young Communist League, or the Komsomol, has a membership of more than 35 million. The Komsomol, says Brezhnev, performs a colossal amount of work. In this organization the young people receive their political education. They are tempered on construction projects, in factories and on state or collective farms, in higher educational institutions, and in students' building teams that work in the most diverse spheres of the economy during vacations.

"Let us recall the many good initiatives the Komsomol has carried into effect," said Leonid Brezhnev at the 25th Congress of the Communist Party of the Soviet Union. "Take the construction of the Baikal–Amur Railway and the high-priority Komsomol construction projects; in the five-year period there were 670 of these, involving more than half a million young men and women. The Komsomol has taken charge of 1,200 land-improvement and rural construction projects in the Non-Black Soil Zone of the Russian Federation. And we all know of the eagerness with which young people seek to join the students' building teams! These teams have been doing very important work. In the Ninth Five-Year Plan period they have done a volume of work worth roughly 5 billion rubles. Nor is it possible to overrate their importance as a school of labor education."

Brezhnev reminds the young people that the tasks they face now are those of the higher school of socialist economics rather than the elementary school of socialist economic management that faced the country in the past. The most important thing today is to acquire up-to-date knowledge and promote scientific and technical progress.

In the Soviet Union exceptional importance is attached to the development of education, including higher education. The all-around development of young people in higher schools is based on an organic combination of education and training designed to bring up educated, ideologically tempered, and spiritually mature young men and women.

Since the establishment of Soviet power the country has built up an extensive network of higher and specialized secondary educational establishments which have trained nearly 35 million skilled specialists. Annually more than 700,000 people graduate from institutions of higher learning.

Brezhnev called on the students to strive for the summits

in their professions. "The loftiest beacon in study," he said, "should be the demands which life makes today on a Soviet specialist, on an active participant in communist construction."

On Brezhnev's initiative the Central Committee of the Communist Party of the Soviet Union and the Council of Ministers of the Soviet Union adopted a decision on the further improvement of general secondary schools, the system of vocational and technical training, and higher and specialized secondary education.

"At the dawn of socialism Lenin dreamed of seeing our homeland become a country of universal literacy," he said. "We solved this task long ago. Now we have reached new horizons and are completing the transition to universal secondary education." In this field the Soviet Union has made spectacular progress. In the period from 1950 to 1975 the number of people with a ten-year education has increased thirteenfold.

The transition to universal secondary education is directly connected with the heightening of the role of the school. Brezhnev devotes special attention to the need to bring the substance of secondary education into greater conformity with the present-day requirements of science, technology, and culture.

Young people are enthusiastically tackling these tasks because the future is in their hands. National contests in physics, chemistry, and mathematics in which millions of schoolchildren participate with great interest have become a tradition. Throughout the country there are societies of senior-grade pupils and centers of young technicians and naturalists.

Since all education is free, all people have access to it. There is being formed a Soviet intelligentsia which, according to Brezhnev, is determined to dedicate its creative energy to the people's cause and to the cause of building a Communist society.

The Increasing Role of Science

Being himself an engineer and an experienced statesman and party leader, Brezhnev has always paid a great deal of attention to promoting the development of science and technology. His name is associated with many achievements in this field. He has always sought to create all the necessary conditions for the development of research. "The life-giving wellspring of technical, economic, and social progress, the growth of the people's spiritual culture, and its well-being—that is what science means to us today." That is how the General Secretary assesses the significance of science for Soviet society.

The Soviet people are genuinely proud of the Soviet Academy of Sciences. Dwelling on the importance of this scientific center, Brezhnev told the 25th Congress, "It is the party's policy to continue showing tireless concern for the promotion of science and for its headquarters, the Academy of Sciences, whose 250th anniversary was widely marked last autumn. In it is concentrated the flower of our science—venerable scholars, founders of scientific schools and trends, and the most talented young scientists blazing new trails to the pinnacles of knowledge. The party highly values the work of the academy and will enhance its role as the center of theoretical research and the coordinator of all scientific work in the country."

The spreading of Soviet science is unprecedented; in the past decade the party has been giving close attention to the organization of regional scientific centers.

This idea was prompted by the need for a more rational distribution of scientists and researchers throughout the vast

Soviet Union, to link their effort closer to the local conditions of economic development and to concentrate material, manpower, and financial resources. This idea splendidly expressed the needs of the evolving "science-industry-agriculture" system in adequate organizational forms.

Scientific centers are being founded or have already been established in the Union Republics. In the Russian Federation there are several successfully developing scientific centers, including the Ural center, which was founded on the basis of 10 major institutes; the Far Eastern center, which unites 13 institutes and coordinates the activities of more than 100 institutes in that territory; and the North Caucasian center, which embraces 40 institutions of higher education and 150 research institutes with a staff of more than 30,000.

All these scientific centers draw on the experience of one of the earliest and biggest of them—the world-famous Siberian Branch of the Soviet Academy of Sciences. Founded in 1957, it has already played a tremendous part in promoting science and developing the productive forces of the Soviet Union, particularly in its eastern areas. The Siberian Branch engages in basic and applied research, and its links with industry and agriculture are becoming increasingly close.

At present the Academy of Sciences' network of institutions has increased by almost 50 percent and includes about 250 centers with 40,000 research workers.

Brezhnev has set science immense tasks. "The party expects the scientists to carry on deeper and bolder research into new processes and phenomena, actively to contribute to scientific and technical progress, searchingly to analyze the arising problems, and to come forward with responsible recommendations on the best ways of solving them in the interests of strengthening the country's might and improving the life of the people, in the interests of building communism."

Economy: Results and Prospects

One of the most important trends in the party's guiding activity is the elaboration of technical policy and the search for such forms of organization and management of the economy as would best contribute to its growth, accelerate scientific and technical progress, and raise the living standard of the Soviet people.

In this respect the October 1964 plenary meeting of the Central Committee of the Communist Party of the Soviet Union, at which Brezhnev was elected General Secretary of the Central Committee, is a historical milestone in the party's activity.

Subsequent plenary meetings of the Central Committee and party congresses adopted important decisions which steeply raised economic management to a qualitatively higher level.

The end of the 1960s witnessed a change in economic management methods with the view to raising the efficiency of production. For many years gross output had been the criterion for assessing the economic activity of an industrial enterprise. Now its performance was to be judged by the volume of sales and profits. Brezhnev, who initiated this change, emphasized that at the current stage the principles underlying the party's economic policy called for "greater emphasis on economic methods and incentives in management, a radical improvement of state planning, more economic independence of and initiative by industrial enterprises and state and collective farms, and an enhancement of their responsibility and larger material incentives for their work."

The very first results of the economic reform confirmed the efficiency of the new system of planning and economic stimulation and its beneficial effect on the entire activity of enterprises. Their personnel became more interested in the results of their work, in getting better results with the least outlay of labor, in economizing means and materials, in fuller utilization of equipment and its timely modernization. The conversion of industrial enterprises to the new system was in the main completed by 1970.

In the formulation of economic policy it is very important to take into account the basic features of each stage in the country's development. Brezhnev stressed this frequently. Comparing, for instance, the current economy with that of the end of the 1930s, he said that today it stands at a much higher level of development, as do socialist social relations and the culture and awareness of the masses. Now a developed socialist society, to which Lenin in 1918 referred as the future of the country, has already been built by force of the Soviet people's dedicated labor. This enabled them to undertake the practical and important task set in the party's program and its recent congresses—that of building the material and technical basis of communism.

The Soviet Union has made great strides in its development since Brezhnev's election to the post of General Secretary of the Central Committee. It has made impressive headway in creating the material and technical basis of communism and consolidating its economic might, and it has secured a considerable rise in the living standard.

As regards the current stage of economic development, it has assumed a new dimension. The progress is truly unprecedented.

It should be recalled that the Soviet Union sustained great losses during the war and the temporary occupation of a part of its territory by the Hitlerites. They killed millions of civilians, and millions of Soviet soldiers laid down their lives on the battlefield. The nazis destroyed and plundered enormous material resources in the temporarily occupied territories.

The enemy fully or partially demolished nearly 32,000 industrial enterprises; plundered 98,000 collective farms, 1,876 state farms, and 2,890 machine-and-tractor stations; and destroyed tens of thousands of schools, hospitals, technical colleges, higher educational establishments, and libraries. All told, the enemy plundered or destroyed material assets to the sum of 679 billion rubles (in prewar prices).

It seemed impossible even to think of rehabilitating the country in just a few years, rebuilding the industry from the ground up and restoring agriculture. But the Soviet people managed. Their heroism in labor was akin to their heroism in battle.

The social transformations carried out in the Soviet Union paved the way for swift progress in all spheres of life.

In 1977, the year of the 60th anniversary of the Soviet Union, the country's potential is bigger than it has ever been. The national income in 1977 is almost 70 times higher than in tsarist Russia in 1913 and more than 100 times higher than in 1917.

The Soviet Union's modern socialist industry turns out 145 times more than Russia's factories did in 1913 and 225 times more than in 1917. Today Soviet industry produces as much in two or three days as was produced in prerevolutionary Russia in a year. In 1913 Russia ranked fifth in the world after the United States, Great Britain, Germany, and France in industrial output, with the United States producing eight times as much as it did. Today Soviet industry holds a firm second place in the world. Its volume of output surpasses the industrial product of the Federal Republic of Germany, Great Britain, and France combined.

Deep-going changes have been wrought in agriculture since the establishment of Soviet power. A large-scale collective-farm economy has been established. In the early period of socialist construction Lenin dreamed of providing

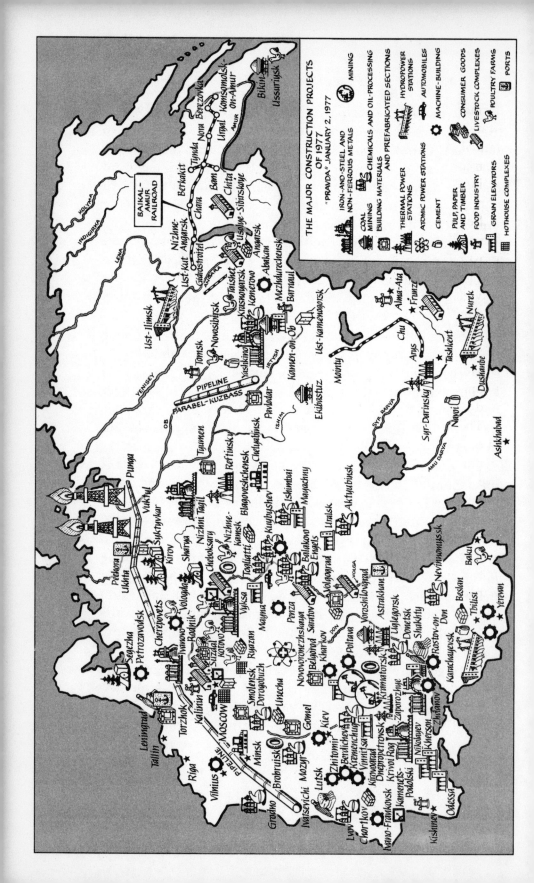

THE MAJOR CONSTRUCTION PROJECTS
OF 1977
"PRAVDA" JANUARY 2, 1977

MINING

IRON-AND-STEEL AND
NON-FERROUS METALS

CHEMICALS AND OIL-PROCESSING
AND PREFABRICATED SECTIONS

HYDROPOWER
STATIONS

COAL
MINING

BUILDING MATERIALS

AUTOMOBILES

THERMAL POWER
STATIONS

MACHINE-BUILDING

ATOMIC POWER STATIONS

CONSUMER GOODS

CEMENT

LIVESTOCK COMPLEXES

PULP, PAPER
AND TIMBER

GRAIN ELEVATORS

FOOD INDUSTRY

PORTS

HOTHOUSE COMPLEXES

BAIKAL–
AMUR
RAILROAD

Bikin
Ussuriysk
Komsomolsk-
on-Amur
AMUR
Urgal
Berezovka
Nora
Tynda
Bam
Chita
Chara
Berkakit
Usolye-Sibirskoye
Gidrostroitel
Nizhne-
Angarsk
Ust-kut
Angarsk
Taishet
Abakan
Mezhdurechensk
Angarsk
ANGARA
Barnaul
Ust-Ilimsk
Krasnoyarsk
Kemerovo
Novosibirsk
Yashkino
Tomsk
Kamen-on-Ob
Ust-Kamenogorsk
IRTYSH
Alma-Ata
Frunze
Chu
Arys
Ekibastuz
Moiyty
Tashkent
Pavlodar
ISHIM
Dushanbe
PIPELINE
PARABEL-KUZBASS
OB
Syr-Darinsky
Navoi
SYR-DARYA
Ashkhabad
YENISEY
Tyumen
Reftinsky
Chelyabinsk
AMU DARYA
Nizhne Tagil
Sharya
Kirov
Cheboksary
Nizhne-
kamsk
Ishimbai
Mayachny
Aktyubinsk
Uralsk
Kuybyshev
Blagoveshchensk
LENA
KOLYMA
INDIGIRKA
Vuktyl
Syktyvkar
Pechora
Ukhta
Saczna
Petrozavodsk
Leningrad
Tallin
Riga
Vilnius
Torzhok
Kalinin
Kirovabad
Ivanovo-
Voznesensk
Vologda
Rodniki
Cherepovets
Togliatti
Maina
Penza
Balakovo
Engels
Saratov
Volgograd
VOLGA
Baku
Nvrimnuyssk
Beslan
Tbilisi
Yerevan
Karachayevsk
Zhdanov
Rostov-on-
Don
DON
Shakhty
Donetsk
Voroshilovgrad
Astrakhan
Uglegorsk
Kommunarsk
Moscow
PIPELINE
Suzdal
Kotovo
Smolensk
Dorogobuzh
Uracha
Ryazan
Vyksa
Novovoronezhskaya
Belgorod
Kharkov
Kramatorsk
Zaporozhye
Poltava
Ivatsevichi
Mozyr
Gomel
Lutsk
Brobruisk
Minsk
Zhitomir
Berdichev
Kremenchug
Vinnitsa
Kirovograd
Dnepropetrovsk
Krivoi Rog
Nikolayev
Kherson
Gradno
Lvov
Chortkov
Ivano-Frankovsk
Kamenets-
Podolski
Odessa
Kishinev

farmers with 100,000 tractors. At present the collective and state farms have 2,400,000 tractors, 700,000 grain harvesters, and almost 1,500,000 trucks. As a result, agricultural production in the year of the 60th anniversary of the October Revolution surpassed the 1913 and 1917 levels by 230 and 340 percent respectively.

Leonid Brezhnev pointed out: "We have managed in only ten years to double the economic potential which it took almost half a century to build up."

There is legitimate pride for the economic successes of the Soviet Union in these words because with a vast, diversified, and extremely complex economy it is vital to be able to look ahead, to focus the people's efforts on the crucial sectors at the right time, and to organize and inspire their work. The Soviet Union's successes are the successes of the Soviet people and the Communist Party, of the Central Committee and General Secretary Brezhnev.

The entire Soviet Union has become a giant construction site. In the past decade work was continued on developing a major oil and gas base in the Tyumen and Orenburg regions, the Komi Autonomous Republic, and the Uzbek and Turkmen Union Republics. A new iron-ore base for the iron-and-steel industry is being developed in the region of the Kursk Magnetic Anomaly.

The world's biggest Krasnoyarsk hydropower station on the Yenisei has gone into operation and attained its rated capacity of 6 million kilowatt. The 2,400,000-kilowatt Konakovo thermal power station near Moscow is also working at full capacity.

The construction of the Ladyzhinskaya and Estonian thermal power stations and the Saratov hydropower scheme with an aggregate capacity of more than 4 million kilowatts has been completed, and the construction of a mighty system of hydropower plants on the great Siberian rivers is in progress.

Following the completion in record time of the Volzhsky car works, the construction of another giant, the heavy-duty truck factory at Naberezhnyye Chelny, on the banks of the Kama, was launched.

The construction of the Baikal–Amur Railway is now in full swing. "This project is tremendously important," Leonid Brezhnev noted. "The Baikal–Amur Railway will cut through the age-old taiga, crossing areas with enormous wealth that must be put at the service of the country. . . ."

The 25th Congress of the Communist Party of the Soviet Union which took place early in 1976 was a major event in the life of the party and of the entire Soviet people. "An Outstanding Result of the Labor of Soviet People," "Economic Progress under Détente," "Brezhnev Speaks about Good Results and Future Plans"—such were the headlines carried by many foreign newspapers in those days.

Guests from abroad and many foreign correspondents noted the spirit of optimism and confidence in the future which reigned at the Congress. It brought together people who had directly participated in accomplishing the tasks of the Ninth Five-Year Plan. Now, in addition to summing up what had been accomplished, they examined and approved the main orientations of the Soviet Union's further development.

The Congress heard Brezhnev's confident voice. In a comprehensive report he analyzed the international position of the Soviet Union and the foreign policy of the Communist Party, the contemporary stage of communist construction in the Soviet Union, the party's domestic policy, and all the areas of its multifarious activities.

Brezhnev reported to the Congress that major progress had been made in creating the material and technical bases of communism and in improving the well-being of the people. The main result of the Five-Year Plan was that the labor of the Soviet people and the guiding and organizing activity of the party had ensured stable economic growth, the fulfill-ment of socioeconomic tasks, and a further rise in the Soviet people's standard of living.

Brezhnev said that the growth of industrial output, capital investments, and state allocations for enhancing living stan-dards had been higher than in any of the preceding five-year plan periods.

He searchingly analyzed the Communist Party's economic strategy, the main orientations of economic development for 1976–80, as well as the economic outlook until 1990. He told the Congress that according to estimates, the country's ma-terial and financial resources in the period from 1976 to 1990 would be almost double those of the preceding fifteen years.

Brezhnev described 1976–80 as five years of efficiency and quality. This will be a period of a rapid rise of labor produc-tivity and a sharp increase in the efficiency of social produc-tion as a whole. "We interpret the problem of quality in very broad terms," he said. "It covers all aspects of economic work. High quality means a saving of labor and material re-sources, growth of the export potential, and, in the long run, better and fuller satisfaction of society's requirements."

The 25th Congress of the Communist Party provided for the economic development of a number of new regions. For instance, development is to be continued, in particular, of the West Siberian complex. In the long term it will account for nearly one-half of the Soviet Union's oil and natural gas output and a considerable portion of its synthetic rubber and plastics output.

It is planned to inaugurate a fundamentally new stage in the development of East Siberia's productive forces. The Sayan complex alone, which will receive its energy from the Sayano-Shushenskaya hydropower station, the world's big-gest, will consist of a number of industrial centers specializ-ing in metallurgy and the engineering industry.

These are only a few of the elements of the imposing plans

discussed at the 25th Congress. "Ahead of us there is great and difficult work," Brezhnev said. "But there is no doubt that our party and our people will cope with it with honor and add yet another stirring page to the chronicle of the building of the first Communist society in the world." All the forces of Soviet society, of the entire Soviet people are oriented on further progress in the creation of the material and technical bases of communism.

"The Five-Year Plan has got off to a good start," Brezhnev said, referring to the first results of the plans drawn up by the 25th Congress.

Already in the first year of the current Five-Year Plan, the country's tenth—that is why Brezhnev called it a jubilee plan—the industry turned out thousands of millions of rubles' worth of production in excess of plan. A record grain harvest of 220 million tons was taken in.

The gigantic work of building new industrial complexes, factories, railways, and oil pipelines was under way.

Glance at the map on page 154!

(The map of new construction projects was published in *Pravda* on January 2, 1977.)

It shows only the most important projects. Let us add that there was room on it for only some of the biggest ones. Many new signs will appear on the map of the Soviet Union toward the end of the Five-Year Plan period.

The impressive plans for the country's development, for building a new Communist society are carried into practice by ordinary people—workers, farmers, the intelligentsia— and they are going about it in a purposeful manner, regarding it as a natural mission and their life's work. Brezhnev spoke of his pride of them. "It has long been noticed that the continuous succession of days that resemble one another, that routine, day-to-day work—and all of us are engaged in this work—often prevents us from fully appreciating the significance and scale of what is taking place around us," he said. "Even spaceflights have become customary and commonplace, to say nothing of the commissioning of new factories or, say, the settlement of new residential districts. That is probably as it should be. Indeed, comrades, that is as it should be. For every morning tens of millions of people begin another and most ordinary working day: they take their places at the workbenches, go down into mines, drive out to the fields, bend over microscopes, computations, and charts. They most certainly do not think of the greatness of their work. But in carrying out the plans charted by the party, they, and nobody else, are raising the Soviet Union to new and ever higher summits of progress. And in calling ours a time of great accomplishments, we pay tribute to those who have made it such—we pay tribute to the working people."

Everything for the Benefit of Man

It is impossible to give a full account of the social progress made by Soviet society in sixty years without referring to the changes in the people's material and cultural levels.

"To create for the workingman the most favorable conditions for labor, study, rest, for the development and the best possible application of his abilities," Brezhnev said, "is the main aim and meaning of the policy which our party consistently pursues." The supreme goal of the policy of the Communist Party of the Soviet Union is to ensure the maximum satisfaction of the material and cultural requirements of the people. And it is with good reason that the phrase "everything for the sake of man, for the benefit of man," written down in the program of the Communist Party of the Soviet Union, has become a catchword in our country.

For many years in their heroic history millions of Soviet people consciously accepted hardships and privations; they

were satisfied with bare essentials and did not consider themselves entitled to demand special comforts. Now the situation has changed fundamentally.

The country's steady economic growth has created new
opportunities for further enhancing the well-being of the Soviet people, improving their working and living conditions,
achieving considerable progress in health protection, education, and culture, in everything that helps mold the new man,
the all-around development of the personality, and the per-
fection of the socialist way of life.

A characteristic feature of Soviet reality is that there is no
unemployment in the Soviet Union. The last of the unem-
ployed got a job back in the early 1930s. Since then the Soviet people have completely forgotten the labor exchange
and what it means to be dismissed. They have confidence in
the future and know that the right to work recorded in the
Constitution is a reality.

The results of the development of Soviet society, particularly in the past decade, show how this course, designed to
raise the well-being of the people to a still higher level, is
translated into reality. A general indicator of progress in this
field is the growth of real incomes—*i.e.,* of the sum total of
material benefits and services for the people. In fifteen years,
from 1961 through 1975, the real per capita income has
nearly doubled. Brezhnev mentioned this at the 25th Congress and stated with pride that the figure reflected a fundamental change in the level and mode of life of the people and
that it was a sort of revolution in their well-being.

The most important factor contributing to the growth of
each family's real income is the rapid rise in wages, the principal source of benefits under socialism. In this period the
average wages of industrial and office workers rose by nearly
100 percent and the remuneration of the collective farmers
by more than 200 percent. It should be noted, for example,

that as a result of special measures, the earnings of 75 million industrial and office workers were increased in the period from 1971 to 1975.

The prices of basic consumer goods are stable. This was so in the past five-year period and will be so in the current five years. The prices of bread, meat, milk, potatoes, and many other food products in state shops are the same as ten years ago.

Electricity and gas charges and subway, tramcar, and trolley bus fares have not been changed for about thirty years.

In addition to wage increases, there has been a sharp growth in payments out of social maintenance funds—of allowances in case of illness and childbirth—and, to an even greater degree, of various pensions. The old-age pension system has become universal in the Soviet Union. While in 1961 old-age pensions were paid out to 5,400,000 people, in 1977 this figure reached 30 million, and it covers practically all veteran workers who have reached pension age. (Incidentally, the pension age in the Soviet Union is fifty-five for women and sixty for men, much lower than in many other countries.) From 1961 to 1977 the total number of pensioners (of all categories) has increased more than twofold, from 22 million to 46 million.

In order to visualize the significance of the increase in the cash incomes of Soviet people, it should be taken into account that the index of state retail prices changed by not more than 1 or 2 percent in the 1960s and 1970s. It is common knowledge that free medical service is available to all in the Soviet Union. The Communist Party (as was reiterated at its 25th Congress) takes into account that "no social task is more important than concern for the health of the Soviet people." One of the most striking indicators of the accelerated development of health protection is the growth of its material and organizational bases and, above all, of the number of doctors and the population under their care. In the last prewar decade the number of doctors increased on an average by 10,000 a year, in the period from 1951 to 1960 by 17,000, and in the past decade by an average of 28,000 a year. The steady growth in the number of doctors has made it possible to improve considerably the public health service. In the early 1950s there were on an average 650 to 700 people per doctor in the Soviet Union, ten years later 500, and now approximately 300 people.

With the cost of medical treatment rising sharply because of the development and widespread use of sophisticated medical equipment, the lengthening treatment courses, and the appearance of new and more complicated ailments, free medical care is coming to play a particularly significant role in the life of society.

It is also hard to overestimate the importance of the system of free education which has existed in the Soviet Union since the establishment of Soviet power. Under conditions of developed socialism it has attained an unprecedented scale. Universal free primary education was introduced in the 1930s, and incomplete secondary education in the 1950s, and at present the Soviet Union has in the main completed the transition to universal secondary education. Practically all children from six to seventeen years of age receive one or another form of secondary education at general schools, secondary vocational and technical schools, technical colleges, and the like.

The Soviet people receive social and cultural services either free of charge or at reduced cost; in addition, they get many extremely important material benefits. Such forms of raising the well-being of the people play an immense role, particularly in solving one of the most complicated social problems—namely, the problem of housing.

The housing problem which our country inherited from

capitalism became even more acute owing to the rapid urbanization that began in the 1930s, and it reached a critical level in the 1940s and 1950s as a result of wartime destruction.

From the 1950s to the 1970s Soviet society made a tremendous effort to solve the housing problem. In the period from 1956 to 1976 the state, as well as the population with the help of state grants and loans, built more than 47 million homes (apartments and cottages). To picture the scope of this construction, it should be borne in mind that there are nearly 60 million families in the Soviet Union.

It should be borne in mind that housing construction in the Soviet Union is mainly state-financed and that the rent is very low. It is, in fact, lower than in any other country and constitutes on an average about 1 percent of the family budget, or approximately 4 percent including the charges for electricity, water, etc.

Brezhnev drew attention to this fact when he said, "Rent has not changed in the Soviet Union since 1928, although the wages of industrial and office workers have increased several-fold in this period and the quality of housing has improved greatly. Rent and utility charges do not cover even a third of the actual cost. Therefore the state annually allocates about 5 billion rubles for housing and utility services. And this practice will continue."

The gigantic scale of housing construction and the socially just distribution of housing give every reason to believe that the housing problem will be fully solved in the foreseeable future.

The state housing fund which constitutes the bulk of the newly built housing is distributed practically free, and its maintenance is paid for with the reduced rent, which covers less than a third of the actual costs, while the state takes care of the rest of the sum. This system makes it possible to provide all sections of the population with comfortable homes. It is noteworthy that in the past two decades approximately 230 million people—*i.e.*, the overwhelming majority of the population—either moved into new apartments or received additional space in old houses.

The Soviet Union occupies one of the top places in the world for the number of apartments built per 1,000 population.

In the preceding Five-Year Plan period 56 million Soviet people had their housing conditions improved.

"The target for the next five years is 550 million square meters of housing," said Brezhnev. "This means that approximately 10 or 11 million people will move into new apartments each year. This is not bad at all. At the same time housing will continue to improve; that is to say, the quality of the apartments, their layout and finishing, will be better."

The entire history of Soviet society attests to a continuous heightening of the living standard of the people. But even so, said Brezhnev, there is nothing in the history of the country to compare with the social program that was put into effect in the Ninth Five-Year Plan period.

"We have not yet attained communism," he noted. "But the whole world sees that our party's activities and its aspirations are aimed at doing everything necessary for the benefit of man, for the sake of man. It is this supreme and humane goal of the party that gives it kinship with the people, creates firm and indissoluble bonds between it and all the Soviet people."

At this juncture it will be interesting to cite the observations of Professor Hans Apel of the University of Bridgeport in an article entitled "Soviet Standard of Living: Results of a Secret Poll" published in the West German *Frankfurter Hefte* magazine (No. 10, 1976). Almost 100 percent of those questioned, writes the author, who spoke to 203 "chance Soviet contacts" in various parts of the Soviet Union, are satisfied with the changes in their lives in the past decade. He stresses that the comparative data about the life of Soviet people, now current in the West, are obsolete and cites several examples of how public opinion in the West is being deceived.

Development of Foreign Economic Relations

Among the key economic objectives there is one acquiring ever-increasing importance—promotion of foreign economic relations. This is a direct result of the rapid growth of our economy, of the far-reaching changes taking place in the world, and of the success of the policy of peace and détente. Brezhnev attaches great importance to these ties. "We regard foreign economic relations as an effective help to carry out political and economic tasks," he said. "The might and cohesion of the community of socialist countries have been growing stronger through economic integration. Cooperation with the developing states is facilitating the restructuring of their economy and social life on progressive principles. Lastly, economic, scientific, and technical ties with the capitalist states are consolidating and broadening the material basis of the policy of peaceful coexistence. . . .

"Like the other countries, we strive to use the advantages of foreign economic relations to increase additional possibilities for the successful fulfillment of economic tasks and saving time, for enhancing production efficiency and speeding up scientific and technical progress."

Currently 115 countries are trading with the Soviet Union. Its foreign trade turnover is increasing rapidly: it was 10.1 billion rubles in 1960, and 51 billion in 1975. In the Tenth Five-Year Plan period—from 1976 to 1980—there will be a further expansion of foreign economic relations. "It is planned," Brezhnev said, "that trade with socialist countries will rise by 41 percent and with industrialized capitalist countries by more than 31 percent."

The industrialized capitalist countries alone purchase from the Soviet Union thousands of machine tools and tractors, tens of thousands of automobiles, millions of tons of coal, tens of thousands of tons of aluminum, hundreds of thousands of cameras and radio sets. It proved advantageous for the French to buy a super-heavy-duty stamping press after they had failed to negotiate a deal with the United States and the Federal Republic of Germany; for the Canadians to buy Soviet-made turbines, machine tools, and tractors; for the Americans to purchase computer parts; and so forth.

Brezhnev emphasized the importance of promoting new forms of foreign economic ties and noted that they "greatly enlarge our possibilities and, as a rule, yield the greatest effect. I have in mind, among other things, compensation agreements under which new enterprises, belonging entirely to our state, are built in cooperation with foreign firms. We are granted credits, equipment, and licenses, and we pay for this with part of the output of these or other enterprises. For the time being, agreements of this kind cover mainly industries producing primary materials and semifinished products. But it is perhaps time to expand the sphere of their operation, so as to include the manufacturing industry and look for new approaches to cooperation in production."

CHAPTER IV

Working for World Peace

Never yet in the history of humanity had so many workers for peace gathered at so representative a forum as the one in Moscow in October 1973. The delegates represented the majority of mankind—the working people, religious groups, the world of science, the political world, women, and youth from 124 countries and all continents. The forum was never equaled in scale.

The 3,000 delegates gave a standing ovation to the man who strode vigorously across the stage of the giant Kremlin Palace of Congresses to the speaker's platform.

On his lapel glittered the golden badge of Lenin Peace Prize Laureate, conferred on him a few months before for his tremendous role in normalizing international relations and bringing about a change of course toward a relaxation of tensions and world peace.

The ovation at the World Congress of Peace Forces on that October day in 1973 was an acknowledgment of his services to all people of goodwill who cherish peace and abhor war.

In the audience were representatives of forty-nine socialist and social-democratic parties and of fifty-eight national-democratic and revolutionary-democratic parties and movements, members of seventy-four Christian-democratic, liberal, agrarian, and other parties and of many pacifist and clerical organizations, and members of the business world and professional groups. About one-fourth of the delegates were Communists.

The audience included 233 members of parliaments, representatives of 308 different trade unions, 84 women's and 104 youth organizations, representing hundreds of millions of people.

Brezhnev's speech was frequently punctuated by applause. Sometime later the prominent Catholic professor Rudolph Weiler, of the theological department of Vienna University, said, "In my view, the important speech made at the Congress by the General Secretary of the Central Committee of the Communist Party of the Soviet Union, Leonid Brezhnev, gives a precise definition of the issues on which a dialogue is possible between groups of different outlooks."

Brezhnev said that for many centuries people had never tired of condemning and cursing war. Nations longed for enduring peace, but in spite of this, the sinister glare of armed conflagrations big and small is reflected on every page of human history.

Now, thanks to the efforts of the peace forces, the international climate has become healthier and the policy of peaceful coexistence and international cooperation is yielding tangible results.

But this, Brezhnev emphasized, was only a beginning. The audience responded enthusiastically to his appeal to make the easing of tension a stable, an enduring, and, even more, an irreversible process.

Much effort had been required to attain even the present level of détente. And tremendous credit for this goes to

Brezhnev. He is putting into effect the policy of consolidating peace among nations and ensuring a just and democratic peace—a policy set in motion by the Soviet state in the very first years of its existence.

I. ON THE BASIS OF
HISTORICAL EXPERIENCE

Peace—how welcome the word has sounded in all ages. But history knows of practically no period when guns were silent and the blood of innocent people was not shed in some corner of the world.

On November 7, 1922, on the 5th anniversary of the October Revolution, the first peaceful year of the Soviet Republic, the newspaper *Izvestia* published a drawing by the then still young and later highly prominent Soviet cartoonist Boris Yefimov. It was a full-length picture of a bricklayer laying the bricks of the foundation of the new society on whose banner were inscribed the words "Peace and Fraternity of All Nations." The first brick represented 1918, the second 1919, the third 1920, the fourth 1921, and the fifth (still held by the worker) 1922.

The bricklayer with a trowel—the epitome of peaceful construction—symbolized the most typical feature of that autumn of 1922, when the Soviet Union, the worker-peasant state that had proclaimed peace and fraternity among nations the immutable basis of its policy, was only just being built under Lenin's leadership. And this in a country of which *Pravda* wrote at the time: "Impoverished, ragged, and hungry, the workers' republic is celebrating the great day of its birth. For four years it was bathed in blood, fields of battle were strewn with the bones of its finest sons, and its last crumbs were sacrificed to ensure victory. Millions of its people are in the deadly grip of hunger. The stacks of hundreds of its factories are belching no smoke. The factory whistles are silent. . . . But the Red Republic stands firm on free land, its own land, having overcome countless hosts of enemies.''

These few years were crucial years for the Soviet people.

The importance of the external factor for the development and the very survival of the world's first socialist worker-peasant state was emphasized by Lenin, its founder. ''From the very beginning of the October Revolution,'' Lenin said, ''foreign policy and international relations have been the main question facing us.'' It is no secret that Soviet Russia's successes were furthered by such international factors as its peaceful and internationalist foreign policy, the support it won among the world's progressive forces, and the mass struggles for peace, democracy, national independence, and socialism, while acts of aggression, the interventions, the continuous danger of an imperialist attack, and the hostile capitalist encirclement worked against it.

The Great October Socialist Revolution showed the unseverable connection between socialism and peace. ''An end to wars, peace among the nations, the cessation of pillaging and violence—such is our ideal,'' Lenin said. Soviet Russia was the first country to withdraw from the World War of 1914–18. In its very first decree, written by Lenin, the great founder of the Communist Party and the Soviet state, Soviet Russia offered peace to all countries and peoples. It tore up and published all the secret treaties concluded by the Allied powers on dividing the territory of other countries.

Peace, Lenin pointed out, was the crucial condition for the advance of the revolution to the stage of peaceful construction and the building of the first socialist society in history.

But the breathing space won by Soviet Russia in 1917–18 proved very short.

Joining hands with the counterrevolutionaries in Russia, fourteen imperialist countries began a campaign, as Winston Churchill put it, to strangle Soviet power in "its cradle."

This was when all Soviet people learned for the first, but not the last, time that the mere wish for peace, no matter how heart-felt and strong, was not enough. They learned that peace had to be defended, that it had to be fought for, and that a flexible policy of principle, an active and purposeful diplomacy, a dependable rear, and trustworthy allies were required to achieve it.

The intervention of the imperialist powers caused a great loss of life, destruction, and suffering. The Soviet government sought to end the war and establish peace with any power that displayed the same desire. Rejecting the calls of Trotskyites and "Left" Communists for an "unintermittent war" against the capitalist states, Lenin firmly declared this policy unacceptable for real Communists. To begin with, it meant that the sacrifices and losses of the peoples of all countries would multiply immensely, that entire states might be destroyed, and even that Soviet power would be lost. Revolution, as well as counterrevolution, cannot be exported. Every nation must decide its own future and determine its own system and way of life, depending primarily on the development and situation of its own country. Countering the advocates of "unintermittent war" between the socialist and the capitalist system, Lenin formulated and elaborated the main aspects of the other alternative—the peaceful coexistence of the two systems and contention and competition between them in an environment of international peace. This alternative was ultimately approved and supported by the whole Communist Party and the Soviet people. The principle of peaceful coexistence thus became the cornerstone of socialist foreign policy and diplomacy.

Apart from the demands of the masses and apart from the humanitarian feeling, the ever broader recognition of this principle in world relations was motivated, as Lenin brilliantly predicted, by the development of increasingly deadly and destructive types of arms and by economic needs and interests. "There is a force greater than the wish, will, and resolution of any of the hostile governments or classes," Lenin said. "It is the force of the common worldwide economic relations that compel them to establish relations with us."

As a faithful Marxist-Leninist, Brezhnev is working continuously for a dynamic foreign policy, for the further development of its basic principles to suit the progressive course of events, the actual realities, and for the effectuation of Lenin's precepts. "The Soviet people," he stressed, "associate their understanding of a just peace and their view of a policy of peace with the name of our leader and teacher, the founder of our party and state, Vladimir Ilyich Lenin. It was Lenin who for the first time in world history linked the theory of scientific communism with the practical conduct of a state's foreign policy. It was this alloy of Lenin's thoughts and Lenin's deeds that gave birth to the principles and methods of socialist policy in international affairs in which we, his disciples and successors, take guidance and will always take guidance."

Brezhnev emphasizes that the foreign policy of the Soviet Union is a consistent policy of peace, security, and international friendship. Socialism has no other aim but to serve the interests of the people. And what this aim implies, above all, is combating war, which, as Lenin said, is the greatest blight for the working people.

Brezhnev's boundless loyalty to the Communist ideals, the leading one being work and peace, along with his own tremendous, often difficult, fighting experience, have made him an active champion and exponent of Lenin's policy of peaceful coexistence.

2 . PROMOTING THE POLICY OF PEACE

In the postwar years Brezhnev took a most active part in high-level discussions of the major problems of Soviet foreign policy and diplomacy as a member and then as a Secretary of the Central Committee of the Communist Party of the Soviet Union and as an alternate and then a full member of the Presidium of the Central Committee. This made him familiar with all the key problems of postwar international relations and gave him valuable experience in dealing with intricate foreign policy issues. He acquired a deep knowledge of the state of affairs in other countries and their position on the world scene, down to the details, first and foremost in relation to the Soviet Union. In a short time Brezhnev became a prominent international figure and one of the main architects of Soviet foreign policy and diplomacy.

After he was elected Chairman of the Presidium of the Supreme Soviet of the USSR in 1960, he shouldered great and responsible duties.

His stay in office was marked by considerable activity in the sphere of foreign policy.

Brezhnev's first mission abroad as Chairman of the Presidium of the Supreme Soviet was to the German Democratic Republic in September 1960. People in other socialist countries, too, got to know Brezhnev, Chairman of the Supreme Soviet Presidium. He visited Hungary, Czechoslovakia, Bulgaria, and Yugoslavia. And his every meeting with the leaders and people of the socialist countries yielded a rich political and economic harvest and became an impressive demonstration of friendship.

Establishing friendly relations with the developing countries, supporting the struggle of their peoples against old and new colonialism and for complete political and economic independence, and helping them in their striving for progress and peace were an important area of Soviet foreign policy. Brezhnev as Chairman of the Supreme Soviet Presidium devoted utmost attention to ensuring that Soviet relations with the developing countries constantly progress along lines of equal, mutually beneficial, and all-around cooperation and friendship. In those years he visited Guinea, Ghana, Morocco, and Sudan in Africa, paid a visit of friendship and peace to India, that great country in Southern Asia, and was received with honors in Afghanistan and Iran. These visits helped strengthen the friendly ties between the Soviet Union and the developing countries of Africa and Asia. Here Brezhnev's activity went counter to the plans of the colonialists. During his state visit to Morocco they made a criminal attempt on his life. When flying over neutral waters, the plane of the Chairman of the Presidium of the Supreme Soviet of the USSR was fired upon.

Faithful to Lenin's precepts, the Soviet Union sought relations of peaceful coexistence with all capitalist countries without exception, big or small.

At the end of September 1961 Brezhnev paid a state visit to Finland. The very fact of the visit showed the importance attached by the Soviet Union to the maintenance of good relations with that country. The visit had a beneficial effect on the further development of Soviet-Finnish good-neighborly relations, which significantly helped strengthen peace in the northern part of the European continent. The personal acquaintanceship and continuous contacts between Brezhnev and Finnish President Urho Kekkonen, dating to 1961, became an important element of the good-neighborly relations of the two countries.

Brezhnev took an active part in drafting many important foreign policy documents. It was under his chairmanship that the Presidium of the Supreme Soviet of the USSR ratified the 1963 Moscow Treaty banning nuclear weapons tests in the atmosphere, in outer space, and underwater, which was one of the first positive signs of change in the long-tense relations between the United States and the Soviet Union and which signified a certain physical and moral purging of the international climate of the more noxious cold war miasma—a treaty which was extended during the Soviet-American meeting in Moscow in the summer of 1974.

3. CONSISTENT CHAMPION OF PEACEFUL COEXISTENCE

The range of foreign policy problems in which Brezhnev engaged grew much broader after the Central Committee of the Communist Party of the Soviet Union elected him its First Secretary in October 1964. Many duties in this field were also retained by him as a member of the Presidium of the Supreme Soviet of the USSR.

Brezhnev became General Secretary of the Central Committee at a time when the international situation had grown more complicated. The struggle of the two opposite trends in world affairs—the peaceful and the aggressive—had become more acute. World reaction had redoubled its subversive activity against the socialist countries and the progressive regimes in an effort to split the socialist community, to drive a wedge between the Soviet Union and its allies and friends, and to isolate it on the world scene. International tension increased.

International affairs, particularly Soviet-American relations, were harmfully affected at that time by the war in Vietnam and by United States interference in the affairs of the Dominican Republic and the Congo.

In Europe the revenge-seeking reactionary elements in the Federal Republic of Germany not only continued to refuse to recognize the results of the Second World War—the postwar European frontiers and the existence of the German socialist state, the German Democratic Republic—but also tried by various means to gain access to nuclear weapons, making use, as Brezhnev pointed out, of "the NATO plans of creating a 'multilateral nuclear force.' "

In the Middle East, Israel launched what came to be known as the Six-Day War against the Arab states on June 5, 1967. The aggressor managed to occupy part of the territories of Egypt, Syria, and Jordan but failed in his main aim—a decisive victory that would enable him to saddle the Arab peoples with his own peace terms. "The situation in the Middle East," Brezhnev noted, "continues to be tense, and everything must be done to prevent the flames of war from blazing up again." In these conditions mankind was asking whether the world would continue drifting toward war or whether there would be a turn for the better in the world situation.

Firmness and single-mindedness were required to counter the hostile designs. Also required were a continuous initiative and flexibility in order to achieve a peaceful settlement of the acute international problems.

This was precisely the approach of the Central Committee of the Communist Party of the Soviet Union. In so doing, the party, the Political Bureau of the Central Committee, and Brezhnev personally devoted their primary attention to an all-around study and assessment of the basic objective and subjective factors and tendencies in world affairs.

These important and acute international problems were discussed at the Central Committee's plenary meetings in December 1966 and July 1967. The initiative in posing them came personally from Brezhnev, who saw to it that the party should always be abreast of world events and that Soviet foreign policy should be built on its collective opinion, experience, and approval, that it should always work in the interests of the peoples of the Soviet Union, of world peace and progress.

"The international activity of the Communist Party of the Soviet Union," Brezhnev said, "is the cause of the whole people. It reposes on the economic and defensive power of the country, on its spiritual potential, on everything created by the Soviet people. Its successes are the fruit of the experience and knowledge, moral powers and strenuous work of many representatives of the party and the state: members and alternate members of the Political Bureau, Central Committee secretaries, members of the Central Committee, a large number of the Central Committee staff, staff members of the Foreign Ministry, the Ministry for Foreign Trade, the State Committee for Economic Relations, and other ministries and departments, high-ranking functionaries and staff members of the Central Committees of the republics, of territorial and regional committees, comrades from city and district committees, and primary party organizations in town and country. . . . In this context, important tasks are performed by members of the Soviet parliament, the central and local organizations of the Soviets, the trade unions, and other public organizations, by people in science and culture, and, of course, by the press, radio, and television. Thousands of Soviet people are employed abroad—in embassies and other missions and as geologists and builders, doctors and teachers, metallurgists and chemists, transport and other specialists."

Great importance in framing Soviet foreign policy was attached to profound scientific analysis of international relations and the situation in individual countries.

Soviet foreign policy took account of the fact that in some countries the ruling circles were obstinately trying, as they still do, to conduct a blatantly hostile policy against the Soviet Union and its allies, while more realistic views were emerging in other countries, reflecting to one or another

177

degree the alignment of world forces and true national interests.

In these conditions Brezhnev again called attention to the urgency and the good chances of directing international relations to the principles of peaceful coexistence and declared the Soviet Union's loyalty to these principles. "The Soviet Union followed and will continue to follow Lenin's policy of the peaceful coexistence of states with different social systems," Brezhnev said. "It is directed to averting a nuclear world war, to settling disputes between states by negotiation, to respecting the right of every people to choose its social and state systems and settle questions of its internal development by itself. . . . Our country is for settling outstanding problems step by step and consolidating peace."

But peaceful coexistence, Brezhnev stressed, is not a simple absence of military operations or a lessening of the war danger. If the peaceful coexistence of states belonging to opposite social systems is to be stable, it must also be based on cooperation and on mutual understanding, confidence, and advantage. "Our policy is a policy of good relations and mutually beneficial cooperation with all states, and our relations with countries that are interested in it are improving from year to year," Brezhnev noted. "We attach great significance to business contacts and the development of relations with the main capitalist powers."

Not only political but also economic imperatives imposed on the capitalist states the policy of establishing and broadening commercial, financial, scientific, and technical ties and exchanges with the socialist countries.

Projecting the thesis of the influence of economic factors on foreign policy, Brezhnev pointed to the set of important factors working in this direction. "One of the specific features of our time," he said, "is the increasing use of the international division of labor for the development of every country irrespective of its wealth and economic level."

Brezhnev observed that there was an ever more visible influence on the entire system of international relations by problems that concerned the interests of all mankind. "Today," he said, "such global problems as those of raw materials or energy, combating the more dangerous and widespread diseases, environmental protection, exploration of outer space, and use of the resources of the World Ocean have become important and topical."

The growing Western understanding of the fact that capitalist states have as great a stake in peace and cooperation as the socialist countries has helped considerably to weaken the position of the exponents of the reactionary aggressive policy and to augment the numbers of the supporters of peaceful coexistence.

The thorough and clear exposition of the Communist Party's standpoint on the main international problems made by Brezhnev at the 23rd Party Congress represented a further development of the principles of Soviet foreign policy.

"At the Congress we can note with gratification the serious successes of our peace policy in the period under review. The Soviet Union has good relations with most countries of the world," Brezhnev said. He noted that the Soviet Union was conducting "its policy under the sign of struggle for an easing of tension, for a stronger peace, for the peaceful coexistence of states with different social systems, for such international conditions where every nation could advance freely along the road of national and social progress. . . . The Soviet Union stands firmly for noninterference in the internal affairs of all states, for respect of their sovereign rights and of the inviolability of their territory. . . . As for the interstate relations of the Soviet Union and the capitalist countries, we want them not only to be peaceful but also to include the broadest possible mutually advantageous ties in the economic, scientific, and cultural spheres."

In his Report to the 23rd Congress, Brezhnev showed the

invariable internationalist essence of Soviet policy, its continuity and the firmness of its basic principles, and, at the same time, its creative, innovative, and realistic character applicable to the changing situations and the vital requirements of the times. His analysis of the current world situation was based on profound insight into the substance of world events and on a knowledge of the objective laws governing humanity's progressive development.

The active and consistent work of the Communist Party under Brezhnev's leadership in the domain of foreign policy helped frustrate imperialist attempts to make cold war an inalienable component of international relations. This consistent activity furthered the shaping of objective and subjective conditions for a visible change for the better in international relations. This, in turn, served as a premise for the major initiative of the Communist Party of the Soviet Union, and its General Secretary personally, in resolving foreign policy and diplomatic problems and in the struggle for peace and social progress.

This initiative found expression in the Peace Program adopted by the 24th Congress of the Communist Party of the Soviet Union and, later, in the Program of Further Struggle for Peace and International Cooperation and for the Freedom and Independence of the Peoples, proclaimed by the 25th Congress.

4. STRUGGLE FOR DÉTENTE

Never in recent decades has any state come forward with so comprehensive a set of concrete proposals on the basic international problems as the Peace Program set out by Brezhnev at the 24th Congress of the Communist Party of the Soviet

Union and adopted by it. It was striking evidence of the innovative spirit, boldness, dynamism, and farsightedness of Soviet diplomacy and fresh impressive evidence of the fact that the Communist Party of the Soviet Union is guided in its activity on the world scene by the interests of the Soviet people, as by those of other nations of the world, that it responds to their aspirations and relies on their support.

The first section of the Peace Program was aimed at the quickest possible termination of the aggressive wars fought at the time and the elimination of existing flash points of the danger of war and at instilling the principle of peaceful settlement in place of force in international relations. The Communist Party of the Soviet Union regarded the following as the first set of objectives in the struggle for peace:

—To extirpate the hotbeds of wars in Southeast Asia and the Middle East and to promote a political settlement in these regions on the basis of respect for the lawful rights of those states and peoples suffering from aggression.

—To repulse all acts of aggression and international violence instantly and firmly. The resources of the United Nations, too, must be used to the fullest extent for this purpose.

—To make renunciation of the use and threat of force in resolving disputes a law of international life. The Soviet Union, for its part, proposed that the countries with this same approach conclude pertinent bilateral and regional treaties.

The course of events confirmed the realism of this approach. The United States aggression in Vietnam and the rest of Indochina had reached a dead end. Most Americans and the world public demanded an end to the unlawful and brutal assault on the rights of the Vietnamese people and other peoples of this region. Further delay of a political settlement meant only additional loss of life and new complications on the world scene and inside the United States.

In the case of the Middle East, the other seat of the danger of war for the world, the futility of the attempts of Israel's rulers to consolidate their hold on the Arab lands seized as a result of aggression had become obvious. The warnings issued by Brezhnev could not be clearer: "The longer a political settlement in the Middle East is dragged out, the greater will be the outrage of the world public, the greater the Arab peoples' hatred of the aggressor and his protectors, and the greater the harm Israel's rulers will inflict on their own people and country."

Brezhnev reaffirmed the sources of international tension surviving since the Second World War. He suggested:

—Recognizing as final the territorial changes that resulted in Europe from the Second World War, effecting a radical turn toward détente and peace on that continent, and ensuring the convocation and success of the European Conference.

—Ensuring in every way Europe's collective security.

Brezhnev called for reaffirmation of the jointly expressed readiness of the signatories of the defensive Warsaw Treaty for the simultaneous annulment of this treaty and the North Atlantic Alliance or, as a first step, fcr dissolving their military organizations.

The Peace Program strongly emphasized the need for renouncing use of force in international relations. It was aimed at limiting and later eliminating the material basis of the policy of aggression, violence, and war. It put forward an all-embracing set of disarmament measures, and this, first of all, in relation to nuclear and other types of mass annihilation weapons liable to inflict grave losses on mankind. The program envisaged treaties banning nuclear, chemical, and bacteriological weapons, ending nuclear weapons tests by all countries everywhere, including underground tests, and establishing nuclear-free zones in different regions of the world. "We are for the nuclear disarmament of all states possessing nuclear weapons," said Brezhnev, "and for the holding for this purpose of a conference of the five nuclear powers—the Soviet Union, the United States, the People's Republic of China, France, and Britain."

The nuclear disarmament proposals were closely tied in with provisions limiting conventional armed forces and with general and complete disarmament. The program set the objective of stepping up efforts to terminate the arms race and convening a world conference to examine all aspects of disarmament. The Soviet Union called for the winding down of foreign military bases, for reducing armed forces and armaments in regions where the military confrontation is especially dangerous, notably Central Europe, and for reducing military expenditures.

These measures would substantially clear the international atmosphere of fear and suspicion and enable the states to devote the tremendous resources released from military budgets to peaceful purposes.

Imbued with concern for the vital interests of humanity, the Peace Program included a special point on combating all forms of national inequality, discrimination, and oppression: "The UN decisions on eliminating the surviving colonial regimes must be put into effect in their entirety. Racism and apartheid should be met with universal condemnation and boycott."

The program also provided for the development of peaceful cooperation with other countries in important specific fields.

"The Soviet Union," it said, "is prepared to deepen relations of mutually beneficial cooperation in all fields with countries that so wish. Our country is prepared to participate jointly with the other interested states in resolving such problems as environmental protection, development of energy and other natural resources, expansion of transportation and communications, prevention and elimination of the more dangerous and widespread diseases, and exploration and development of outer space and the World Ocean."

The force and effectiveness of the Peace Program derived from a set of interconnected factors: it expressed the real needs that grow out of the state of international relations in the present epoch, that these needs were embodied in concrete and realistic aims of practical policy, and that the Soviet Union, in close cooperation with the fraternal socialist countries, had mounted consistent and purposeful actions to put this foreign policy program into effect.

A few years later, in May 1973, the New York *Times* acknowledged the outstanding services rendered by Brezhnev in elaborating and advancing the Peace Program and described him as the "initiator of the newest policy of relaxing tension."

The 24th Congress of the Communist Party of the Soviet Union devoted considerable attention to relations between the Soviet Union and the United States. Brezhnev stressed that in the opinion of the party Congress relations with the United States could be improved. Soviet policy in relation to the capitalist countries, including the United States, is centered on consistent and full "implementation in practice of the principles of peaceful coexistence, development of mutually beneficial ties, and, with countries prepared for this, on cooperation in consolidating peace, making relations with them as stable as possible." Brezhnev stressed the necessity of determining in each case whether the Soviet Union was dealing with those who really wanted to settle problems at the negotiating table or with those trying to conduct a policy "from positions of strength."

Thus, the Soviet Union in clear terms expressed through the leader of its ruling party its readiness to negotiate an improvement of relations with the United States.

The Program of the 24th Congress was taken a step further at the 25th Congress, which adopted the Program of Further

Struggle for Peace and International Cooperation and for the Freedom and Independence of Peoples.

With many of the objectives of the Peace Program successfully achieved, Brezhnev developed and extended the provisions formulated at the previous Congress and came forward with new important initiatives in world affairs. The two programs blended into one foreign policy complex, as it were, determining the Soviet Union's steady policy of détente and its realization and of its struggle against the arms race.

As noted by Brezhnev, the main objectives required in the present conditions in the interests of peace, international security, and the progress of mankind are the following:

—To increase the active joint contribution of the fraternal socialist states to the consolidation of peace, while steadily strengthening their unity and developing their all-around cooperation in building the new society.

—To work for an end to the growing arms race, which is endangering peace, and for going on to a reduction of the accumulated stockpiles of arms and to disarmament. For this purpose:

• Do everything to complete the preparation of a new Soviet-American agreement on limiting and reducing strategic armaments and to conclude international treaties on universal and complete termination of nuclear weapons tests, on banning and destroying chemical weapons, on banning development of new types and systems of mass annihilation weapons, as well as on banning modification of the natural environment for military or other hostile purposes.

• Launch new efforts to activate negotiations on the reduction of armed forces and armaments in Central Europe. Following agreement on the first concrete steps in this direction, continue in the years ahead to promote military détente in the region.

• Work for a change from the present continuous growth

of the military budgets of many of the states to their systematic reduction.

• Take all measures to ensure the earliest possible convocation of the World Disarmament Conference.

—To concentrate the efforts of the peace-loving states on eliminating the remaining seats of war and, first of all, on implementing a just and durable settlement in the Middle East. In connection with such a settlement the states concerned should examine the question of helping end the arms race in the Middle East.

—To do everything to deepen international détente and to embody it in concrete forms of mutually beneficial cooperation between states. Work vigorously for the full implementation of the Final Act of the European Conference held in Helsinki and for greater peaceful cooperation in Europe. In accordance with the principles of peaceful coexistence, continue consistently to promote relations of long-term mutually beneficial cooperation in various fields—political, economic, scientific and cultural—with the United States of America, France, the Federal Republic of Germany, Britain, Italy, Canada, Japan, and other capitalist countries.

—To work for ensuring security in Asia on the basis of joint efforts by the states of that continent.

—To work for a world treaty on the nonuse of force in international relations.

—To consider as crucial the international task of completely eliminating all vestiges of the system of colonial oppression, infringements on the equality and independence of peoples, and all seats of colonialism and racism.

—To work for eliminating discrimination and all artificial barriers in international trade and all manifestations of inequality, diktat, and exploitation in international economic relations.

The implementation of the Peace Program had its results.

For the first time in the postwar decades mankind shook off the burden of the cold war.

The relaxation of international tension began to acquire realistic outlines.

"What is détente? What do we mean by it?" Brezhnev said. "To begin with, détente means overcoming the cold war and going over to normal and balanced relations between states. Détente means readiness to settle differences and disputes not by force, not by threats and saber rattling, but by peaceful means, at the negotiating table. Détente means definite trust and the ability to reckon with one another's legitimate interests.

"Developments have shown that the atmosphere of international relations can be visibly changed in a short time. Contacts between countries have expanded in the political, economic, cultural, and other fields. And, most important of all . . . the danger of a new big war has receded. People can breathe more freely and are looking to the future with more hope.

"This is what détente means, and those are its tangible results."

The Soviet Union's policy of promoting the principles of peaceful coexistence in international relations, of easing international tension, was and is being conducted in close cooperation with the other socialist countries.

Together with the Other Socialist States

As the General Secretary of the Central Committee of the Communist Party of the Soviet Union, Brezhnev participates in person in most of the bilateral and multilateral meetings and negotiations between leaders of Communist and workers' parties of the socialist countries working out a common position in world affairs.

187

Brezhnev stresses the special nature of the relations with the fraternal socialist states and describes the socialist community as "a new social and historical community of states and peoples." These relations are keynoted by trust and solidarity, equality and unity, which are features never before seen in history. They rest on the community of not only national but also class interests and on identity of a social and economic system and ideology. And since the interests are those of socialist nations and laboring classes, they are of especial endurance and constancy and are directed to a common aim—the building of the new society. The emergence of these relations opened an important chapter in world history and heralded the shaping of international relations of the new socialist type.

Analyzing the development of the socialist community, Brezhnev said, "The emergence and development of this alliance took time and considerable collective effort. We had to find the answer to many fundamentally new questions of theory and practice and to react intelligently and promptly to various turns of events. And the facts have confirmed convincingly that given the correct Marxist-Leninist approach, we resolved and can resolve even the most complicated of problems in a way that contributes to the strengthening of each socialist country and the socialist community as a whole."

The principles of socialist internationalism encompass all the aspects of relations between the Soviet Union and the fraternal socialist countries. These relations are based on fraternal cooperation, complete equality, respect for territorial integrity, state independence, and sovereignty, and noninterference in one another's internal affairs. These principles are practiced, first of all, by the ruling Communist and workers' parties of the socialist states, which are united by the Marxist-Leninist ideology and act in constant and close contact with one another. Their cooperation enriches the parties with mutual experience and enables them jointly to work out the fundamental problems of building socialism and communism, to find the most rational economic ties, collectively to chart a common line in foreign affairs, and to exchange opinion on work in the ideological and cultural fields.

It is natural for Brezhnev to rejoice at the successes of any nation in national development and social progress. He is convinced that all the fraternal socialist countries must act together and rely on mutual support in overcoming all difficulties and scoring ever new victories.

"We want to see every fraternal country a prospering state that harmoniously combines rapid economic, scientific, and technical growth with the flowering of socialist culture and a continuous rise in its people's well-being," Brezhnev said. "We want the world socialist system to be a friendly family of peoples jointly building and defending the new society and enriching one another with experience and knowledge. We want it to be a close-knit and strong family in which people all over the world would see the prototype of the future worldwide community of free peoples."

Coordinating the activities of the fraternal socialist parties and states in foreign affairs is of the utmost importance. Concluded as a counterweight to the Paris and London agreements on the remilitarization of the Federal Republic of Germany and its admission to NATO, the Warsaw Treaty and the organization formed on its basis are a dependable foundation for the further coordination of the efforts of the socialist countries in strengthening peace and achieving détente. The organization's Political Consultative Committee, in which Brezhnev takes part as the head of the Soviet delegation, is convened at regular intervals to discuss common attitudes and work out initiatives. The Political Consultative Committee's 1966 Bucharest Declaration, 1969 Budapest Appeal, 1970 Berlin Statement, 1972 Prague Declaration, and 1974 Warsaw Communiqué contained important initiatives to further international peace and security. The proposals worked out by the Warsaw Treaty countries' Political Consultative Committee at its session in Bucharest in November 1976 are of the utmost importance for the deepening of détente and for cooperation in combating the arms race.

Economic cooperation, extending and diversifying economic ties, holds an important place in the relations between socialist countries. Their scientific, technical, and cultural contacts are growing continuously, and the Council for Mutual Economic Assistance (CMEA) is playing an ever bigger role in the economic development of both its permanent members and the countries that systematically participate in some areas of its work. The CMEA has never been a closed body and affords ample opportunities for all countries that wish to take part in its activity and, at the same time, for extending its own ties and accords with all the other countries of the world.

From separate and simple elements of mutual assistance, the economic cooperation of the socialist states has gradually progressed to increasingly complex and comprehensive forms.

Brezhnev has done a great deal to promote major advances in the specialization and cooperation of production, trade, finance, and scientific-technical research among the CMEA countries in recent years. Much has also been done to coordinate their economic plans, to put their cooperation on a long-term basis, and to extend it to ever new economic fields. The comprehensive program for the further deepening and improvement of cooperation and for the development of socialist economic integration of the CMEA countries, adopted by its session of 1971, was drawn up with Brezhnev's direct participation. As a result of measures aimed at the economic development of each country and of the community as a whole, the CMEA countries have now grown into a dynamic economic world force, and their share in world industrial output now approaches one-third.

Socialist integration is practiced in the interests both of each separate country and of the community as a whole on the basis of complete equality and mutual interest and advantage. It is aimed at facilitating the all-around development of the socialist community as a whole and of each participating country, complementing their national effort of building a peaceful and prosperous economy.

Known throughout the world are many of the large-scale joint projects of the socialist countries, such as the gas pipeline from the Soviet Union to Eastern Europe, the Druzhba oil pipeline, which annually transports tens of millions of tons of oil, the Mir power system, and the joint construction of enterprises for the extraction and processing of various minerals, enterprises making electronic computers, the CMEA Investment Bank, etc.

Formed at first to coordinate the economic effort of several countries of Eastern Europe and the Soviet Union, the CMEA subsequently expanded the scale of its activities, its composition, and its ties with many other states. It was joined by the Mongolian People's Republic and by Cuba. The Democratic People's Republic of Korea, the Socialist Republic of Vietnam, and Yugoslavia participate regularly in the work of many of its agencies. And it has cooperation agreements with other countries, including Asian, African, and Latin American nations, and with various international and interstate organizations and associations.

"The member states of the Council for Mutual Economic Assistance," Brezhnev stressed, "are active champions of equal and mutually beneficial economic cooperation between countries belonging to different social systems. This basic approach follows from their devotion to peace and is an in-alienable element of the policy of easing international tension.''

Brezhnev has always been a welcome guest in the socialist countries of Eastern and Central Europe. Their people know and appreciate his tireless work for peace, strengthening the socialist community, and improving the life of the mass of the people.

During his visits to the fraternal countries Brezhnev meets and talks not only with its leaders but with the general public—workers and farmers, people in science and the arts, engineers and doctors. All of them retain fond memories of these meetings and some approach him personally, as the leader of the Communist Party of the Soviet Union and as an old friend, at some later date in connection with some event or question.

During one of his visits to the Hungarian People's Republic Brezhnev spoke to the gifted folk writer Márton Pálné, a peasant woman and narrator of folk tales, at a meeting of the Hungarian-Soviet Friendship Society in Budapest. A few years later she sent a letter to him in Moscow, saying that a museum of folk art and history had been organized on her initiative in her native village. Among the many exhibits in this museum—domestic utensils, clothes, artifacts, ancient instruments, historical documents, and pictures—were many depicting the hardships of old-time village life in Hungary and the grim days of the fascist regime in that country.

"Thirty years ago," wrote sixty-year-old Márton Pálné to Brezhnev, "the heroic soldiers of the Red Army brought us freedom and happiness. I address you as a representative of the nation to which we owe our good life."

Deeply touched by the artless and heartfelt words of the elderly Hungarian peasant woman, Brezhnev thanked her warmly for her letter, which brought back recollections of their meeting in Budapest. "I was happy to learn," Brezhnev wrote to Márton Pálné, "that you have opened a museum in your native village. Socialism inherits all the best elements created in the long history of national and world culture and puts this wealth at the disposal of the people. Mastering the cultural heritage is a very important, necessary, and useful thing." Brezhnev congratulated Márton Pálné and her fellow villagers on the opening of the museum and wished them health and happiness and new success in building a prosperous socialist Hungary.

Meeting working people in the fraternal socialist countries, addressing them at meetings, Brezhnev always finds heartfelt words that evoke a warm response in his audience. He stands before them as their contemporary, as a man whose life is linked with theirs, with their past and present.

Czechoslovakia, 1973. Speaking in Prague, Brezhnev said, "Many pages in my life are associated with your beautiful country. My acquaintance with Czechoslovakia began during the war, when the Soviet people and the patriots of Bohemia and Slovakia were engaged in hard-fought battles against the nazi invaders for the honor, freedom, and independence of our countries. The men of Ludvik Svoboda's Czechoslovak Corps were our great friends. The glory of those days will never fade from my memory. And later, too, my contacts with Czechoslovakia were practically uninterrupted. I remember well, for example, how as secretary of the party's Dnepropetrovsk Regional Committee in the Ukraine I had the privilege of meeting Comrade Klement Gottwald, the outstanding leader of the Czechoslovak Communists, and spending several hours with him in a congenial comradely atmosphere."

Brezhnev has visited all the countries of the socialist community, some of them several times.

During these visits, as well as when leaders of these countries came to the Soviet Union, important questions were discussed and far-reaching political decisions were made. "With a sense of deep gratification," Brezhnev said at the 25th Congress of the Communist Party of the Soviet Union, "I report to the Congress that the leaders of the Communist parties of the socialist community maintain constant contact with one another. Systematic multilateral as well as bilateral meetings enable us to consult on all major problems and, as they say, share in each other's joys and sorrows and jointly map our further advance."

In its policy of détente the Soviet Union takes account of the interests of, and consults and coordinates its activity with, those two outposts of socialism: the Socialist Republic of Vietnam, in Southeast Asia, and Cuba.

The peoples of the Soviet Union and the fraternal socialist countries aided the war effort of the Vietnamese people against the aggressor, combining this with support for the peace efforts of the Democratic Republic of Vietnam and the National Liberation Front of South Vietnam.

In negotiations and contacts with American statesmen, the Soviet government invariably emphasized the futility of imposing an outside will on the Vietnamese people by force of arms.

A major part in this was played personally by the General Secretary of the Central Committee of the Communist Party of the Soviet Union. He did not spare himself and participated in all meetings and negotiations, and this yielded good results. The termination of the foreign armed intervention in the affairs of the peoples of Indochina was a historic milestone which in many ways facilitated the positive change of course in international relations in the first half of the seventies.

Bonds of friendship prevail between Leonid Brezhnev and Fidel Castro and other leaders of socialist Cuba. The General Secretary's visit to the island in January–February 1974 was of tremendous importance not only for the further strengthening of the socialist countries' common positions on the world scene but also for further progress in the battle for peace. While in the vicinity of the United States, Brezhnev deemed it necessary to reiterate that "the incipient improvement of Soviet-American relations is beneficial for world peace." And he amplified: "We shall continue to follow this line in our relations with the United States, provided, of course, the other side reciprocates."

The visit attracted the attention of the North American and Latin American press, radio, and television. It gave fresh impetus to the movement for the annulment of the Organization of American States' decisions on blockading Cuba.

In the United States an increasing number of public leaders, Senators and Congressmen, political observers, and the general public began to speak out against continuing the senseless efforts to "isolate" Cuba and called for the establishment of normal relations with Fidel Castro's revolutionary government.

The Soviet Union and the Third World

The good progress of Soviet relations with the Asian, African, and Latin American countries is an important contributing factor to international détente and its realization. Brezhnev devotes considerable attention to these questions.

Soviet relations with the developing countries are expanding steadily. "The Soviet Union's ties with countries that have flung off colonial dependence or, as they are also called, the developing countries have expanded and grown stronger," Brezhnev said at the 25th Party Congress. The socialist world renders them moral, political, economic, scientific, technical, and, when necessary, other aid. Relations are making good progress because, among other things, the interests of the socialist and the developing countries coincide or are very close on a wide range of current international problems.

The socialist countries and many of the developing states act in unison in efforts to restrain the arms race and promote disarmament, to further the establishment of atom-free zones and the winding down of military blocs and foreign bases, to reduce military expenditures and transfer part of the thus released resources to peaceful economic needs. They condemn foreign interference in the internal affairs of other countries, colonial and neocolonial policies, racism, and apartheid. The peoples of the world gratefully acclaim their efforts against the spread of seats of the danger of war of a local as well as global character and for the security of peoples and peace. Their voice is heard in the United Nations and at other international forums. More and more often the Soviet Union, the fraternal socialist countries, and most of the developing states take joint action to extirpate the remnants of colonialism, to end economic exploitation and the arms race, and to promote independence and progress and peaceful and equal cooperation among all nations. The Soviet Union, Brezhnev said at the Central Committee plenary meeting of the Communist Party of the Soviet Union in October 1976, actively supports the legitimate demands "of the developing Asian, African, and Latin American countries that international economic relations should be reconstructed on a basis of equality, ending all forms of exploitation by the capitalist countries of their weaker partners in the third world. In this field, as in many others, the interests of the socialist and developing countries coincide." In an interview with the editor-in-chief of the Japanese newspaper *Asahi* in June 1977, Brezhnev said, "Our standpoint is clear on this score. The Soviet Union supports the developing countries' demands for recasting international economic relations along just and democratic lines. This means, first of all, that the process of extirpating colonialism must be spread to the economic sphere, that an end must be put to the multinational imperialist monopolies' oppression and the developed capitalist countries' exploitation of the natural resources and manpower of the developing states.''

Referring to Soviet foreign policy in relation to the African, Asian, and Latin American countries, Brezhnev often stressed that the Soviet Union does not interfere in the internal affairs of other countries and peoples, that it seeks no unilateral advantages, does not hunt for concessions, and wants no political domination or any military bases. "Respect for the sacred right of every people or country to choose its own way of development is an immutable principle of the Leninist foreign policy," Brezhnev said. "But we make no secret of our views. In the developing countries, as everywhere else, we are on the side of the forces of progress, democracy, and national independence; we regard them as our friends and comrades in arms.''

Brezhnev is making a major personal contribution to the development of this cooperation.

At about 11 A.M. on November 26, 1973, shouts of "Brezhnev-Druzhba" resounded at Palam Airport in New Delhi. There was a display of impatience among the many hundreds of guests and guests of honor in the enclosures and even attempts to break through the lines. And when the Il-62 touched down at 11:21 A.M., a rousing reception was given to the high Soviet guest.

Within an hour of his stay in India Brezhnev formulated the purpose of his visit to this great Asian country in lucid terms: "The peoples of the world expect statesmen and political leaders to take concrete action in furtherance of the peaceful cooperation of countries. It is safe to say, I think, that our negotiations will work in precisely this direction.

197

These days the friendship of the great peoples of the Soviet Union and India is of no small significance for peace and security in Asia and the rest of the world. A further strengthening of this friendship and an expansion of cooperation between the two countries are the main purpose of our visit.''

The Indian press hailed Brezhnev as an outstanding statesman, peace fighter, and the initiator of the battle for détente in the whole world.

Here, for example, is what *Link* wrote on December 2, 1973: ''The close-up of the man, provided for the people in the Capital, shows a personality that is perceptive but daring, cautious though dynamic. . . . The resonance of his voice matched the strength of character writ large over the thick eyebrows below a prominent forehead. . . . Another point that struck many New Delhi observers was the language—lucid and sometimes poetic—that Brezhnev used in dealing with complex problems. There was no worn-out jargon to cover lack of clarity in expression. Even while using such oft-repeated phrases as 'peaceful co-existence' or 'economic co-operation,' he showed the capacity to invest it with rich content of far-reaching impact.''

During Brezhnev's visit to India the Soviet Union and the Republic of India concluded a treaty of peace, friendship, and cooperation.

Drawing on the experience and long struggle of the peace-loving Asian countries, the Soviet Union, whose own territory extends across both Europe and Asia, has thoroughly substantiated the concept of Asian collective security. It was put forward as far back as 1969. Collective security, Brezhnev said, must repose ''on such principles as renunciation of the use of force in relations between states, respect for sovereignty and for the inviolability of frontiers, noninterference in internal affairs, and broad economic and other cooperation on the basis of complete equality and mutual advantage. We advocate and will continue to advocate such collective security in Asia and are prepared to cooperate in furthering it with all other states."

It is clear from Brezhnev's words that the Soviet proposal for an Asian collective security system is in the interests of all those who aspire to peace, independence, and equal security and who oppose war, intervention, and territorial expansion.

The idea of ensuring security in Asia and the Middle East is embodied in the treaties of friendship concluded by the Soviet Union with India and Iraq, the Declaration on the Principles of Relations with Turkey, the renewal of the nearly half-century-old Treaty of Neutrality and Nonaggression with Afghanistan, and a number of important documents signed with other Asian countries.

Many of these documents formalize the commitment of states to work for the maintenance of peace in Asia and the rest of the world, to promote détente and disarmament, to further a lasting and just peace, to prevent the use or threat of force, and to refuse the use of their territories for acts of aggression or subversion against other countries, and the like.

In his interview with the editor-in-chief of *Asahi* in June 1977, Brezhnev dwelt on Soviet policy in Asia at the present stage. He said, "Our country was and continues to be indissolubly connected with the Asian continent historically, economically, and geographically. It is natural, therefore, that we are seriously interested in consolidating peace in this region of the world. We hold that détente, which has become the dominant trend in world affairs, must not bypass the Asian continent, the home of more than half of humankind. Following the historic victory of the people of Vietnam and the establishment of the Socialist Republic of Vietnam, that large peace-loving state, following the settlement of the conflict in Southeast Asia and the withdrawal of United States troops from Indochina as a whole, more favorable conditions have appeared, as we see it, for ensuring lasting peace and security in Asia through the joint efforts of all the states of this continent. The Soviet Union favors precisely this course of events in Asia.''

The friendly relations between the Soviet Union and the African states have made further headway in recent years.

Relations with the countries that won their freedom as a result of their peoples' victory over Portuguese colonialism are being shaped in a spirit of sincere friendship and mutual understanding.

The development of ties between the Soviet people and the peoples of Africa was highlighted by the many top-level African delegations received in the Soviet Union in 1976 and 1977.

Brezhnev described the treaty of friendship and cooperation concluded by the Soviet Union and Angola in October 1976 as a new step forward—a big and convincing step—in consolidating the great friendship between the socialist world and the young liberated states. Angolan President Agostinho Neto's visit to the Soviet Union laid an enduring foundation for the further development and deepening of relations between the two countries. President Samora Machel's visit to the Soviet Union testified to expanding ties between the Soviet Union and the young Republic of Mozambique. And in May 1977 a state delegation of socialist Ethiopia, headed by Lieutenant Colonel Mengistu Haile Mariam, chairman of the Provisional Military Administrative Council, paid an official friendly visit to the Soviet Union.

The Soviet Union has sincere sympathy for the peoples of southern Africa fighting to root out the remnants of the system of colonial and racial oppression.

Stating the Soviet Union's position in relation to the African countries, Brezhnev said, "We have no 'special interests,' nor can we have any, either in the south or the north or in any other part of Africa, and we seek no advantages for ourselves there. All we want is for the sacred right of every nation to determine its future and choose its own way to be recognized. . . . We hold that a free people cannot but want other peoples to be free and cannot but support all those who fight for freedom. And we are sure that if all the peoples of Africa, all the oppressed peoples without exception, won freedom and independence, world peace and international security would only benefit from it."

This thought is reaffirmed in Brezhnev's replies to questions put by *Le Monde* in June 1977. "The Soviet Union," he said, "is firmly opposed to interference in the internal affairs of the African countries. We seek no advantages or privileges in Africa for ourselves. On that continent, too, our policy is directed to building peaceful and friendly relations with all peoples and to helping them successfully follow their chosen path of independence and progress."

Our country, Brezhnev stresses, regards as just, and will continue to support as before, the struggle of the peoples of the African continent for freedom and independence, for the right to choose their own way, and against the disgrace of racism and apartheid.

May Europe Be a Peace Zone

Brezhnev works for the solution of the most complicated international problems with his usual energy and perseverance. This applies, among others, to the problem of European security.

At different times—before and after the Second World

War—the Soviet Union's means of struggle for European security changed to suit the changing opportunities. But the persistent striving to strengthen peace on the Continent and to extend business relations with the European states of the other system has been consistent.

"Our party," Brezhnev says, "has always devoted paramount attention to ensuring European security. And the reasons for this are entirely understandable if you consider Europe's importance in world affairs."

Who can forget that it was Europe where the two World Wars originated, causing frightful devastation? The Second World War, which was the most destructive of all wars, claimed more than 20 million Soviet lives and destroyed nearly a third of the country's national wealth. Other European nations, too, suffered tremendous losses. And it is in Europe that the biggest forces of the two different groupings—NATO and the Warsaw Treaty—confront each other today; a vast number of missiles and of nuclear and conventional arms is concentrated there.

Europe is the most densely populated continent. Nearly 660 million people are crowded there into a relatively small area. More than half of them belong to the working class, the chief productive force of society and the leading class of the present epoch.

Europe is a treasure house of incalculable material and spiritual wealth—magnificent cities, the most up-to-date industrial enterprises, centers of scientific and technical thought, unique and precious works of art, and monuments of culture and antiquity.

This concentration in a limited area presages for Europe, and, above all, for its central and western parts, especially heavy losses in the event of a nuclear war. In sum, Europe needs relations based on genuine détente and mutual confidence.

All activities related to the establishment of an effective system of European security and cooperation are these days associated most directly with Brezhnev's name.

It was with his active involvement that the initial outlines of a European model of peace were worked out at the conference of Warsaw Treaty countries in Bucharest in July 1966 and the Conference of European Communist and Workers' Parties in Karlovy Vary in April 1967. The contours of European peace, as conceived by the participants in these conferences, included the following conditions: inviolability of European frontiers, renunciation of the use or threat of force and settlement of international disputes exclusively by peaceful means, development of mutually beneficial good-neighborly relations on the principles of the peaceful coexistence of states with different social systems, convocation of a European conference to discuss security and peaceful cooperation in Europe, and lessening of military tension, including dissolution of military alliances.

"The central question of European security," Brezhnev said in Karlovy Vary, "is that of the inviolability of European frontiers as they took shape as a result of and following the Second World War."

At present, these proposals formulated by Brezhnev have been formalized in treaties concluded by the Federal Republic of Germany with the Soviet Union and other socialist countries and in the Final Act of the Conference on Security and Cooperation in Europe.

Soviet diplomacy attached great importance to the convocation of the European conference. The socialist countries worked tirelessly to have the idea of the conference put into practice, leaning for support on the peace forces in the rest of Europe. And these efforts were crowned with success: the several-years'-long preparations for the Conference on Security and Cooperation in Europe were completed by the summer of 1975. The leaders of thirty-three European countries, the United States, and Canada gathered in Helsinki to sum up the results of the conference and affix their signatures to its Final Act.

There has been no more representative conference more important for European peace in history, and it is universally acknowledged that Brezhnev made a tremendous contribution to its success—from advancing the idea for it right up to its culmination at summit level. The General Secretary of the Central Committee of the Communist Party of the Soviet Union said in his Helsinki speech, "Expectations and hopes that no other collective action since the well-known Allied decisions of the postwar period can equal are associated with the results of this conference.

"The historic significance of the conference is especially clear to people who belong to the generation that experienced the horrors of the Second World War. Its aims are also dear to the hearts and minds of the generation of Europeans who grew up and are living in conditions of peace and who rightly consider that this is as it should be."

Everything must be done to prevent these expectations and hopes from being disappointed, Brezhnev said, and he called for "joint efforts to ensure Europe's conversion into a continent that would never see any more military upheavals."

Brezhnev noted that "the results of the conference are a carefully considered balance of the interests of all the participating states. If there are compromises, these compromises are justified, of the kind that benefit peace without obliterating the distinctions in ideology and social system."

While commending the Final Act and the results of the conference, Brezhnev was already looking to the future and urging that its provisions should not be turned into a scrap of paper but should be put into effect. He stressed that détente must be increasingly filled with material content. "Precisely the realization of détente is the substance of the matter . . ." he said. "It is very important to proclaim the correct and just principles of relations between states. And it is no less important to consolidate these principles in present-day international relations, to translate them into practice and make them a law of international life that no one is allowed to violate."

The Helsinki Conference influenced the entire course of events in Europe and many other regions of the world. Summing up the past and proceeding from the prevailing conditions of the present, it was directed to the future. "The results achieved," Brezhnev said at the 25th Congress of the Communist Party of the Soviet Union, "are worth the expended effort. The participants in the conference have collectively confirmed the inviolability of the existing frontiers. A body of principles has been elaborated for guiding interstate relations; they are entirely consonant—in letter and spirit—with the requirements of peaceful coexistence. . . . The perspectives of peaceful cooperation have been outlined in a number of fields—the economy, science and technology, culture and information, and contacts between people. Some other measures have also been defined to build confidence between states, including in the military sphere."

With the same tireless energy, consistency, and initiative that he displayed in fighting for the convocation of the Conference on Security and Cooperation in Europe, Brezhnev is now working for the complete and all-around implementation of the Final Act. He urges stepped-up efforts in this area, denounces the enemies of détente, and has authored new concrete initiatives.

Brezhnev takes advantage of every public appearance to attract the attention of the world public to questions of European security and cooperation.

Speaking at the 7th Congress of the Polish United Workers' Party in Warsaw in December 1975, he said, "We are in
favor of consistently fulfilling the specific provisions of the
Final Act. In saying so, we would like to stress that it is very
important to see and understand the significance of this document as a whole, and of all its parts, and not succumb to
the temptation of taking separate pieces from it out of context just because someone considers them tactically more advantageous."

Setting an example of the constructive approach to the
Helsinki accords, Brezhnev has made the proposal of convening European congresses and intergovernmental conferences on cooperation in such fields as environmental protection and the development of transportation and energy,
which could, among other things, discuss the idea of a united
transportation and power system stretching from the Urals to
the Pyrenees.

Speaking at the Conference of Twenty-nine Communist
and Workers' Parties of Europe, Brezhnev presented the
Soviet Union's extensive program for implementing the
Helsinki accords in spirit and letter. In the same terms and
with the same sense of conviction as at official negotiations
with Western leaders, he referred at this European Communist forum to the importance of ensuring lasting peace
in Europe and creating the "material fabric of peaceful
coexistence."

Brezhnev hailed the progress of détente on the European
continent but called attention to obstacles and to attempts at
using the Helsinki document for interference in the internal
affairs of the Soviet Union. "The socialist countries," he
said, "are not a 'closed society.' We are open to everything
that is truthful and honest and are prepared to multiply contacts, making the most of the favorable conditions created by
détente. But our doors will always be closed to publications

propagating war, violence, racism, and hatred, and doubly so to emissaries of foreign secret services and the anti-Soviet émigré organizations sponsored by them. . . . I feel that since the recent scandalous exposures of CIA activities everyone will agree that, mildly speaking, there are valid reasons for our approach.

"As we see it, cultural exchange and the mass media must serve humane ideals and peace and friendship among nations. Yet subversive radio stations that have usurped names such as 'Liberty' and 'Free Europe' are operating in the territory of some European countries. Their very existence is a wanton challenge to the letter and spirit of the Helsinki accords."

Brezhnev is seeing to it that the Soviet Union should scrupulously fulfill all the accords and principles of the Helsinki Conference and all its other international commitments. And he wants all the other participants in the conference to abide by the letter and spirit of the Final Act and to put its provisions into effect in their policies and in bilateral and multilateral relations with other countries.

Unlike some Western countries, the Soviet Union published the full text of the Final Act in about 20 million copies—in *Pravda* and *Izvestia* and in the languages of the Union Republics. Acting on the provisions of the Helsinki accords, the Soviet Ministry of Defense has made a practice of inviting observers from neighboring countries, including members of NATO, to military maneuvers in the Soviet Union. Together with other socialist countries, the Soviet Union has come forward with new constructive proposals that substantially take into account the Western powers' position at the talks on reducing armed forces and armaments in Central Europe, with drafts of an agreement on principles of relations between the Council for Mutual Economic Assistance and European Economic Community, on organizing

European cooperation in energetics, on enlivening cultural exchange (in UNESCO), and the like. The Soviet Union has begun, on a reciprocal basis, to grant multiple exit visas to permanently accredited journalists and has extended their range of movement in the country.

The following UNESCO data are enough to show the Soviet Union's broad approach to cultural cooperation: the Soviet Union publishes four times as much translated literature as the United States; more than 300 American, 150 British and as many French, and hundreds of works by other foreign authors are published annually in the languages of the Soviet peoples in tens of millions of copies.

The International Institute of Journalism (based in Finland) estimates that for every three Western programs shown on television in the socialist countries, Western television shows only one program from the socialist countries. As many as 130 modern foreign plays are running in Soviet theaters, while modern Soviet plays are few and far between on the Western stage. In Soviet secondary and higher schools 12 million people are learning English, 11 million German, and 2.5 million French, whereas in the West an infinitely smaller number are learning Russian.

"On the whole," Brezhnev pointed out at the October 1976 plenary meeting of the Central Committee of the Communist Party of the Soviet Union, "the work of implementing the Helsinki accords has now been parceled into tens, even hundreds, of practical measures. They may not always be conspicuous, but they amount to party and government work of the utmost importance. And we Soviet people appreciate the efforts of those who are working in the same direction."

At the end of November 1976, after his visits to Yugoslavia and Rumania, Brezhnev took part in a conference of the Political Consultative Committee of the Warsaw Treaty countries held in Bucharest. There the Soviet Union and the other socialist countries again displayed their resolution to promote détente and cooperation and to strengthen peace and security in Europe and the rest of the world. Noting the tremendous importance of, and the significant progress made in, carrying out the Final Act, the Political Consultative Committee made important new proposals to further its implementation. The socialist countries proposed, in particular, that all the participants in the Helsinki Conference should conclude a treaty on not being the first to use nuclear weapons against one another. Reaffirming their readiness for the simultaneous dissolution of the Warsaw Treaty and North Atlantic Treaty organizations and, first of all, their military establishments, they furthermore suggested that admission of new members to the existing military alliances of the socialist and capitalist states be suspended.

In June 1977, answering questions put by *Le Monde*, Brezhnev said, "Today, I think, no one will contest the fact that the Helsinki accords contain a great potential of positive influence on relations between states and on the situation in Europe and beyond its borders. More, the Final Act signed in Helsinki has already become a weighty political reality of international life and is being put into effect quite actively. Much has already been done, though the degree of progress is naturally different in different areas. After all, and the participants in the European Conference agree on this point, the Final Act is a broad and long-term program of action by states to strengthen European peace. I would like to emphasize that this program will be all the more successfully implemented in future if there are fewer attempts to poison the climate of relations between states."

Brezhnev considers the Final Act one of the most important achievements of the policy of peaceful coexistence and spares no effort to promote its consistent and all-around im-

plementation and to ensure a just democratic peace in
Europe.

Soviet-French Relations

Soviet-French relations are an important element in building the European collective security system. Substantial con-
tributions were made to this by the Soviet-French meetings
in the latter part of the sixties, the meeting in Moscow in the
fall of 1970, the visits to France by the General Secretary of
the Central Committee of the Communist Party of the Soviet
Union in October 1971, June 1973, and December 1974;
Brezhnev's meetings with the late President Georges Pompi-
dou in Zaslavl, near Minsk, in January 1973 and in Pitsunda
on the Black Sea in March 1974; and his meetings with President Giscard d'Estaing in October 1975 in Moscow and in
June 1977 in France.

"The Franco-Soviet friendship has deep roots in history,"
wrote Geneviève Tabouis, the veteran French journalist. "It
has always been in the national interests of France and the
USSR to work together for peace and security in Europe and
the rest of the world."

The Soviet people, who hold in high esteem the glorious
historical traditions of the French nation and its national
character, industry, and culture, have always favored broad
political, economic, and cultural ties with France.

Brezhnev said on this score, "I must confess that my first
encounter with Paris awakens special emotions in me. It was
to have taken place much earlier—more than twenty-six
years ago. At that time I was in the Soviet Army, which had
just completed its final operations against the nazis in the
heart of Europe. In those spring days of forty-five, still fresh
in the memory of our generation, one of my army friends and
I nursed this dream of visiting Paris." He explained that

their wish was motivated by a sense of deep respect for their comrades in arms, the patriots of France. They felt drawn to France by the reverence and interest alive in every Russian for the country "that has given the world great enlighteners and revolutionaries and great men of the arts and of science. I had already made concrete plans for a trip to the French capital but had to give it up at the last minute.

"I had the honor of being invited to participate with my front comrades in the Victory Parade in Moscow's Red Square and had to prepare for this big and happy event. Then came other things and other concerns. This is how it happened that my encounter with Paris was put off until more than a quarter of a century later. Now I am deeply gratified that it has finally taken place and that it is keynoted by the growing friendship of the Soviet Union and France."

Tokens of friendship were in evidence at every step during Brezhnev's stay, beginning with the warm reception at Orly Airport and right up to the signing of the Principles of Soviet-French Relations on the day he departed.

Brezhnev's visit to France in December 1974 for a working meeting with Valéry Giscard d'Estaing, the new French President, reaffirmed the stability of the policy of concord and cooperation prevailing between the two countries. In many respects this policy has become an essential factor of détente and the reshaping of international relations on the principle of the peaceful coexistence of states with different social systems.

The results of Brezhnev's talks with the President of France showed that Franco-Soviet cooperation was an important factor contributing to the deepening of détente and the consolidation of international security. Giscard d'Estaing noted the General Secretary's great personal contribution to the Soviet-French dialogue and concord. He said he was "simply astounded by the cordiality, frankness, and informality that highlighted the talks with M. Leonid Brezhnev. At these negotiations, I must say, he showed a very clear understanding of the issues, a very deep knowledge of the problems, and at the same time displayed extraordinary frankness in expounding them. I tried to reciprocate."

The French President spoke of his impressions again at a televised news conference.

He said to the journalists gathered in his conference room, the Gold Salon of the Palace d'Élysée, adjoining his study, "I really have the impression that I am dealing with a man guided by a genuine desire for peace." Brezhnev, the French President said, cannot conceive Soviet foreign activity as something that could or can be accompanied by armed interference.

Soviet-French relations were given fresh impetus during President Giscard d'Estaing's official visit to Moscow in October 1975, when he had another exchange of opinions with Brezhnev. "Soviet-French summit meetings," Brezhnev said at the dinner in honor of the French President in the Grand Kremlin Palace, "are invariably filled with great political content and have invariably ensured progress in the relations between our two countries."

The negotiations culminated in the signing of the Declaration on the Further Development of Friendship and Cooperation Between the Soviet Union and France and in agreements on scientific, technical, and industrial cooperation in civil aviation and the aircraft industry and on cooperation in energetics and in tourism. In July 1976 the two countries also concluded an important agreement on preventing the accidental or unauthorized use of nuclear arms.

In October 1976 the Soviet Union and France began exchanging television programs giving viewers a better idea of life in either country, of its culture, art, scientific achievements, and the like. The start for this exchange was given by

Brezhnev and Giscard d'Estaing in their addresses respectively over French and Soviet television.

Answering the questions of Yves Mourousi, the well-known French television commentator, whom he received in his Kremlin office, Brezhnev commended the results of the Franco-Soviet dialogue. "Soviet-French cooperation," he said, "has yielded visible benefits to both countries and has, at the same time, contributed many fresh and original elements to international practice, to relations between states with different social systems. . . .

"We cherish the growing friendship and cooperation of the Soviet and French peoples, which is a very valuable common asset."

In concluding his interview, Brezhnev expressed trust in the consistency and future of Soviet-French cooperation and in its steady progress. He said that there were still many untapped possibilities, especially in the political field—eliminating the danger of war and promoting disarmament and Europe's conversion into a continent of lasting peace.

Answering the questions of *Le Monde* on the eve of his visit to France in June 1977, Brezhnev cast a retrospective glance at the development of relations between the Soviet Union and France.

The beginning of the road traveled jointly by the Soviet Union and France, he said, goes back to the meeting of the Soviet leaders with General Charles de Gaulle in 1966. It brought about a radical change in Soviet-French relations— with the sights being set on developing cooperation in many different spheres. Since then good results have also been achieved in bilateral relations and as concerns the two countries' interaction on the international scene.

"Among the many agreements and protocols signed by our two countries in this period," Brezhnev said, "I should like to single out the agreement on preventing the accidental or unauthorized use of nuclear weapons. Its importance extends beyond our two countries, and it may be safely described as a substantial contribution to world peace. It would be a good thing if other actions by our two countries would follow, aimed at eliminating the risk of a nuclear conflict and at easing and ending the arms race.''

Brezhnev continued: "I have already had occasion to refer to the successful development of Soviet-French economic ties. In a way, they are the material foundation of relations between our countries. In the past we set and reached the objective of doubling our commodity turnover. Now we are going further—our aim is to treble it. And judging by the results of the past two years, this, too, will be achieved. . . .

"Many good things could be said about the scientific, technical, and cultural ties of our two countries. They enrich the peoples of both countries and promote better mutual understanding and a friendly atmosphere. We have many achievements in this field. . . .

"In short, we in the Soviet Union," Brezhnev said in conclusion, "take a positive view of the traversed path and hold that a good foundation has been laid for stable long-term relations in the years to come. At present it is important to maintain and augment the momentum of our cooperation.''

The importance of Brezhnev's visit to France in June 1977 far transcended the framework of Soviet-French relations. Key issues of current international affairs were raised at the talks—consolidation of peace and détente, elimination of the seats of the danger of war, ending the arms race, and eliminating the danger of a nuclear war. The joint statement on international détente expressed the resolve to follow the path charted at the Helsinki Conference and to work for peace, security, and equal cooperation. Great importance is attached to the Soviet-French declaration on the nonproliferation of nuclear weapons. Other important political documents were signed, including a number of agreements furthering and deepening Soviet-French political, commercial, industrial, scientific, and technical cooperation.

Soviet-West German Relations

The improvement in Soviet-West German relations is another significant factor strengthening European security and peace. This is confirmed by the entry into force of the treaties between the Soviet Union and the Federal Republic of Germany. Treaties have also been concluded between the Polish People's Republic and the Federal Republic of Germany and between Czechoslovakia and the Federal Republic of Germany. There is the quadripartite agreement on West Berlin and the treaty on the principles of relations between the German Democratic Republic and the Federal Republic of Germany.

The Soviet-West German treaty ended a long period of strain between the two countries created by the revenge-seeking policy of the West German rulers.

The treaty laid the necessary political and legal foundation for peaceful and mutually beneficial cooperation between the Soviet Union and the Federal Republic of Germany in the interests of the peoples of the two countries and of peace in Europe.

Systematic meetings at summit level have become a significant form of Soviet-West German cooperation. "Experience shows," Brezhnev said at a dinner in honor of the Federal Chancellor on May 21, 1973, "that when top political leaders join competent experts in various fields in developing relations between two countries, this acts as a stimulant for all concerned to work more effectively and promptly. But the main thing, I hold, is that the participation of political leaders vested with supreme responsibilities makes for a broad long-term view of the whole complex of relations; that is, it ensures a greater range of vision and more certain progress.''

After receiving Federal Chancellor Willy Brandt in Moscow in 1970 and in Oreanda in 1971, Brezhnev paid a visit to the Federal Republic of Germany in May 1973 and received in the Soviet Union the new Federal Chancellor, Helmut Schmidt, in October 1974 and West German President Walter Scheel in November 1975.

At the end of 1975, responding to a request by the weekly *Vorwärts* to say a few words on the 5th anniversary of the Moscow Treaty and the 20th anniversary of Soviet-West German diplomatic relations, Brezhnev observed that ''the normalization of relations between the Soviet Union and the Federal Republic of Germany is one of the most important developments in Europe's postwar history. . . . In a short time, the Soviet Union and the Federal Republic of Germany have radically reconstructed and advanced their relations. Regular political consultations at different levels, broader economic and commercial ties, and intensive scientific, cultural, and tourist exchanges—all this is concrete evidence of the favorable changes in the relations between our two countries. . . . We see the future of our relations with the Federal Republic in the context of peaceful coexistence and cooperation. This policy, consonant with the vital interests of our peoples and states, has stood the test of time and proved its merits. The Soviet Union is resolved to continue following the same course.''

Speaking at the 25th Congress of the Communist Party of the Soviet Union, Brezhnev stressed that the normalization of relations between the Soviet Union and the Federal Republic of Germany reposed ''on the only possible basis of renouncing claims to tearing down the existing European frontiers.'' Brezhnev noted at the same time that in the Federal Republic of Germany the policy of normalizing relations with the socialist countries was being attacked by right-wing forces, which were in effect pursuing a revenge-seeking course. Their pressure was evidently affecting certain aspects of Bonn government policy. The General Secretary noted in particular that not enough was being done as yet to ensure strict observance of the agreement on West Berlin and for its conversion from a source of disputes into a constructive element of peace and détente.

The forces attacking the "Eastern policy" of the government from an anti-Soviet and flimsily disguised revenge-seeking angle were especially active during the Bundestag elections in the fall of 1976. In the circumstances the Soviet government deemed it necessary to issue a special policy statement. The Soviet guidelines were summarized thus: the Soviet Union welcomes the change in its relations with the Federal Republic of Germany and their normalization; it regards the Federal Republic of Germany as a major international partner; it welcomes the rise in the international prestige of the Federal Republic of Germany as a result of the realism displayed by the Brandt-Schmidt governments in their relations with the socialist countries; it urges strict observance of the quadripartite agreement on West Berlin; it emphasizes that the opponents of détente are unable to offer any alternative to peaceful coexistence; it steadfastly seeks closer long-term cooperation with the Federal Republic of Germany in the political, economic, scientific, and cultural fields, a further lessening of international tension, disarmament, and peaceful development in Europe, with which the future of the Federal Republic of Germany is intimately associated.

Referring to Soviet-West German relations at the October 1976 plenary meeting of the Central Committee of the Communist Party of the Soviet Union, L. I. Brezhnev noted that in the opinion of the Soviet Union the majority of the West

German population is in favor of peace and détente and a further improvement of relations with the socialist states. This should facilitate the normal development of all-around mutually beneficial, long-term, and large-scale cooperation between the Soviet Union and the Federal Republic of Germany. As far as the Soviet side is concerned, the General Secretary stressed, "our position is clear: we are in favor of it."

In June 1977 L. I. Brezhnev received Hans-Dietrich Genscher, Deputy Federal Chancellor and Federal Minister of Foreign Affairs, in the Kremlin. During their talk they stressed the importance of steadily expanding cooperation between the Soviet Union and the Federal Republic of Germany. Brezhnev emphasized the constancy of the Soviet policy of deepening international détente and making it stable and irreversible.

Relations with Other European Countries

Brezhnev has worked very hard for the development of positive relations with other European countries. Special mention should be made of the Soviet-British summit meeting in Moscow in February 1975. As a result of the talks between the Soviet delegation, headed by L. I. Brezhnev, and Harold Wilson and James Callaghan, a dependable and constructive foundation was laid for Soviet-British relations. Broad opportunities were created for mutually beneficial cooperation between the Soviet Union and Britain, which had lost pace for some years owing to the unconstructive attitude of the Conservative government. Recalling the wartime alliance of the Soviet Union and Great Britain and their successful cooperation despite the differences in their social systems, Brezhnev stressed that Britain could be a good partner in the drive to consolidate peace and peaceful coexistence.

During the talks Brezhnev devoted much attention to Soviet-British economic ties. He was gratified to note, he said,
that a further expansion of Soviet-British economic cooperation would create new jobs for thousands upon thousands of
Britain's workers and give fresh impetus to its economic
growth.

The Soviet-British summit meeting was assessed by the
Political Bureau of the Central Committee of the Communist
Party of the USSR, the Presidium of the Supreme Soviet of
the USSR, and the Council of Ministers of the USSR as
highly important for the promotion of stable relations between the Soviet Union and Great Britain on the principles
of peaceful coexistence. Furthermore, they pointed out, its
results were a positive contribution to the consolidation of
international peace and security, especially in Europe.

Having made gigantic progress toward a more dependable
peace in a relatively short time, Europe is becoming one of
the chief factors in exercising a benign influence on world
affairs. Beyond the European horizon of security and cooperation there will inevitably open broader perspectives of
peace and security in other regions of the world.

Referring to the necessity of spreading détente to the
whole world, Brezhnev expresses deep faith that the policy
of peaceful coexistence will take deep root and go from success to success. "It is still too early to say, of course," he
said, "that a lasting foundation for peace has already been
laid in Europe, let alone the world. That would be a prema-
ture judgment. But what has already been done and what is
being done to this end are opening hopeful prospects." And
he added, "But very many difficult problems must still be
solved if these prospects are to become reality."

CHAPTER V

To Be Good Neighbors

The Soviet Union is developing businesslike cooperation and mutually advantageous relations with capitalist countries. Notwithstanding deep-going differences with the United States on a number of global political issues, the Soviet Union believes normal Soviet-American relations to be both possible and desirable—but not, it goes without saying, by renouncing any of its principles, not to the detriment of its friends and allies, and not at the expense of any other countries or peoples.

This is a principle that Brezhnev has always championed and champions today. He carefully follows the state and development of Soviet-American relations and invariably displays a readiness to take any actions that would improve them, such as corresponding, meeting, and negotiating with the top leaders of the United States.

"Neither economic or military might nor international weight," Brezhnev has said, "gives our countries any additional rights, but they do impose upon them a special responsibility for the fate of world peace, for preventing war. In its approach to ties and contacts with the United States, the Soviet Union is fully aware of this responsibility."

In his advocacy of normal relations between the Soviet Union and the United States, Brezhnev is motivated by a deep understanding of the vital needs of the Soviet, American, and other peoples of the globe, and is acting in the spirit of the behests of the founder of the Soviet state, Lenin.

I. A BRIEF EXCURSION INTO HISTORY

The complexity and importance of the relations between the Land of Soviets and the United States were appreciated by Lenin at a time when Washington would not hear of recognizing revolutionary Russia in general, let alone conduct negotiations or conclude agreements with it.

Lenin strongly censured the policy of hostility toward the young Soviet Republic followed by the most reactionary, conservative forces in the United States and the active part they played in the military intervention against Soviet Russia and in imposing a blockade on the country and refusing to accord it diplomatic recognition. In the summer of 1918 American troops—together with those of Britain, France, and Japan—landed in Murmansk and Vladivostok and seized Archangel and part of the Soviet Far East and Siberia. Everywhere the forces of foreign intervention dealt brutally with the civilian population and sought to carve up Russian territory into spheres of influence.

While calling on the Red Army and the Soviet people to give a forceful rebuff to the American and other foreign interventionists, Lenin at the same time spoke highly of the progressive Americans—intellectuals and industrial workers—who had launched the "Hands Off Russia!" campaign in the United States and were urging that food supplies and other relief be sent to the Soviet working people and that American-Soviet relations be normalized.

Lenin considered it necessary to work for peace with the United States. He advanced the idea of peaceful coexistence with the United States and, for that matter, with other capitalist countries, too. His appeal for peace was contained in the famous Decree on Peace, the very first document adopted by the Bolsheviks after they came to power in Russia in 1917.

Throughout the struggle against the forces of foreign intervention and domestic counterrevolution Lenin invariably reaffirmed the Soviet government's desire and readiness for peace with the United States. A message to the Congress and administration of the United States sent by the All-Russia Central Executive Committee at his initiative on March 20, 1921, said, "Ever since its inception Soviet Russia has hoped that friendly relations might speedily be established with the great North American republic and has counted on the creation of close and stable ties between the two republics to their mutual benefit."

The great founder of the Soviet state was explicit and frank in speaking of the principles for relations with the United States. When, on February 18, 1920, a correspondent of the New York *Evening Journal* asked him what he considered the basis of peace with America could be, Lenin replied, "Let the American capitalists leave us alone. We shall not touch them. We are even ready to pay them in gold for any machinery, tools, etc., useful to our transport and industries. We are ready to pay not only in gold but in raw materials too."

When the American correspondent asked what the obstacles to such a peace were, Lenin said, "None on our part; imperialism on the part of the American (and of any other) capitalists." *

* V. I. Lenin, *Collected Works*, Vol. 30 (Moscow: Progress Publishers, 1974), pp. 365–66.

Despite the persistent refusal of the American ruling circles of the time to establish normal diplomatic and economic links with Soviet Russia, Lenin invariably expressed his faith in a better relationship between the two countries and their peoples in the future.

In February 1920 Lenin regarded it as heartening that "some American manufacturers appear to have begun to realize that making money in Russia is wiser than making war against Russia. . . ." †

Although tremendously busy and suffering increasingly from ill health, Lenin invariably gave earnest attention to the state and prospects of Soviet-American relations. He personally dealt with all matters connected with these relations, supporting any initiatives that could improve them. In 1922, for example, he received Armand Hammer, the prominent American industrialist, who had proposed closer economic cooperation with Soviet Russia. Lenin urged that every possible assistance be given to Hammer and other American businessmen from the Soviet side.

Lenin's principles for the peaceful coexistence of the two systems in general and for relations with the United States in particular invariably remain basic to Soviet foreign policy. However—and this was particularly true in the early Soviet years—their implementation depended on the general international situation and the postures of the major Western powers, which were hostile to the young republic. Consequently, over the course of many years there were lengthy periods of a "freeze" in Soviet-American relations.

"In the past," Brezhnev said in his television address in the United States on June 24, 1973, "the relations between our countries have developed very unevenly. There have been periods of stagnation, there have been ups and downs,

† *Ibid.*, Vol. 42, (Moscow, Progress Publishers, 1971), p. 176.

but I will probably not be mistaken if I say that the significance of good relations between the Soviet Union and the United States of America has always been clear to the more farsighted statesmen.''

This was most strikingly confirmed during World War II, when the Soviet and American peoples fought side by side, in the ranks of the United Nations, against the fascist aggressors. This comradeship in arms clearly confirmed that states with different social systems can cooperate.

Although after the Second World War, too, there were always people in the United States supporting good, mutually advantageous relations with the Soviet Union, for a long time they did not attain a decisive role in shaping official policy. Until recent years the numerous peace moves and proposals of the Soviet Union were either rejected or ignored altogether in Washington, or else they met with only a feeble and short-lived response.

2 . WINDS OF CHANGE

Signs of a change in Soviet-American relations became evident at the beginning of the seventies, when the Soviet Union, backed by the changes taking place in the correlation of world forces, launched an all-out peace offensive.

The Peace Program put forward at the 24th Congress of the Communist Party of the Soviet Union provided for the settlement of the key international issues of our times, including an improvement in Soviet-American relations.

"Elements of realism in the policies of many capitalist countries are becoming ever more pronounced," Brezhnev said at the end of 1972, "as the might and influence of the Soviet Union and the fraternal socialist countries increases, as our peace policy becomes more vigorous, and as other

At a harvester combine plant in Krasnoyarsk

Visiting an enterprise in Frunze, the capital of Kirghizia

Inspecting the Novorossiisk factory built in cooperation with Pepsico of the United States

Among workers at the Lomonosov porcelain factory in Leningrad

Visiting the experimental fields of an agricultural research institute in the Altai Mountains

Among Young Pioneers in the city of Kiev

Visiting collective farmers in Turkmenia

Addressing the 25th Congress of the Communist Party of the Soviet Union

At the World Congress of Peace Forces in 1973

In Belgrade

In the German Democratic Republic, Brezhnev is presented with a teddy bear, symbol of Berlin

In Cuba

At a mass meeting in Delhi

The head of the Soviet delegation signing the Final Act of the Helsinki Conference

Signing Soviet-French documents during the 1977 visit to France

Leaving for home from Orly Airport

Receiving Helmut Schmidt in the Kremlin

With Urho Kekkonen

Receiving representatives of Keidanran, the Japanese federation of economic organizations, in the Crimea

Talking with American journalists in Moscow

In Washington on June 18, 1973

At a White House dinner on the same day

Meeting members of the United States business world in Washington

Receiving American and Soviet spacemen of the joint Apollo-Soyuz project, Moscow, 1976

The first meeting of the Presidium of the Supreme Soviet of the USSR after Brezhnev's election as its Chairman, June 17, 1977

At a reception of diplomatic envoys accredited in Moscow, July 8, 1977, Brezhnev converses with United States Ambassador Malcolm Toon

At polling place during elections to local Soviets, June 1977

At the office

Resting

important progressive processes make headway in the contemporary world. . . . In other words, our consistent policy of peace and the entire course of events are gradually causing the capitalist world to recognize the necessity of dealing with the socialist states on a footing of peaceful coexistence."

The Soviet-American summit meeting in Moscow in May 1972 produced a number of important documents, above all the Basic Principles of Relations Between the USSR and the USA. In it the two sides declared that in the nuclear age there was no alternative to conducting Soviet-American relations on the basis of peaceful coexistence.

The Moscow meeting graphically demonstrated the decisive fact that despite the profound differences between the social systems and ideologies of the two great powers, improved Soviet-American relations were possible and necessary both in their own interests and for universal peace.

The principles of peaceful coexistence were for the first time in the history of Soviet-American relations recorded and given enactment in terms of international law. Both sides undertook to settle disputed issues by negotiation and to refrain from the use or threat of force.

The Soviet-American agreements signed in Moscow covered many fields: cooperation in space, environmental protection, public health, science and technology, the prevention of incidents on the high seas, and others.

Especially important were the first agreements on strategic arms limitation, for these are matters that affect every human being in the world. Any detail relating to these agreements, no matter how minor, is appreciated by people everywhere.

The treaty on limiting strategic defensive arms was signed in the Vladimir Hall of the Grand Kremlin Palace on May 26. The texts of the treaty—the Soviet text in a red folder and the American text in a blue folder—were placed on a table covered with a white fringed cloth in the middle of the hall. Two white gold-trimmed armchairs stood beside the table. Brezhnev invited President Nixon to come to the table. Leaders of the Communist Party and Soviet government and members of the American delegation gathered around them.

This was a historic moment. The Soviet leader picked up a pen from the table and signed the texts of the treaty on behalf of the Union of Soviet Socialist Republics. The American President signed likewise. Both of them then rose and exchanged texts. There was loud applause, and champagne glasses were filled. The treaty had been concluded.

The Treaty on the Limitation of Anti-Ballistic Missile Systems was concluded for an unlimited duration. In it each side undertook not to deploy antiballistic missile (ABM) systems throughout its territory. The Soviet Union and the United States agreed, in the treaty, that each could have only two ABM system deployment areas.

This meant that the United States was giving up the Safeguard Program, which it had adopted in March 1969. This program, if fully carried out, would have established fourteen ABM complexes and would have cost American taxpayers a colossal sum (from 50 to 100 billion dollars, according to experts). At the same time it would not have assured the American population of its security but would merely have meant a new round in the strategic arms race. The deployment of similar systems in the Soviet Union was likewise halted.

The Interim Agreement on Certain Measures with Respect to the Limitation of Strategic Offensive Arms, which was signed with the treaty, provided for a five-year "freeze" on the number of strategic intercontinental ballistic missile launchers and submarine launchers.

The New York *Times* said the Moscow summit had accomplished more than the pessimists had expected. On the positive side, it had substantially improved the atmosphere of relations between the United States and the Soviet Union. And the newspaper added that it also made a historic beginning toward ending the nuclear weapons race.

In the months that followed, steps were taken to carry out the treaties concluded at the summit, and new agreements were also reached by the Soviet Union and the United States. For example, in October 1972 agreements were signed on certain matters concerning marine shipping, on the settlement of lend-lease accounts, on the reciprocal granting of credits, and on trade. The latter agreement provided that each side would grant the other most-favored-nation treatment, thereby ending discrimination against Soviet commodities on the American market.

Without waiting for the long-delayed ratification of this agreement by the Congress of the United States, many American businessmen hurried to Moscow to conclude mutually advantageous deals with Soviet organizations.

Armand Hammer, who had been received by Lenin many years earlier, visited Moscow again and was received in the Kremlin once more. Brezhnev had a long talk with him about economic cooperation between the Soviet Union and the United States and other matters. "It is symptomatic," Hammer said afterward, "that Brezhnev received me in the same building where I had met with Lenin fifty-two years earlier."

In speaking of his impressions of his meeting with the General Secretary, Hammer noted in particular his keen, penetrating mind. "I regard him as an outstanding leader," Hammer said. "Brezhnev's bold policy has contributed greatly to the East-West détente. In this sense Brezhnev is going straight along the road begun by the great Lenin."

The improvement of Soviet-American relations gave a powerful new impetus to the trend toward general interna-

tional détente. That, in turn, created a favorable climate for a
visit by Brezhnev to the United States.

Brezhnev's efforts to improve and develop Soviet-American relations and his determination to do everything possible
in this field met with understanding and support among many
American statesmen and public leaders, among broad sections of Americans. They openly expressed their approval
and backing.

When, for example, Americans learned of the forthcoming
visit by this distinguished guest, letters began to pour into
the Soviet Embassy in Washington, inviting him to come to
various towns and small communities, factories and farms.

The writers of these letters knew that the General Secretary's visit would be a working visit, that every hour of his
short stay in the United States would be taken up by important negotiations, and that it would be physically impossible
for him to accept their invitations. Yet they kept on sending
such invitations as a way of expressing their friendly feelings
and their hospitality.

"More than 6,000 of our city's most prominent citizens
will gather to talk to you," said a letter from Los Angeles. "I
would be greatly honored to meet you in Detroit and show
you our plants," wrote Richard C. Gerstenberg, chairman of
the board of General Motors. Morris Frey of Vernon, Massa-
chusetts, wrote that he did not know Brezhnev's itinerary in
the United States and did not know whether he would have
even a single hour free from affairs of state, but if he had
one free evening, Morris Frey would very much like the honored guest to drop in on them. All the inhabitants of his small
town would come out to meet him. He assured him that they
would have a good time, and Brezhnev would be pleased.
They would have a heart-to-heart talk, without any politics
or diplomacy, the way ordinary people who respect one another talk among themselves.

These invitations, ranging from the businesslike to the

emotional, indicated the profound personal respect of Americans for the Soviet leader, their obvious desire to relegate the cold war to the past, and their hopes associated with Brezhnev's visit for a better future in the relations between the two great nations—the Soviet Union and the United States.

3 . MEETING WITH AMERICA

On June 16, 1973, an Il-62 airliner with Brezhnev on board landed at Andrews Air Force Base near Washington. The long flight and the seven-hour time difference called for a rest before beginning the official meetings and negotiations. The government residence at Camp David was put at Brezhnev's disposal for this purpose.

The opening ceremony of the official visit was held on the White House lawn on the morning of June 18 after United States Air Force helicopters had brought the Soviet guest and his party there. General Secretary Brezhnev was welcomed by President Nixon, Secretary of State Henry Kissinger, and other prominent personalities.

The officials, newsmen, and Washingtonians who had gathered on the White House grounds burst into warm applause when they saw the Soviet leader. They cheered his gestures and greetings and his statement that a specific kind of relativity operates in politics—that notwithstanding the unchanging geographical reality of 10,000 kilometers between Moscow and Washington, the distance between the Soviet Union and the United States "is shrinking not only because we are flying in modern aircraft along a well-traveled route but also because we are united by a big goal: assuring a durable peace between the peoples of our countries and consolidating security on our planet."

A few minutes later the Soviet-American talks got under

way in the Oval Room, the President's office. In the evening the President gave a dinner in the White House in honor of the General Secretary. It was attended by leading American political figures, members of the Cabinet and Congress, officials of the White House, and representatives of the business community and the labor unions.

On June 19 the General Secretary met with Senators William Fulbright, Mike Mansfield, Hugh Scott, and other members of the Senate Foreign Relations Committee. At the meeting Brezhnev spoke in detail about the principles and goals of Soviet foreign policy and replied exhaustively to questions.

Senator Howard H. Baker, Republican, said of the meeting that he was greatly impressed by the Soviet leader's deep interest in improving relations between the United States and the Soviet Union, as well as his wish to make the international climate sounder as a whole.

Senator George McGovern, Democrat, referred to Brezhnev as a strong personality, a calm, very impressive man, who is firmly at the helm of leadership and leads a truly profound spiritual life.

American press comment on the meeting with the Senators emphasized Brezhnev's political acumen in correctly appreciating the important role that Congress plays in American public and political life and in devoting appropriate time and attention to meeting its leading members concerned with foreign policy.

Negotiations with the President were resumed immediately after the meeting with the Senators. That day they were devoted to trade and economic relations. After noting the considerable progress made in that field, the parties to the talks examined possible ways of further expanding the commercial and economic relations between their countries on a large-scale, long-term, and mutually advantageous basis.

The second day's talks, which lasted until evening, ended

on board the presidential yacht *Sequoia* on the Potomac. After that the Soviet guests and their American hosts flew by helicopter to Camp David.

It was there that the talks were continued on June 20 and the morning of June 21. They dealt mainly with international problems and SALT progress in Geneva. The General Secretary and the President then returned to Washington.

On June 22 Brezhnev received representatives of the American business community at Blair House, his residence during his stay in Washington. They included Secretary of the Treasury George P. Shultz, Secretary of Commerce Frederick Dent, President of the National Association of Manufacturers Edgar D. Kenna, President of the U.S. Chamber of Commerce Edward Rust, President of the Board of the New York Stock Exchange James Needham, and the top executives of a number of leading banks and corporations.

Brezhnev had a thorough discussion with the businessmen, who represented more than forty banks and companies that were either already doing business with the Soviet Union or intended to do so. They expressed an interest in such practical matters as possible spheres of cooperation and trade and ways of expanding them. The consideration of economic matters went beyond the framework of figures and calculations. It touched on the basic economic policies of the two countries, an inseparable part of their overall political courses. There was much interest in Brezhnev's statement at the meeting. In this brief statement he pointed out that "the old forms of economic relations no longer meet the requirements of the times. The economies of individual countries have attained a new scale. The scientific and technological revolution . . . is going ahead at full speed. There have been big cultural and educational strides. This irresistible progress gives birth to a tremendous growth in people's needs and requirements and calls for an increasingly broad international division of labor, for an extension of commercial, economic, scientific, technical, and cultural contacts between countries. . . .''

On the subject of Soviet-American relations, Brezhnev said, "The Soviet Union and the United States are the countries with the biggest economic potentials. We have vast natural riches. We often admit that in some respects you Americans are in the lead. But in some things we have outstripped you. And if we unite our efforts and approach the matter broadly, on a big scale, with a view to the long-term prospects, for about twenty years ahead, we will see enormous possibilities opening up.''

Brezhnev concluded his speech with these words: "I always believed and believe that man's intellect, his mind and talent, triumph over darkness. It is intellect, a constructive approach, and prudence that have brought our peoples to an understanding of the fact that we have to take the road of improving our relations and removing everything that cast such a dark shadow upon them.''

The businessmen listened with intense interest, and Brezhnev's speech was punctuated with applause.

The captains of American business present, noted the New York *Post,* commented favorably on Brezhnev's businesslike and constructive approach to the basic issues of American-Soviet relations. James Needham, president of the board of the New York Stock Exchange, said after the meeting that Brezhnev had not dealt with any specific deals but had merely wanted to be understood by the businessmen and had spoken in the friendly manner that was his nature.

Not only businessmen but ordinary Americans—specifically, the members of a number of labor unions—urged normalizing and developing American-Soviet relations, including trade. For instance, a convention of the West Coast longshoremen's and warehousemen's union passed a resolution stating that the sharp improvement in trade between the United States and the socialist countries was a heartening sign for American workers. It expressed the view that Congress should grant the Soviet Union the same trade status that is given to other countries and should abolish discriminatory tariffs.

After receiving the businessmen, Brezhnev met at the Soviet Embassy in Washington with Henry Winston, national chairman of the Communist Party of the United States, and Gus Hall, its general secretary. The American Communist Party leaders said that Brezhnev's official visit was of great significance in bringing about a turn in American-Soviet relations and a general relaxation of international tensions. They made the point that the visit signified new successes for the policy of peaceful coexistence, that it opened up new possibilities for cooperation between the American and Soviet peoples, and that it was meeting with broad support among democratic Americans.

On the evening of June 22 General Secretary Brezhnev and the American President, together with their parties, flew from Washington to California.

June 23 was another full day of wide-ranging talks. In the evening there was a warm and friendly meeting with California political leaders, businessmen, and intellectuals, as well as with Hollywood film directors and stars.

Brezhnev was very pleased to meet the Californians. He warmly congratulated the President and people of the United States on the successful conclusion of the heroic flight by the Skylab crew. And he expressed his hope that joint work by Soviet and American spacemen to fathom the secrets of the universe would be one of the many aspects of Soviet-American cooperation.

The working part of Brezhnev's visit to the United States ended, in the main, in California on June 24. Prominent

American leaders, representatives of the local public, and the newsmen covering the visit were invited to the President's residence at nine o'clock in the morning. The final joint Soviet-American communiqué, summing up the impressive results of the visit, was signed at a table placed under age-old trees on the shore of the Pacific.

The General Secretary's visit to America made a major new contribution to the peaceful coexistence of countries with different social and political systems. The visit greatly aided the process of changeover from the cold war to a normalization and further development of Soviet-American relations.

At their meetings the leaders of the Soviet Union and the United States discussed many important problems of Soviet-American relations and world affairs. Nine new agreements were signed—more than at any other summit meeting.

The agreements cover a broad range of problems: cooperation in agriculture, transportation, the study of the World Ocean, the peaceful uses of nuclear energy, and the extension of contacts and exchanges in science, technology, education, culture, and other fields.

Of great significance is the document entitled Basic Principles of Negotiations on the Further Limitation of Strategic Offensive Arms, in which it was stated that these limitations could apply both to their quantitative aspects and to their qualitative improvement.

June 22 could be described as a history-making day not just for the Soviet and American peoples. That day witnessed an act of importance for the whole of mankind. Along with a number of other new Soviet-American documents, the Agreement on the Prevention of Nuclear War was signed on that day. The signing ceremony was attended by leading members of the administration and Congress, the members of the Soviet delegation, and 100 newsmen. It took place in the East Hall of the White House, adorned with portraits of two great Americans, George Washington and Abraham Lincoln. When the prolonged applause had subsided, Brezhnev heartily thanked everyone present for expressing their support of this extremely important act. The Soviet Union and the United States, guided by the objective of strengthening world peace and international security and conscious that nuclear war would have devastating consequences for mankind, agreed that they would act in such a manner as to rule out an outbreak of nuclear war between them and between either of the sides and other countries.

The two powers undertook to refrain from the threat or use of force against each other, or against allies of the other party, or against other countries in circumstances that might endanger international peace and security.

This agreement, Brezhnev said, is "the best proof that Soviet-American relations are not standing still, but are moving forward. . . ."

"What the Soviet and American leaders have agreed upon," said the New York *Times,* "is a code of ethics for governments which have the unquestioned power to destroy each other—and the rest of the globe as well. This is hardly a feat to be belittled.

There was a worldwide welcome for the fact that political détente in Soviet-American and international relations had begun to be supplemented with military détente. As Brezhnev has repeatedly pointed out, political détente cannot develop successfully without military détente, for the existence of enormous arsenals, the confrontation of the armed forces of states belonging to opposite social systems, the continued arms race, and the existence of seats of military danger jeopardize world peace and are incompatible with the relaxation of international tensions.

The Soviet Union seeks to make the improvement of the

international situation, including Soviet-American relations, as broad, stable, and irreversible as possible and to draw in as many countries as possible.

Far from being aimed against any other countries, the development of Soviet-American contacts presupposes respect for their legitimate interests and corresponds to them.

"We see the improvement of Soviet-American relations not as an isolated phenomenon," Brezhnev said, "but as an organic—moreover, highly important—part of a broad process of fundamental normalization of the international atmosphere. . . . We will welcome it if our efforts to improve Soviet-American relations help draw more and more new countries, whether in Europe or Asia, in Africa or Latin America, in the Middle East or the Far East, into the process of détente."

A mere listing of the international problems on which the Soviet Union and the United States agreed to work together reveals how much the whole of mankind stands to gain from cooperation between the two powers bearing a major responsibility for world peace.

In their joint communiqué the Soviet Union and the United States stated "their readiness to consider additional ways of strengthening peace and removing forever the danger of war, and particularly nuclear war," and "their readiness to move ahead jointly toward an agreement on the further limitation of strategic arms."

They declared that they "attach great importance to joining with all states in the cause of strengthening peace, reducing the burden of armaments, and reaching agreements on arms limitation and disarmament measures" and reaffirmed "that the ultimate objective is general and complete disarmament, including nuclear disarmament, under strict international control."

The Soviet Union and the United States "expressed their

deep satisfaction at the conclusion of the Agreement on Ending the War and Restoring Peace in Vietnam,'' and they ''reaffirmed their stand that the political futures of Vietnam,
Laos, and Cambodia should be left to the respective peoples
to determine, free from outside interference.''

The leaders of the Soviet Union and the United States examined matters relating to the Conference on Security and
Cooperation in Europe and stated that it would enhance the
possibilities for the process of détente and that the two countries would ''conduct their policies so as to realize the goals
of the conference and bring about a new era of good relations
in this part of the world.'' They further stated that it would
be a good thing ''if the relaxation of political tensions were
accompanied by a reduction of military tensions in Central
Europe.'' In this context they attached ''great importance to
the negotiations on the mutual reduction of forces and armaments and associated measures in Central Europe.''

''The return visit to the USA of the General Secretary of
the Central Committee of the CPSU, L. I. Brezhnev, and the
talks held during the visit'' were summed up in the joint
communiqué ''as an expression of their mutual determination to continue the course toward a major improvement in
Soviet-U.S. relations.'' And it was decided ''to take further
major steps to give these relations maximum stability and
to turn the development of friendship and cooperation between their peoples into a permanent factor for worldwide
peace.''

At the signing of the communiqué the General Secretary
and the President made speeches, which were televised. The
whole of America watched them sign the document and
heard them speak.

Brezhnev said that his meetings and talks in America had
strengthened his conviction that ''the American public are
aware of the importance of the steps which we have taken

2 3 7

toward further development of Soviet-American relations. That is why," he said, "we are leaving the United States with light hearts. What has been achieved will give us added strength and new energy to continue our work for peace."

Soon after the signing of the joint communiqué Brezhnev took his leave of the Californians. Many local personalities came to San Clemente to see him off. Before his departure, astronauts Charles Conrad, Joseph P. Kerwin, and Paul J. Weitz, just back from their space mission, were introduced to the Soviet leader, who warmly congratulated them and wished them further successes in the advancement of science.

The final leg of Brezhnev's journey in America was the helicopter flight from San Clemente to the El Toro Marine base, from there the flight aboard the *Spirit of '76* to Washington, and then another helicopter flight, this time to Camp David.

It was at that time that two major American TV networks—the National Broadcasting Company and the Columbia Broadcasting System—screened Brezhnev's broadcast to the American nation.

From their TV screens Brezhnev conveyed to the citizens of America the greetings and friendly feelings of the millions of Soviet people, who hoped that this summit meeting would be fruitful in improving relations between the two countries and strengthening universal peace.

Brezhnev expressed his satisfaction with the business results of the visit and said, "Personally, I am also pleased that this visit has afforded me an opportunity to gain a firsthand impression of America, to become acquainted with some aspects of American realities, to meet your country's noted statesmen and public figures, and to come into contact with the life of Americans."

The General Secretary gave Americans a detailed picture

of the Soviet people's life, work, plans, and hopes and spoke of their tremendous desire for peace and good relations with all peoples, the Americans included.

"The Soviet people, perhaps better than any other people," Brezhnev said, "know what war is. In the Second World War we achieved a victory of worldwide historical importance. But more than 20 million Soviet citizens died in that war; 70,000 of our towns and villages were razed to the ground. One-third of our national wealth was destroyed.

"The historical path we have traversed," he continued, "has not been an easy one. Our people take pride in the fact that in a short historical period following the victory of the socialist revolution, a backward Russia was transformed into a major industrial power, which has achieved outstanding success in the scientific and cultural fields.

"We have great plans for the future. We want to raise considerably the living standards of the Soviet people. We want to achieve further success in the spheres of education and medicine. We want to make our towns and villages more convenient for living in and more beautiful. And every Soviet person knows full well that the realization of these plans requires peace above all."

Brezhnev pointed out that the Soviet people's ardent desire for peace determined the peaceful orientation of Soviet foreign policy, was reflected in the Soviet Peace Program, and had brought him to the United States.

"On the whole we can say," he stated, "that much has already been accomplished in the development of Soviet-American relations. But we are still standing at the very beginning of a long road.

"We must show constant concern to protect and nurture the fresh shoots of good relations. Tireless work is needed to determine the most necessary and most suitable forms of cooperation in various spheres. Patience is needed to understand this or that specific feature of the other side and to learn to do business with each other.''

People all over the world followed Brezhnev's visit to the United States with unflagging interest. They welcomed the visit and its outcome as completely harmonizing with their desire for peace.

Inside the United States itself the vast majority of people highly approved of the visit and of the American-Soviet talks and agreements. There were various hostile, anti-Soviet maneuvers by a few, but at times highly influential and vociferous, supporters of the cold war. But they were not representative of the mood prevailing in the United States.

Highly indicative was the statement of the *Wall Street Journal* that ''Leonid Brezhnev comes to the United States as a living symbol of Soviet-American détente.''

Similar comments appeared in other periodicals. Brezhnev's stay in the United States, said *Time* magazine, was aimed at erasing in American minds the cold war image of Russia as antagonist and replacing it with a vision of a peaceful, stable and sophisticated trading partner.

In a Harris Poll reported on the day before the conclusion of the Brezhnev visit, 66 percent of the Americans polled voiced the view that the United States and the Soviet Union had taken the path of improving their relations and concluding agreements important to both countries and the whole world. They expressed support for further American-Soviet summits. Of the Americans polled, 78 percent expressed approval of the results of Brezhnev's visit and talks in the United States.

These sentiments were reflected in a statement by Senate minority leader Hugh Scott, who expressed deep satisfaction with what had been accomplished. Senator Scott said he felt a surge of optimism when he reflected on what had been recorded in the agreements and what could be achieved in the future to reduce the danger of nuclear war and strengthen mutually rewarding confidence and mutually beneficial cooperation between the United States and the Soviet Union. The main thing, Senator Scott felt, was that following Brezhnev's visit to the United States, international tension would undoubtedly drop several more degrees.

As they watched, with the aid of ubiquitous television, every step and gesture made by the General Secretary and listened to every word he spoke, Americans could see that this "Communist No. 1" was a friendly peace-loving person and an outstanding political leader.

What Brezhnev told them about his country was comprehensible and convincing, though much of it was unusual to ordinary Americans. For many of them had been steeped in absurd fabrications and prejudices—throughout the long years of the cold war they had been fed incorrect notions about the Soviet Union and about socialism.

Typical were reactions such as those of Mr. and Mrs. Brook of Salt Lake City. They said they had been teenagers when World War II had broken out. Their youth had been darkened by the advent of nuclear weapons. They had matured as the cold war had set in. They were now gray-haired, and their children had grown up, but the fear of a nuclear catastrophe was always with them. It was only now, they said, that they really believed that reason was stronger than madness. They fully agreed that if faith in reason were lost, if it were replaced by a blind reliance on strength alone, on the power of nuclear or some other weapons, then human civilization—and mankind itself, for that matter—would face a pitiful destiny.

Young as well as old Americans assessed the results of the Brezhnev visit highly. A poll of college and university students in the country illustrated this graphically. Asked how they felt about the results of the visit, 91 percent of the young people polled gave an affirmative reply (31 percent described the results as "excellent," 42 percent as "very good," and 18 percent as "good"). Personal impressions were 97 percent favorable (39 percent described them as "excellent," 47 percent as "very good," and 11 percent as "good").

"We certainly are fortunate," said one Oregon University freshman, "that TV gave us a chance to see him [Brezhnev] face to face. It took a lot of the mystery out of Soviet-American relations."

Soviet men and women, of course, followed the Brezhnev trip to America with tremendous interest. At one accord they approved of the visit, its results, and the whole of Brezhnev's purposeful foreign policy activities.

In letters and telegrams to Communist Party and government bodies, to newspapers, television and radio stations, in speeches at meetings and press interviews, men and women, workers and scientists, farmers and students, engineers and technicians expressed wholehearted support of all the agreements signed at the Soviet-American summit.

They said that Brezhnev's activities were fully in keeping with their thoughts and hopes and with their desire for peace, friendship, and cooperation with other nations, including the people of America.

Many Soviet citizens expressed thanks to Brezhnev personally. They thanked him for his creative and highly principled approach to world problems and for his diplomatic skill, and they expressed approval of his enormous work for the good of the people in the Soviet Union and elsewhere.

This enthusiastic backing, both in the Soviet Union and in the United States, of the results of Brezhnev's visit revealed the great fund of good-feeling among both peoples for each other and showed that further steps to normalize relations would be welcomed by them.

4. CONSOLIDATING AND BUILDING ON WHAT HAD BEEN ACCOMPLISHED

The Brezhnev visit to the United States helped to consolidate and further the positive turn in Soviet-American relations. With international tension reduced and relations between the Soviet Union and the United States improved, the danger of local conflicts escalating into an all-out war became much smaller.

When, in October 1973, a conflict flared up in the Middle East, caused by Israel's stubborn refusal to withdraw its forces from the Arab territories it had occupied, the Soviet Union and the United States cosponsored a motion in the United Nations Security Council proposing a cease-fire. They thereby helped localize and speedily halt this conflict, which in the absence of contacts and mutual understanding between the Soviet Union and the United States could have assumed much more dangerous dimensions.

Brezhnev's meetings and talks with members of the administration, Congress, and business world in the United States did much to promote trade, and scientific, technical, and cultural exchanges between the two countries.

The road was thus cleared for new summit meetings. The next one took place in Moscow and the Crimea in the summer of 1974.

5. THE 1974 MOSCOW SUMMIT

The decision taken during Brezhnev's visit to the United States to place Soviet-American summits on a regular footing imparted stability and continuity to the dialogue between the two great powers and paved the way for the next such meeting, which was held in Moscow and the Crimea during President Nixon's visit to the Soviet Union in the summer of

1974. A number of significant agreements were signed during that meeting. Highly important was the understanding reached on further efforts to work out a new agreement on the limitation of strategic offensive arms, which should cover the period until 1985 and deal with both quantitative and qualitative restrictions on strategic nuclear arsenals.

A protocol to the 1972 treaty on limiting strategic defensive arms was signed, stipulating that each side would have a single deployment area for ABM systems instead of two such areas.

The Soviet Union and the United States concluded a Treaty on the Limitation of Underground Nuclear Weapon Tests. They undertook to end all underground nuclear weapon tests having a yield exceeding 150 kilotons at any place under their jurisdiction or control, beginning on March 31, 1976, and to limit the number of tests to a minimum.

Later, in his speech in Warsaw on July 21, 1974, Brezhnev said that the Soviet Union, which had long been ready to end nuclear weapon tests completely, regarded this agreement as a step toward an eventual all-inclusive, universal ban on nuclear weapon tests.

Agreements were concluded providing for extensive programs of cooperation between the Soviet Union and the United States in the fields of energy, housing construction, and public health. An agreement was also signed on long-term economic cooperation, intended to facilitate ever broader mutually advantageous trade between the two countries.

There were detailed discussions on major international problems at the 1974 Moscow meeting. The points set down in the joint communiqué indicate that here, too, it proved possible to make considerable progress, although substantial differences remained in the approach of the Soviet Union and the United States to quite a number of issues.

We have every reason to say, Brezhnev pointed out in a

speech at a dinner in the United States Embassy on July 2, 1974, that the results of the Moscow meeting "can be described as constructive and weighty."

He explained that he was referring, first of all, "to the new steps in a field which may rightfully be called central in Soviet-American relations—the field of lessening the risk of war and restraining the arms race."

In the Joint Soviet-American Communiqué both sides said they were "deeply convinced of the imperative necessity of making the process of improving U.S.-Soviet relations irreversible." That was how the term "irreversibility of détente" became part of the international vocabulary.

The Politburo of the Central Committee of the Communist Party of the Soviet Union, the Presidium of the Supreme Soviet, and the Council of Ministers of the Soviet Union, after examining a communication by the General Secretary on the results of the 1974 Moscow summit meeting, summed them up as "important to strengthening the relations between the Soviet Union and the United States and to the cause of peace and international security" and said that the Soviet people backed them with full accord.

There was worldwide public approval of the results of the Moscow meeting. A poll conducted by the New York *Times* showed that the agreements reached with the Soviet Union had helped strengthen the trust of Americans in the Soviet Union and its policies. Asked whether the United States administration should continue seeking accommodation with the Soviet Union, 72 percent replied affirmatively.

The leader of the group of American astronauts who were training for a joint flight with Soviet cosmonauts and were in Moscow during the summit, Brigadier General Thomas Stafford, said he was "deeply pleased" that this meeting would promote further progress in American-Soviet cooperation in diverse fields of life.

General Stafford said the radical turn in the relations between the two countries had enabled their spacemen, too, to establish friendly cooperation and to train effectively for the joint Apollo and Soyuz flight.

Stafford said he had been in space on three occasions and had often, when looking down on our blue globe, reflected on how much more precious it was to him than any other planet or star. At such times his thoughts involuntarily turned to problems of war and peace. And he was glad, he said, that the third summit meeting had resulted in further steps toward détente.

6. JOINT EFFORTS MULTIPLY

Victor Hugo once said, "An idea whose time has come is irresistible." As a result of the political initiatives that had taken place, the idea of Soviet-American cooperation—which would have seemed utopian in the years of the cold war—had gained ground.

In many areas of agreed-upon cooperation—economics, science and technology, medicine, urban construction, agriculture, the study of the World Ocean, environmental protection, etc.—joint Soviet-American commissions and councils were set up and began working on joint research programs.

Cooperation and exchanges between the Soviet Union and the United States in science and technology have acquired broad scope, and American scientists and engineers have often had occasion to see for themselves that Brezhnev was right when he said that the Soviet Union is an equal partner of the United States.

The General Secretary underscored the cardinal fact that both parties benefit equally from their cooperation, which not only is desirable but is a natural result of the present-day scientific and technological revolution and the international division of labor.

A spokesman for General Electric, one of America's largest corporations, Lowell Steele, expressed the view of many American businessmen when he said, "The total Soviet technical effort and technical resources are very large by any standard. Particularly in the areas of interest to General Electric, we know, for example, that they have large and effective programs in metallurgy, especially in fields such as welding, in superconductivity, in hard metals for cutting, and in equipment for metal fabrication. They have active programs in engineering plastics and are doing good work in organic-metallic chemistry. Their massive potential in hydro-electric power has led the Soviets to develop great strength in hydrogeneration and in a.c. and d.c. high-voltage transmission from remote sites. They have also provided pioneering advances in fusion research which have strongly influenced work in this field throughout the world."

Many other American companies besides the General Electric Corporation have signed agreements on cooperation with Soviet scientific and technical organizations.

They include Brown and Root, Inc. (management and organization methods and technical facilities in designing and construction), Hewlett-Packard (medical electronics, scientific measuring instruments, and minicomputers), Kaiser Industries (ferrous and nonferrous metallurgy, coal mining, etc.), Control Data and Burroughs (computers), the Singer Company (information gathering, processing, and transmission, aviation and marine navigating equipment and instruments, garment manufacture technology, knitwear machinery, etc.), International Telephone and Telegraph, and the Stanford Research Institute.

The Soviet-American Agreement on Cooperation in the Field of Peaceful Uses of Atomic Energy provides for joint activities in three areas: controlled thermonuclear fusion, fast breeder power reactors, and research on the fundamental properties of matter. Within the framework of this agreement, Soviet scientists are taking part in joint research at the National Accelerator Laboratory in the United States.

Soviet-American cooperation in the field of public health is making good headway. Soviet and American medical specialists have held many meetings and conferences and made reciprocal visits to acquaint themselves with each other's work.

For example, Soviet cardiologists are working with American specialists to learn more about the causes and mechanisms of the atherosclerotic process. Joint efforts have been undertaken against cancer, one of man's most formidable diseases. A special agreement on cooperation in developing an artificial heart has been concluded.

Within the framework of the Soviet-American Agreement on Cooperation in the Field of Environmental Protection, public health bodies of the two countries are studying the biological effects of chemical pollutants when they enter the human body with inhaled air or with ingested food or by a combination of ways. In general, they are investigating the possible consequences of changing environmental conditions and environmental pollution for human health.

The cooperation in various fields begun as a result of détente has thus acquired a mutually beneficial character, serving as a two-way street.

The deep-rooted processes of strengthening Soviet-American cooperation and the basic desire to promote it made for continuity of this political course when the United States administration changed in 1974.

On becoming President of the United States, Gerald Ford said in one of his first foreign policy statements that he would remain true to the policy followed toward the Soviet Union in the preceding years.

The President said, "To our two peoples, and to all mankind we owe a continued effort to live, and, where possible, to work together, in peace; for in a thermonuclear age there can be no alternative to a positive and peaceful relationship between our nations."

The President's statement evoked a positive response in the Soviet Union. "We have noted with satisfaction," Brezhnev said in one of his speeches, "President Ford's statement that he personally and his administration intend to continue following the course of further developing the relations between our countries in the same direction."

With a view to the usefulness of continued contacts and in order to form a personal acquaintance, Brezhnev and Ford agreed to a new Soviet-American summit at the end of 1974 on Soviet territory—in the vicinity of Vladivostok, a picturesque city with a population of half a million, resembling, as the Washington *Post* remarked, San Francisco or Seattle.

Vladivostok and the entire Soviet Far East are beginning to play an ever more appreciable role in the growth of trade and transportation between the Soviet Union and the United States, as their general relations improve. Business links with the Soviet Far East, Mayor Wes Uhlman of the American seaport of Seattle has said, for example, are becoming routine in the life of the city. After all, he added, Seattle–Vladivostok is a short route between the United States and the Soviet Union.

7. THE VLADIVOSTOK UNDERSTANDING AND THE FURTHER DEVELOPMENT OF CONTACTS

Brezhnev arrived in Vladivostok on November 22. The following day he warmly welcomed President Ford as the latter alighted from his aircraft. As soon as they became acquainted, the two leaders got down to business, and even on the train taking them to their official residence they began talks both on the general world situation and Soviet-American relations.

The talks continued after their arrival at the residence, which was situated in the midst of the picturesque wooded hills in the environs of Vladivostok.

General Secretary Brezhnev and President Ford soon became acquainted and gained an appreciation of each other's qualities. As the President noted when interviewed by *Newsweek* on his return, the atmosphere at the talks was friendly from the outset.

Ford said that the Vladivostok meeting had given him an opportunity to become acquainted with Brezhnev as a leader and a person. And he went on to say that Brezhnev "is a person who can be alternately very jovial, very pleasant, he will kid a lot, and then he can get deadly serious and be extremely firm . . . I was impressed with him. He is a strong person. . . . He was firm in what he wanted, and yet he could understand our point of view. . . .

"He started out almost at the beginning in saying that we had a serious—speaking of them as well as ourselves—a serious obligation to try and reach an agreement to stabilize the problems between the two major nuclear powers. He took a very broad view.

On the second day of the working summit a Soviet-American joint communiqué and joint statement were adopted. Secretary of State Henry Kissinger summed up his impressions of the outcome of the Vladivostok meeting by saying that the parties to the talks had found a common language.

In their joint communiqué the Soviet Union and the United States "reaffirmed their determination to develop further their relations in the direction defined by the fundamen-

tal joint decisions and basic treaties and agreements concluded between the two states in recent years."

Special consideration was given in the course of the talks
to a pivotal aspect of Soviet-American relations: measures to
eliminate the threat of war and to halt the arms race.

At Vladivostok General Secretary Brezhnev and President
Ford reached a new understanding of paramount importance
on limiting strategic offensive arms. In their joint statement
they reaffirmed their intention of holding further negotiations
and concluding a new agreement in this field based on the
following provisions:

"1. The new agreement will incorporate the relevant provisions of the Interim Agreement of May 26, 1972, which will
remain in force until October 1977.

"2. The new agreement will cover the period from October
1977 through December 31, 1985.

"3. Based on the principle of equality and equal security,
the new agreement will include the following limitations:

"a) both Sides will be entitled to have a certain agreed
aggregate number of strategic delivery vehicles;

"b) both Sides will be entitled to have a certain agreed
aggregate number of intercontinental ballistic missiles and
submarine-launched ballistic missiles equipped with multiple
independently targetable warheads.

"4. The new agreement will include a provision for further
negotiations beginning not later than 1980–1981 on the question of further limitations and possible reductions of strategic
arms in the period after 1985."

At a dinner honoring the distinguished American guest in
Vladivostok on November 24, Brezhnev said that their joint
attention had been concentrated, in the first place, "on such
a vitally important problem as reaching agreement on further
restricting and then reducing arms, especially what it has
now become customary to call strategic arms." This is es-

251

sential, Brezhnev said, if we really want to help eliminate the threat of the outbreak of a nuclear missile war, with all its dire consequences. Brezhnev then added this point: "International détente must be backed up by détente in the military sphere if it is to become really stable. Further progress in this respect will have tremendous significance for world peace. It seems to me we have done useful work in Vladivostok in this respect."

This appraisal was seconded by the most farsighted statesmen and public personalities, military and political leaders, and press, radio, and TV commentators.

The historic meeting near Vladivostok, the Baltimore *Sun* commented, for example, was the most encouraging demonstration of common sense that the world had seen in recent years.

At his news conference on December 2, 1974, President Ford stressed the point that at his talks with General Secretary Brezhnev they had agreed on maximum limits of strategic forces that were "well below the force levels which would otherwise have been expected over the next 10 years, and very substantially below the forces which would result from an all-out arms race over that same period."

The President declared further, "What we have done is to set firm and equal limits on the strategic forces of each side, thus preventing an arms race with all its terror, instability, war-breeding tension and economic waste.

"We have in addition created the solid basis from which future arms reductions can be—and hopefully will be—negotiated. . . . But we have made a long step forward toward peace, on a basis of equality, the only basis on which agreement was possible." The President expressed his confidence that this agreement would be approved by the American people.

In the course of the Vladivostok meeting there was also an

exchange of views on a number of international issues. Special attention was given to negotiations designed to remove existing sources of tension and to strengthen international security and world peace.

Brezhnev and Ford agreed that there were good chances for the early successful conclusion of the Conference on Security and Cooperation in Europe. They proceeded from the assumption, as was said in the communiqué, "that the results achieved in the course of the Conference will permit its conclusion at the highest level and thus be commensurate with its importance in ensuring the peaceful future of Europe."

The Soviet Union and the United States reaffirmed their intention to make every effort to promote a solution of the key issues of a just and lasting peace in the Middle East on the basis of UN Security Council Resolution 338, taking into account the legitimate interests of all the peoples of the area, including the Palestinian people, and respect for the right to independent existence of all states in the area.

General Secretary Brezhnev and President Ford emphasized the special importance they attached to further progress in the field of commercial, economic, scientific and technical ties, especially cooperation on a long-term basis, including large-scale projects. They noted the progress made in implementing agreements on developing ties and cooperation between the Soviet Union and the United States in the fields of science, technology, and culture.

Senate majority leader Mike Mansfield said he was glad the Brezhnev-Ford meeting in Vladivostok had been so fruitful. The Senator hoped the agreements reached during the talks would be put into practice and new agreements would be reached, further reducing the burden of arms and diminishing the danger of a thermonuclear conflict.

Senator Mansfield said that as Democratic majority leader

in the Senate he intended to give the President maximum support in successfully carrying out the course that the United States was adopting in its foreign policy.

The success of the American-Soviet summit, said General Secretary Gus Hall of the Communist Party of the United States, confirmed the significance of the consistent struggle for peace that Brezhnev had constantly advanced.

The Politburo of the Central Committee of the Communist Party of the Soviet Union, the Presidium of the Supreme Soviet, and the Council of Ministers of the USSR fully approved Brezhnev's activities in Vladivostok and the significant political results of his first meeting with President Ford.

This meeting, they stated in their official announcement, reflected a striving to assure continuous progress in the development of Soviet-American relations and to make this process irreversible. The documents adopted at the Vladivostok meeting provide a good basis for taking future steps in this direction.

The Politburo of the Central Committee of the Communist Party of the Soviet Union, the Presidium of the Supreme Soviet, and the Council of Ministers of the USSR stated that "the Soviet people, unanimously supporting the party's Leninist foreign policy, regard the meeting near Vladivostok as a new major step along the road of implementing the Peace Program charted by the 24th Congress of the Communist Party of the Soviet Union. The Soviet people attach great importance to the results of the talks and the contribution made to this cause by the General Secretary of the Central Committee of the Communist Party of the Soviet Union, Comrade L. I. Brezhnev."

After the conclusion of the official talks, Brezhnev and Ford toured Vladivostok. Brezhnev then saw Ford and his party off at the airfield, where they took off for the United States.

President Ford's trip to the Soviet Far East, said Speaker Carl Albert of the House of Representatives, had shown all Americans that the idea of improving relations between the United States and the Soviet Union lived on and that the new administration had not swerved from the course charted during the earlier summits. The success of the Vladivostok talks, he added, reaffirmed that this was a sensible and the only correct course. Many other leading Representatives spoke out in the same vein, as did Senator Frank Moss, Democrat, a member of the Senate Commerce Committee, who said he was deeply convinced that meetings of the Soviet and American leaders should continue.

Along with meetings with Presidents of the United States, very important, too, were the systematic meetings and talks of Brezhnev and other Soviet leaders with the Secretaries of State, Commerce, and the Treasury of the United States, as well as with other high-ranking officials. At these business-like and frank meetings there were discussions of great practical value on many complicated problems of Soviet-American relations and on various proposed agreements and arrangements between the two powers.

Highly important, too, considering the decisive role of the Supreme Soviet of the USSR and the Congress of the United States in deciding matters of war and peace and in shaping foreign policy generally, were the meetings of the legislators of each country with their counterparts and with the top leaders of the other.

In 1974–75 there were reciprocal official visits by parliamentary delegations for the first time in the history of the Soviet Union and the United States. In May 1974 the United States was visited by a delegation of the Supreme Soviet headed by Boris N. Ponomarev, Candidate Member of the Politburo, Secretary of the Central Committee of the Communist Party of the Soviet Union, and Chairman of the Foreign Affairs Commission of the Soviet of Nationalities of the Supreme Soviet of the USSR. At a meeting with members of the Senate Foreign Relations Committee, Ponomarev said on behalf of his delegation:

"As you remember, when speaking to members of the U.S. Congress last year, General Secretary Brezhnev spoke of how important it would be to establish closer contacts between the United States Congress and the Supreme Soviet of the USSR. We are deeply satisfied that our visit, so to speak, fills one of the gaps that existed in relations between the Soviet Union and the United States. Mutual contacts between legislators are a necessary and important matter."

In July and August 1975 delegations of the Senate and the House of Representatives paid return visits to Moscow and met with Soviet legislators. Both delegations were received by Brezhnev, who told the Senators and Representatives in detail about Soviet domestic and foreign policies, and answered their many questions.

On July 2 when he received the Senate delegation in the Kremlin, Brezhnev noted the importance of the turn toward better relations and fruitful cooperation between the Soviet Union and the United States, achieved in recent years through efforts on both sides. At the same time he drew attention to increased activities by the opponents of improved Soviet-American relations in the United States and condemned their provocative attacks on the Soviet Union and calls for a further stepping up of armament building.

Both parties emphasized the importance and necessity of further developing and deepening Soviet-American relations on a basis of equality, noninterference in internal affairs, and mutual advantage.

The Washington *Post* reported many Senators as saying after the meeting with Brezhnev that they had been impressed with the Soviet insistence that nuclear weaponry must be curbed and the arms race somehow slowed, and with the General Secretary's emphasis on the idea of strengthening peace.

American political and public personalities, Senators and businessmen who have met Brezhnev have repeatedly noted how profoundly dedicated he is to the cause of peace, well informed about the international situation and United States policies, and sincerely desirous of promoting mutual understanding and contacts between the two countries and their peoples. Former United States Ambassador to Moscow Averell Harriman, a prominent figure in the Democratic Party, said, for example, after his latest visit to Moscow, in September 1976, that he was deeply convinced that Brezhnev was dedicated to the idea of détente and of improving Soviet-American relations and that he attached great significance to the talks on limiting strategic offensive arms.

United States Treasury Secretary William Simon, who took part in the meetings of the US-USSR Trade and Economic Council in Moscow in 1974 and 1976, said that the General Secretary was playing an exceedingly important role in promoting the policy of détente and in strengthening cooperation between the Soviet Union and the United States. Secretary Simon paid tribute to Brezhnev's wisdom in championing a policy of world peace based on mutual cooperation. He added that those who had been fortunate to work with him in this cause and to know him personally regarded the General Secretary as an outstanding world leader.

Meetings with many Americans visiting the Soviet Union—Cabinet members, Senators, businessmen, and scientists—help Brezhnev to keep abreast of Soviet-American relations, to know the mood of the American leaders and public, and to take a realistic view of American domestic and foreign policies.

8. USEFUL RESULTS OF COOPERATION

Top-level meetings, negotiations, and correspondence have played a most important part in developing the relations between the Soviet Union and the United States. "Practice, including that of Soviet-American relations," Brezhnev has said, "has shown the usefulness and fruitfulness of summit meetings, when each of the parties strives for a constructive, businesslike dialogue." The top leaders of the two powers, vested with the necessary powers and authority, have been able not only to subject all problems of bilateral and international relations generally to a profound and comprehensive review but also to take political decisions of principle or to lay down the guidelines for the successful solution of these problems.

The results of a number of consecutive summit meetings and negotiations—as well as of contacts through diplomatic channels and between various government, public, and other organizations in the Soviet Union and the United States— have clearly shown that despite the profound differences between the social systems of the two countries and despite their different and even opposite attitudes to several issues, an improvement in the relations between the two great powers is possible and necessary both in their own interests and to assure world peace.

"In recent years our relations with the United States have been developing in many areas," Brezhnev said at the 25th Communist Party Congress. "There is a frequent exchange of delegations, including parliamentary, and cultural exchanges have become more active. Many Soviet-American agreements have been concluded, envisaging expansion of mutually beneficial cooperation in various economic, scientific, technical, and cultural areas. Most of them have already come into force and are being put into practice to the obvious benefit of both sides and, more important still, of mutual understanding between the Soviet and American peoples.''

All in all, the treaties and agreements concluded between the Soviet Union and the United States—which have reached the impressive figure of forty—have laid a sound political and legal groundwork for the development of mutually beneficial cooperation between the Soviet Union and the United States on the principles of peaceful coexistence. To a certain degree, they diminish the danger of a nuclear war. In this lies the main result of the development of Soviet-American relations in recent years.

Besides diminishing the danger of a new world war, the change for the better in Soviet-American relations has also led to advances in other fields.

There has been a colossal increase in direct personal meetings and contacts between Soviet and American citizens, ranging from the regular and constructive exchanges of views between the leaders of the two powers to tourist trips by Soviet citizens to the United States and by Americans to the Soviet Union.

Despite difficulties and obstacles, there has been a steady expansion in exchanges of material and cultural values, scientific and technical knowledge, athletic and tourist groups, information, etc. Such exchanges enrich both peoples and promote greater understanding and trust between them, with due respect for sovereignty, customs, and noninterference in each other's internal affairs.

The General Agreement Between the Union of Soviet Socialist Republics and the United States of America on Contacts, Exchanges, and Cooperation and the program of cultural exchanges for 1974–76, signed during Brezhnev's visit to the United States, were a source of much pleasure to the many lovers of the arts in both countries.

Notable events, for example, were the United States tour by the Bolshoi Theater opera and ballet groups, the exhibition of Scythian treasures and paintings from the collections of the Leningrad Hermitage, and the performances by the choreographic group of the Soviet Peoples Art Festival directed by Igor Moiseyev and featuring all the nations of the Soviet Union. American audiences have admired not only the virtuoso performances of many Soviet artistes but at times also their courage in carrying on with their performances notwithstanding threats and provocations by enemies of friendship between the Soviet and American peoples.

In the Soviet Union there have been successful performances by the Children's Theater of the State University of New York in Albany, the Grand Ole Opry, the *Holiday on Ice* revue, the New York Philharmonic, the New York Jazz Repertory, the San Francisco American Conservatory Theater, etc. Soviet men and women highly appreciated the fact that very rare and valuable pictures from United States museums were selected for showing in the Soviet Union, tracing the evolution of the fine arts in the country from colonial times almost to the present day.

Literary critic Maxwell Geismar has said, for example, that he feels every thinking American citizen should and will welcome improved Russo-American relations and the policy of peaceful coexistence after so long a period of tension and artificially fanned hostility. He personally welcomed this as a blessing for American culture, which he described as casting off dire cold war constraints, illusions, and restrictions. Maxwell Geismar added that, as he had already pointed out before, "containing Russia" in American foreign policy had actually meant containing American cultural advancement.

The scope and advanced forms of exchanges achieved in higher education (likewise on the basis of the 1973 general agreement and the 1974–76 program) are immeasurably more in keeping with the requirements of the parties than was the situation following the conclusion of the first Agreement on Exchanges in the Fields of Culture, Technology, and Education, signed in 1958. Exchanges of young researchers for short training periods have become a very important form of cooperation involving postgraduate students—and, most frequently, young instructors and researchers—working on topical problems in laboratories or archives under the supervision of highly qualified scientists or scholars.

The annual exchange of leading professors and instructors of universities to conduct scholarly research is another form of cooperation between Soviet and American universities and colleges in the sciences, technology, and the humanities. Highly important, too, is the exchange of professors and specialists for lectures in accordance with the wishes of the receiving side for periods ranging from one semester to a full academic year, which has been operative since 1974.

In recent years there has also been growing cooperation in the study of the language of one country in the other, which is especially important in promoting all-around contacts and mutual understanding between the Soviet and American people. It is noteworthy, in this context, that in the Soviet Union English ranks first among the foreign languages in the number of people studying it. In Soviet general educational and higher schools alone there were about 12 million people studying English in 1974. In the United States the scope of Russian language studies is much more modest: only 130,000 people are engaged in all forms of Russian-language studies. As one measure toward righting this "imbalance," a mixed Soviet-American group of authors has been set up to compile a set of Russian textbooks for United States educational institutions (two elementary-course books, seven grammar and lexicology books, one book of conversational Russian, several readers, and a book about the Soviet Union and its literature).

Highly important to the training of Russian- and English-language teachers, and to improving their qualifications, is the annual exchange of Soviet and American students and instructors.

These growing links and exchanges of scientists and scholars, cultural and artistic personalities, teachers and instructors are only one instance of the all-around and promising cooperation between the Soviet Union and the United States.

Several government, public, and private organizations have been established to normalize and expand economic exchanges between the Soviet Union and the United States: the US-USSR Trade and Economic Council, the Trade Representation of the USSR in Washington, the Commerce Bureau of the USA in Moscow, the KAMA Purchasing Commission in New York, and the offices of more than twenty American corporations and banks in Moscow. The export and import activities of Amtorg, whose council embraces more than 300 American and Soviet firms and organizations, have become more active in recent years.

Experience has shown that the Soviet Union, with its powerful scientific and technological potential, dynamic and recession-immune economy, rich natural resources, and steadily growing domestic market, is a promising customer for American products and exporter of goods needed by the United States. From 1973 to 1975 the Soviet Union bought more than 1 billion dollars' worth of industrial plant, machinery, and other industrial manufactures on the American market. At the same time the Soviet Union increased its purchases of American farm produce and consumer goods.

Elements of a long-term character have gained significance in the economic relations of the two countries, and in some areas business has acquired a measure of stability and considerable scope. An important practical step in the development of the forms of Soviet-American links has been the conclusion of large-scale contracts on a compensation basis. Other forms of cooperation are also being developed: the joint production of goods for domestic markets and for export to third countries, etc.

At the same time there is no denying that the scope and forms of Soviet-American trade still fall far short of its potentialities and of the rapidly growing scale and pace of the Soviet Union's cooperation with other Western countries, which, unlike the United States, do not seek to link economic cooperation with attempts to interfere in the Soviet Union's domestic and foreign policies, do not deny it trade credits, and do not place it in conditions of obvious discrimination on their markets.

At a dinner he gave in the Kremlin on November 30, 1976, in connection with the fourth meeting of the US-USSR Trade and Economic Council in Moscow, Brezhnev said this of the problems of Soviet-American trade: "Future prospects, too, could be not bad—if normal conditions were created for this on the American side. On the whole, we propose to boost trade with the developed capitalist countries in this five-year period—that is, by 1980—by more than 30 percent. According to the estimates of our organizations, the volume of our trade with the United States just in industrial products, including raw materials, could run to about 10 billion dollars, if not more. We would be prepared to develop economic, technical, and industrial cooperation with you, including compensation deals, in many industries: the automobile, oil and gas, chemical, paper and pulp, machine tools, electrical engineering, nonferrous metallurgy, shipbuilding, etc.

"But, of course, this will be possible only if the main problem is solved—if discrimination against the Soviet Union in matters of trade and credits in the United States is ended."

In June 1977, at a meeting of the Executive Committee of the US-USSR Trade and Economic Council, the Soviet side reaffirmed its invariable attitude with respect to trade and economic relations between the two countries, as outlined by the General Secretary on November 30, 1976.

Soviet-American cooperation in environmental protection has no precedent in ranging over various aspects of this problem and is central to the international efforts against disturbances of the ecological balance in individual countries, regions, and the entire world. In the Soviet Union more than twenty-five all-Union ministries and government departments and about seventy large research, designing, and industrial establishments are involved in implementing the agreement. Under the agreement work is in progress on about forty specific joint projects, including projects to evaluate the response of various ecosystems to environmental pollution, to simulate water and atmospheric pollution processes, to assess possible climatic changes under the influence of human activities, to gauge possible genetic changes and general effects on human health resulting from changes in the environment and its pollution, to preserve vanishing species of animals and plants, to improve earthquake prediction techniques, to control environmental pollution through better purification of effluents and waste products, and to protect nature preserves and establish national parks.

The work of the US-USSR Joint Committee on Cooperation in World Ocean Studies has resulted in joint activities in such highly important areas as the large-scale interaction of the ocean and the atmosphere, ocean currents on a planetary scale and other problems of ocean dynamics, the geochemistry and hydrochemistry of the World Ocean, its biological productivity, and geological, geophysical, and biochemical investigations.

A tropical Atlantic experiment was concerned with the study of the physical processes governing the structure of the upper mixed ocean stratum, which interacts with the boundary layer of the atmosphere, and the system of equatorial currents and its dependence on wind intensity. Expedition work aboard research vessels has been supplemented with surveys conducted by special buoys, aircraft, and earth satellites.

Soviet scientists are taking part in the work conducted aboard the American vessel *Glomar Challenger* to study the structure, composition, origin, and history of the oceanic basins and their interaction with the continents, to verify the hypothesis of the expansion of the seabed, continental drift, etc.

The Soviet oceanographic vessels *Mikhail Lomonosov* and *Vityaz* and the nonmagnetic schooner *Zarya* have repeatedly called at ports on the East and West coasts of the United States, while the American vessels *Oceanographer, Atlantic II,* and *Kellar* have called at the Soviet ports of Odessa, Novorossiisk, Murmansk, and Nakhodka.

People all over the world closely followed and acclaimed the joint Soviet-American Soyuz-Apollo spaceflight in July 1975. The Soviet and American spacemen Alexei Leonov, Valeri Kubasov, Thomas Stafford, Donald Slayton, and Vance Brand not only successfully docked their craft and paid each other "visits" in orbit but also carried out a series of joint observations and experiments important to science and technology. The remarkable coordination and clockwork precision achieved by the organizers and executors of this flight—illustrating the great potentialities of Soviet-American cooperation in space—are borne out by its entire record: the successful preparations for the launching of the spaceships from two launch complexes thousands of miles apart, the fine interaction of the two mission control centers, the overcoming of the language barrier, etc.

In his personal message to the Soyuz and Apollo crews, Brezhnev pointed out that the conditions for this first international spaceflight had been created by détente and by the favorable changes in Soviet-American relations. "New possibilities are opening up," he said, "for the broad and fruitful development of scientific ties between countries and peoples for the good of the peace and progress of the entire human race."

Soon after the conclusion of the six-day Soyuz-Apollo flight in earth orbit, the crews of the two spacecraft went on a joint tour of cities in the Soviet Union and the United States, visiting Moscow and Washington, Leningrad and New York, Kiev and Chicago, Novosibirsk and Los Angeles, Volgograd and San Francisco, Sochi and Salt Lake City, etc. Everywhere they were welcomed by hundreds of thousands of people, who expressed their admiration of the spacemen's courage and acclaimed this striking example of joint efforts by the Soviet Union and the United States in space exploration, this example of trust and cooperation between them.

On September 22, Brezhnev heartily greeted the Soviet and American spacemen in the Kremlin. They presented to him a plaque commemorating the first international docking of manned spacecraft in orbit. The plaque had been put together during the joint flight from parts carried aboard the Soyuz and Apollo spacecraft.

In the course of the warm and friendly conversation that took place, Brezhnev congratulated the spacemen on the success of their history-making experiment, asked about their condition and impressions of the flight, and wished them further successes, good health, and personal happiness. He emphasized the great scientific and technical importance of this first international spaceflight in history and spoke highly of the courage and skill displayed by Leonov, Stafford, Kubasov, Slayton, and Brand and of the work of the many groups of scientists, specialists, and workers in the Soviet Union and the United States, who had made the flight possible.

Brezhnev then said that the success of the Soyuz-Apollo joint flight provided graphic evidence of the improvement in the relations between the Soviet Union and the United States and of the increased trust and understanding between them. The flight, he said, embodied and promoted the Soviet and American peoples' desire for peaceful cooperation.

Brezhnev had a discussion with the Soviet and American spacemen and specialists on the further development of cooperation between the Soviet Union and the United States in the exploration and use of outer space.

Soviet-American cooperation in many major areas of human life and activity, in society and man's relations with the world around him, with nature, not only accords with present-day world economic, scientific, technological, and ecological requirements and the interests of the Soviet, American, and all other peoples but also provides a very important material foundation for the improvement of mutual understanding and trust between the Soviet Union and the United States and cements their relations, promoting the security and well-being of both countries and the whole of mankind.

9. PROBLEMS OF DISARMAMENT AND SOVIET-AMERICAN RELATIONS

In his speech at the conference in Helsinki on July 31, 1975, Brezhnev emphasized that in the struggle for the realization of détente the Soviet Union "gives the highest priority to . . . the task of ending the arms race and achieving tangible results in disarmament."

With his characteristic concern for peace and realistic thinking and with growing insistence and increasing frequency, Brezhnev is drawing the attention of leaders and peoples of other countries to the urgent need for supplementing political with military détente. He has noted that the relaxation of international tension cannot become stable or irreversible without material progress in restraining the arms race. Disarmament is a fundamental task in the realization of détente, in strengthening world peace. Brezhnev has stressed on many occasions that the two opposed processes—political détente and the arms race—cannot proceed along parallel courses indefinitely. Sooner or later they are bound to collide, and one of them will have to stop and even throw the other one back.

"Despite the persistent efforts of the Soviet Union and the other socialist countries, which have long been insisting on a reduction in military spending and military preparation," Brezhnev said at a Kremlin Palace of Congresses meeting on the 30th anniversary of the Soviet people's victory in the Great Patriotic War on May 8, 1975, "an arms race of unprecedented proportions continues in the world.

"Meanwhile, this stockpiling of weapons, including mass destruction weapons, is becoming ever more absurd. The starting of a nuclear missile war would spell inevitable annihilation for the aggressor himself, to say nothing of the vast losses for many other countries and peoples not even formally involved in the war. It is also clear that it is impossible for a long time to have a parallel development of international détente and a constant buildup of military spending and improvement and stockpiling of weapons.

"That is why it is not enough to talk about disarmament, it is time to go on to concrete agreements on a reduction of the military preparations of states. That is what the Soviet Union is working for."

Slightly more than a month later, addressing his electors on the eve of elections to the Supreme Soviet of the USSR,

Brezhnev again referred to the task of halting the arms race and made a proposal which immediately attracted the attention of the public and of statesmen. "I should like to stress one important question," Brezhnev said. "It has not yet been reflected in the agreements between states, but it is assuming, in our opinion, ever greater urgency with each passing day. What I have in mind is that the states and, above all, the big powers should conclude an agreement banning the development of new weapons of mass destruction and new systems of such weapons.

"The level of present-day science and technology is such that there arises the serious danger of weapons' being developed that are still more frightful than nuclear ones. The reason and conscience of mankind dictate the need for raising an insurmountable barrier to the development of such weapons."

In recent years on Brezhnev's initiative the Soviet Union made other important proposals to slow down the arms race and to further disarmament. These are addressed to all states, but primarily to the United States of America—the leading military power of the capitalist world. Soviet diplomacy is using all ways and means to discuss and implement any disarmament measure based on the principles of equality and security of all contracting parties. Devoting tremendous attention to the bilateral talks with the United States in Geneva on the limitation of strategic offensive arms, the Soviet Union is, at the same time, actively discussing with the United States and a number of other countries in Vienna the reduction of armed forces and arms in Central Europe and the prohibition of chemical weapons and other lethal types of weapons in the Disarmament Committee, in the United Nations, etc.

"Efforts to end the arms race and to promote disarmament," Brezhnev emphasized at the 25th Congress of the

269

party, "have been and remain—as the Peace Program requires—one of the main trends in the foreign-political activity of the Central Committee of the Communist Party of the Soviet Union and the Soviet government. Today this objective is more vital than ever. Mankind is tired of sitting upon mountains of arms, yet the arms race spurred on by aggressive imperialist groups is becoming more intensive. . . .

"The Soviet Communists," Brezhnev continued, "are proud of having undertaken the difficult but noble mission of standing in the front ranks of the fighters striving to deliver the peoples from the dangers ensuing from the continuing arms race. Our party calls on all the peoples, all countries, to unite their efforts and end this perilous process. General and complete disarmament has been and remains our ultimate goal in this field. At the same time the Soviet Union is doing all it can to achieve progress along separate sections of the road leading to this goal.

"An international convention on banning and destroying bacteriological weapons, based on a draft submitted by the Soviet Union and other socialist countries, was drawn up, was signed, and has entered into force. In effect, it is the first real disarmament measure in the history of international relations. It envisages removal of a whole category of highly dangerous mass annihilation weapons from the military arsenals of states.

"The sphere of operation of the Treaty on the Non-Proliferation of Nuclear Weapons has expanded. Recently other large states, including the Federal Republic of Germany and Italy, have become party to it. But further effective measures to prevent the spread of nuclear weapons all over the planet are still a most important objective. The Soviet Union is prepared to cooperate with other states in this matter. . . .

"On our country's initiative," Brezhnev continued, "the UN General Assembly has in recent years adopted a number of important resolutions on questions of restraining the arms race and banning development and manufacture of new types of mass annihilation weapons, of new systems of such weapons.

"The task is to have these resolutions implemented. . . .

"Therefore, special importance attaches to the proposal supported by the vast majority of UN member states to convene a World Disarmament Conference."

On May 28, 1976, the General Secretary of the Central Committee of the Communist Party of the Soviet Union and the President of the United States signed at one and the same time in Moscow and Washington, respectively, the Treaty on Underground Nuclear Explosions for Peaceful Purposes. "Taken in conjunction with previously achieved agreements," Brezhnev said, "the treaty is another link in the chain of measures to hold down the stockpiling of armaments, to achieve universal prohibition of nuclear weapons."

The expiration in 1977 of the five-year interim agreement on the limitation of the levels of offensive strategic arms of the United States and the Soviet Union lends special urgency to finalizing the talks between the two powers on substituting another agreement for this one for a new term on the basis of the Vladivostok arrangements. The conclusion of this agreement would help prevent another round of the senseless race in nuclear missile armaments and would reduce the danger of war.

The Soviet Union's clear and precise stand on this question was outlined by Brezhnev at the end of 1976 in his replies to the American political observer J. Kingsbury-Smith.

Brezhnev said, "We are for completing as soon as possible the work on a Soviet-U.S. agreement limiting strategic arms, on the basis of the understanding reached in Vladivostok in 1974.

"For our part there were, are and will be no obstacles to this matter, which is the concern of all mankind.

"A Soviet-U.S. agreement would now, undoubtedly, be a

very important step toward bringing the arms race to an effective halt.

"Carrying out this task is most closely linked with the main goal of our time—to prevent nuclear war.

"Conversely, any delay in reaching agreement, at a time when even more terrible varieties and systems of weapons continue to be developed, is filled with new threats to peace, international stability and security. . . .

"By achieving a relaxation of political tension, we have also opened the way to taking up in earnest the cardinal questions of arms limitation and disarmament.

"I want once again to say most definitely: the Soviet Union does not threaten anyone, and does not intend to attack anyone.

"Instead of scaring oneself with mythical threats one needs to discuss in a businesslike and constructive way the problems and possibilities existing in this area.

"Nor can a continuing arms race be justified by allegations that limitation of arms carries risks to national security.

"A far greater risk to general security today lies in inactivity, in permitting the arms race to continue unbridled."

Brezhnev made it perfectly clear that "our country is determined to pursue the policy of further improving Soviet-American relations, which meets the interests of the American and Soviet peoples, and also the interests of world peace."

Unfortunately the positive developments in disarmament proved to be less than what they could and should have been. At the time of the election campaign in the United States in 1976 and in the first months of the new administration certain difficulties arose in Soviet-American relations, and the improvement of the political climate slowed down. This immediately affected the approach to questions of disarmament. For all practical purposes the United States administration went back on the understandings reached with its predecessors and thereby reneged on the principle of continuity. Its stand on disarmament and, first of all, on strategic arms limitation was a rejection of the commitments assumed by the United States in Vladivostok and during subsequent diplomatic talks. Having considerably complicated the conclusion of further agreements on limiting strategic arms, the new administration had set its sights on triggering a new round of the arms race. It was precisely from this angle that one viewed the decisions on the cruise missiles and the development of a new means of mass annihilation—the neutron bomb.

The position taken by the Soviet Union in this connection was clear and precise. The Soviet Union was guided by the desire to surmount through new initiatives the barriers raised intentionally or unintentionally on the road leading to a further improvement of Soviet-American relations. And as before, the leading part in setting this course belongs to Brezhnev. He continually stresses that the Soviet Union is prepared to advance further along the road of lessening the nuclear war threat in cooperation with the new United States administration if the latter shows intent to act in the same spirit.

In his speech in Tula in January 1977, which attracted the close attention of the world public by its wealth of ideas on international issues, Brezhnev exposed once again the absurdity and groundlessness of the allegations that the Soviet Union is going farther than required for its defense, that it is seeking superiority in armaments in order to deliver a "first strike." The Soviet Union always was and continues to be a convinced opponent of any such concept, Brezhnev emphasized. The efforts of the Soviet Union are directed precisely to averting any first or second strike, to averting nuclear war in general.

Further, Brezhnev said, "We are prepared jointly with the new administration in the United States to accomplish a new major advance in relations between our countries.

"First of all, we are convinced, it is necessary to complete in the nearest future the drafting of the agreement on limiting strategic armaments on the basis that we reached in Vladivostok at the close of 1974. Some politicians in Washington now express regret that this agreement has not yet been signed. But whatever the regrets, lost time cannot be regained, and it is important that practical conclusions be drawn from this.

"In the United States, too, they are asking themselves what will happen if these conclusions are not drawn. An influential United States newspaper wrote recently that in this event the Soviet Union and the United States will start developing a new generation of nuclear weapons which it will be practically impossible to control.

"Such a prospect does not suit us. I repeat that time will not wait and the conclusion of the agreement must not be postponed.

"Naturally, the Soviet Union is prepared to go even farther in the matter of limiting strategic arms. But at first it is necessary to consolidate what has already been achieved and to implement the accord reached in Vladivostok, and the more so since the interim agreement expires this October. Then we could immediately pass on to talks on more far-reaching measures. Otherwise, it may happen that by adding new questions to those that are being currently discussed, we will only further complicate and delay the task as a whole.

"The need is ripe to prevent the proliferation of nuclear weapons more reliably, to make more effective the regime of nonproliferation established by the known treaty. We are prepared to conduct definitive talks on this score.

"We would like to reach an early agreement on the reduction of armed forces and armaments in Central Europe. We have no objections to discussing the related questions at any level and at any venue: in Vienna, in Bonn, in Washington, in Moscow—anywhere."

The problems of limiting the arms race and furthering disarmament were analyzed by Brezhnev in detail in his speech at the 16th Congress of Soviet Trade Unions in March 1977. Among the concrete and realistic tasks Brezhnev listed completing the preparation of and signing a new agreement on the limitation of strategic offensive weapons essentially prepared in 1974 and moving farther on this basis to a mutual reduction of arms with the strict observance of the principle of equality and equal security. Brezhnev also referred to possible joint initiatives of the Soviet Union and the United States regarding the prohibition and liquidation of the most dangerous lethal types of chemical weapons and other measures of curbing the arms race and strengthening international security.

In his television speech in May 1977 Brezhnev expressed concern about the continuing arms race, including that in strategic arms, owing to the line taken by the new United States administration. This line, Brezhnev said, is plainly geared to obtaining unilateral advantages for the United States. Quite naturally, this line will not help the preparation and conclusion of a new long-term agreement on the limitation of strategic arms between the Soviet Union and the United States, the drafting of which has already been delayed beyond measure. Noting a certain coming together of positions as the result of the talks conducted in Geneva by Andrei Gromyko, Minister of Foreign Affairs of the Soviet Union, and United States Secretary of State Cyrus Vance, Brezhnev emphasized: "But I must say frankly that no serious advance has so far been achieved in view of the unconstructive line of the United States. Clearly, great efforts will be required in this area. But the most important thing of all is that the United States administration should shift fully to a realistic stand and proceed from the principle of equality and equal security.''

Questions of struggle against the arms race were outlined by Brezhnev in his interview with the editor-in-chief of *Asahi* early in June 1977. Brezhnev said, "Our country has always been in favor of completely banning nuclear weapons—it has been so from the moment they appeared. In 1972, as you know, on the Soviet Union's initiative, the UN General Assembly adopted a decision on the nonuse of force in international relations and on the simultaneous banning forever of the use of nuclear weapons. It will also be recalled that the UN is now considering a draft World Treaty on the Non-Use of Force in International Relations submitted by the Soviet Union, which envisages that states should renounce the use of all types of weapons, including nuclear. Unfortunately little progress is being made because the attitude of some states has been negative. I want to say very definitely: the Soviet Union is ready to sit down at the negotiating table at any time with all the other nuclear powers jointly to elaborate practical ways to resolve the nuclear disarmament problem.''

Brezhnev continued: "For several years the Soviet Union has been holding talks with the United States on limiting strategic arms. We believe that important results have been achieved. These talks are still going on and are based on the well-known Vladivostok accord. We are striving for the earliest fruitful completion of the talks. This is quite possible if our partners, of course, do not try to secure unilateral advantages for themselves. We will not sign any agreement that could jeopardize the security of the Soviet Union and our allies.''

Explaining again and again the stand of the Soviet Union on its relations with the United States, Brezhnev said, "Our policy regarding the United States is not a matter of convenience; it is calculated not for months but for years and decades. We wish the Soviet Union and the United States to have really stable peaceful relations for the sake of our peoples and world peace without any damage to the interests of third countries."

But Soviet-American relations, Brezhnev emphasized, must be based "on principles of equality, mutual respect of interests, and noninterference in one another's internal affairs, and disputes must be resolved in the interests of détente and cooperation between the peoples of the Soviet Union and the United States."

10. NO ALTERNATIVE TO PEACEFUL COEXISTENCE

The development of cooperation and growth of understanding and contact between the Soviet and American peoples could be much more rapid and on a greater scale if they did not run into various natural or intentionally created difficulties, complications, and obstacles.

Some of these difficulties and complications are quite understandable and, if one may say so, natural. Any change in politics, especially a turn from open cold war hostility and confrontation to normal peaceful relations between the two greatest world powers, is an intricate matter that requires preparation and time, tremendous effort and work, the breakup of old dogmas and notions, etc. And this is doubly difficult if it concerns the relations between two states personifying the two opposite social and political systems—socialist and capitalist. Besides having different social-economic and state-political systems, the Soviet Union and the United States have absolutely different histories, which deeply influence the thinking of their peoples. Since the Civil War of 1861–65 for more than 100 years there have been no large-scale hostilities on United States territory proper. As for the Russian people and the other peoples of Russia, and subsequently the Soviet Union, they were involved in their land in this century in the First World War of 1914–18, the Civil War and the foreign intervention of 1917–22, and the Great Patriotic War of 1941–45. These wars took a toll of tens of millions of lives. It is only natural that having paid this terrible price to liberate and defend their Motherland and to make it a developed, great, and advanced power, all Soviet people devote special attention to the all-important problems of war and peace, security and cooperation.

This is why the Soviet people cannot put up with the attempts at belittling the importance of détente. "One can't help being surprised," Brezhnev said in this connection, "upon hearing some seemingly responsible people in the West speculate whether détente is useful or harmful, in other words whether it is good or bad to live in the conditions of a more solid peace and a lessening of the danger of war.

"We are told sometimes that attempts to question the benefits of détente are made for purely tactical internal reasons of winning the support of right-wing elements in certain countries. Frankly speaking, we hold that the strengthening of peace is much too serious a matter for the present and future generations to subordinate it to some transient considerations or moods."

There is no doubt that the entire process of reconstruction, normalization and improvement of relations, the building of comprehensive cooperation between such vast, complex, and specific government and social entities as the Union of Soviet Socialist Republics and the United States of America is a matter not only of great importance but also of considerable difficulty from the point of view of internal and international politics, from the legal, economic, and even purely technical point of view. The negotiations and agreements on practically any question between the Soviet Union and the United States touch upon national, state, departmental, and private interests; they are related directly or indirectly to other problems and encompass hundreds and thousands of points; and they require the reconciliation of differing views not only in each country but in many cases with its allies.

It takes time to prepare and conclude every agreement and to implement it, to obtain the results desired by each side. There are cases in which, after the signing of a treaty which establishes general principles of Soviet-American cooperation in different spheres, it is necessary to work out detailed ways and means of implementing the treaty.

But there are obstacles of another, clearly artificial character to Soviet-American rapprochement.

It is no secret that in the United States of America there are numerous overt and covert opponents of better Soviet-American relations and détente in general. Though the most intractable among them are clearly in a minority, their influence is out of proportion to their number. Wielding in some cases considerable power and resources, being well organized and active, they exert a visible pressure on the country's political life and have broad access to the mass media. At times they succeed in winning to their side those individuals and public elements in America who while favoring, in the main, Soviet-American cooperation, particularly on the crucial questions of peacekeeping and disarmament, disagree with one or another aspect of Soviet foreign or home policy. The opponents of normalizing Soviet-American relations take advantage of this and of everything else and raise a hue and cry over some concocted or secondary issue and associate it with the entire policy of détente to hinder, restrict, or even torpedo it altogether.

As far back as the end of 1974 the opponents of progress in Soviet-American cooperation wrecked a trade agreement concluded between the Soviet Union and the United States in 1972. The coalition, which was formed in the United States Congress and which included both conservatives with narrow egoistic political designs or those still loyal to the heritage of the cold war and some "liberals," ventured to make the granting of trade credits and most-favored-nation treatment to the Soviet Union dependent on absolutely impermissible attempts at intervening in a matter related to the sphere of Soviet internal jurisdiction—the emigration of Jews from the Soviet Union. It is only natural that such attempts were bound to fail; the Soviet side repeatedly warned the American side about this.

Speaking at a dinner in the Kremlin on October 15, 1974, on the occasion of the second session of the US-USSR Trade and Economic Council, Brezhnev drew attention to the fact that "the economic benefits that accrue to our planning and foreign trade bodies from some transactions with American firms are less than those from similar transactions with firms in other Western countries." Addressing the American participants in the session, the General Secretary of the Central Committee of the Communist Party of the Soviet Union said, "This is due to the fact that there are still in the United States a number of laws that discriminate against the Soviet Union, laws left over from the cold war epoch. These discriminatory laws impede the export of our goods and, to some extent, limit the possibilities of financing the exports of your American goods to the Soviet Union. Credit for financing American deliveries to the Soviet Union is now granted, now frozen for an indefinite period. Needless to say, this kind of inconsistency does not contribute to stable business ties. . . .

"Finally, attempts to tie the development of trade and economic bonds with the Soviet Union to demands on matters totally unconnected with the trade and economic field and lying fully within the domestic competence of states are utterly irrelevant and unacceptable. It is high time to understand clearly that such interference in internal affairs can do nothing but harm. . . ."

When the United States Congress approved the Jackson-Vanik amendment to the 1974 Trade Bill—a wanton attempt at interfering in Soviet domestic affairs and a violation of the principles and spirit of Soviet-American relations—the Soviet Union was compelled to refrain from putting into operation the trade agreement with the United States. This again demonstrated that good relations between the Soviet Union and the United States can develop only on a principled, completely equal, and mutually advantageous foundation that precludes any attempts to interfere in the partner's domestic affairs, to impose terms upon him, or to engage in impermissible mixing of international and domestic issues of either country. As was repeatedly stated by Brezhnev when he spoke of the desire of the Soviet side to improve and widen relations with the United States, complete reciprocity is essential for any progress in the development of cooperation between the Soviet and American peoples.

The artificial restriction of the Soviet-American trade potential is damaging to the interests of numerous American businessmen, who have been deprived of profitable orders, to the workers, who suffer from a decline in employment, and, what is particularly important, to the overall improvement of Soviet-American relations and the creation of a particularly favorable climate for them. This is openly recognized by businessmen, high-ranking members of the administration, and legislators, including those who voted for the Jackson-Vanik amendment. It is said that ways are being sought now to remedy the situation. But the damage to Soviet-American relations has been done, and this, indeed, has been and still is the objective of those who oppose an improvement in relations.

The enemies of the policy of peace and cooperation with the Soviet Union tried in the past and continue efforts to justify their position and their attacks on this policy by alleging that it gives unilateral advantages to the Soviet Union. They assert that it is therefore necessary to make the Soviet Union pay for détente by concessions in international politics and moreover in questions of its own home policy.

The error of these claims is clear to any unbiased person. Facts and logic and the realities of life show that an improvement in Soviet-American relations and likewise an easing of international tension are needed and profitable for both sides. Given modern means of warfare, at a time when peace is indivisible and the country is no longer strategically invulnerable, the United States has no less interest than the Soviet Union in preventing a nuclear war, in not being involved in any international conflict which might lead to a confrontation between the two great powers. The United States too needs the maintenance of universal peace, the peaceful settlement of the sharpest international problems, peaceful coexistence.

On the other hand, at a time of the further internationalization and progress of the world's division of labor, the aggravation of the critical situation in energy, raw materials, food, economic, and other problems, in the face of growing unemployment and inflation, the United States needs multilateral and bilateral cooperation in trade, economy, and technology no less than does the Soviet Union.

American politicians who are out to destroy détente and the improvement of Soviet-American relations and those who connive in this or yield to their pressure for the sake of convenience are assuming a grave responsibility. They overlook the fact that far from yielding the expected results, the "positions from strength" policy the United States' rulers pursued at the time of the cold war brought about a number of grave defeats and critical situations in American society. By placing their narrow and transient domestic political or other considerations above the truly national and state interests of the United States and the worldwide humanitarian interests of security, peace, and cooperation, and probably not always aware of the real or potential dangers and consequences of their anti-Soviet and bellicose actions, they are unable to offer any realistic alternative to the policy of peaceful coexistence because no such alternative exists.

CHAPTER VI

The Head of the State

Previous chapters have given you an idea of the truly gigantic work being done by Brezhnev. This work is multifaceted and rich in content and extends into both internal and foreign politics.

It is safe to say that all current achievements of the Soviet Union are associated with Brezhnev: in economic progress; in the further improvement of the socialist state and of democracy; in the progress of culture; in raising the people's standard of living. Behind this there is the very real daily effort of a leader of such stature as Brezhnev.

Brezhnev is one of the most prominent international leaders. On many occasions he has represented the Soviet Union abroad at summit-level talks on fundamental questions of strengthening peace and ensuring the security of the peoples. His signature is affixed to many highly important documents of present-day international relations.

Thus, for many years, Brezhnev has in fact been acknowledged by the Soviet people and by the world to be the most influential representative of the Communist Party and the Soviet state. This reflects Brezhnev's personal qualities, his extensive merits and prestige, as well as the enhanced role of the Communist Party in the society of developed socialism in the Soviet Union.

Developments have put on the order of the day the question of formalizing the new situation in the structure of the leadership of the state.

For this reason, the plenary meeting of the Central Committee of the Communist Party of the Soviet Union on May 24, 1977, unanimously recognized it as desirable for Leonid Ilyich Brezhnev, General Secretary of the Central Committee, concurrently to assume the office of Chairman of the Presidium of the Supreme Soviet of the USSR.

This is a highly responsible office, since under the Fundamental Law of 1936 and the new Constitution the Presidium of the Supreme Soviet is vested with very broad powers.

Three weeks later the Supreme Soviet of the USSR— the highest representative organ of the Soviet state—met in session.

At 10 A.M., June 16, 1977, members of both chambers filled the Grand Kremlin Palace. The first item on the agenda was: "Concerning the Chairman of the Presidium of the Supreme Soviet of the Union of Soviet Socialist Republics."

Deputy M. A. Suslov, member of the Politburo of the Central Committee and Secretary of the Central Committee, made a thoroughly substantiated statement in which he highly commended Brezhnev's work for the good of the party, the Soviet people, détente, and international peace, and moved a draft decree of the Supreme Soviet of the USSR:

"The Supreme Soviet of the Union of Soviet Socialist Republics *decrees:*

"Comrade Leonid Ilyich Brezhnev shall be elected Chairman of the Presidium of the Supreme Soviet of the Union of Soviet Socialist Republics."

The decree was unanimously approved by the deputies.

Then Brezhnev went up to the rostrum. He thanked the deputies for the confidence they had in him, electing him for the second time to the office of Chairman of the Presidium of the Supreme Soviet. In his brief speech Brezhnev said in part, "I shall do all I can for our dear country to grow stronger and to prosper, for the life of Soviet people to improve more and more, for world peace to grow stronger, and for international cooperation to increase."

Brezhnev's election to the post of Head of State was acclaimed all over the world. This showed that Brezhnev's unrelenting struggle for international détente, lasting peace, and social progress has won him prestige and respect among all people of goodwill. Leaders, progressives, the press in many countries expressed profound satisfaction that the most prestigious representative of the Communist Party and the Soviet state has been elected to the highest office in the Soviet Union. The press in different countries stressed that the event was important both for the life of the Soviet people and internationally.

Congratulations addressed to Brezhnev came from all continents.

The party and state leaders of the socialist countries referred to Brezhnev in their messages as to an individual who has played an exceptional part in furthering the friendship and cooperation of the socialist countries, in their joint struggle for socialist and communist construction, in strengthening socialist internationalism, in the struggle for peace.

Messages from developing countries stressed his intolerance to colonialism, racism, and apartheid and his warm and friendly feelings for the peoples of Asia, Africa, and Latin America.

Many congratulations came from Western countries. They referred to the deep respect enjoyed by Brezhnev and said that his election to the new office would further the relations of the Soviet state with the respective countries.

Irrespective of their political beliefs and ideological views, all those who congratulated Brezhnev noted his profound dedication to peace.

"Your name is associated with the most urgent task of worldwide importance—prevention of a third world war, the building of peace in the world," read the telegram from Fidel Castro, First Secretary of the Central Committee of the Communist Party of Cuba, Chairman of the State Council and of the Council of Ministers of the Republic of Cuba.

"Under your leadership, the Soviet Union has made a decisive contribution to the strengthening of international peace and security. We are confident that your work for world peace will continue to be your guiding star," wrote Urho Kekkonen, President of Finland, in his message of congratulations.

"I am happy to recall the part you have always had in world affairs and your active contribution to the persistent search for peace and international security," pointed out Houari Boumedienne, President of the Algerian People's Republic and Chairman of the Revolutionary Council.

The election of Brezhnev to the office of Chairman of the Presidium of the Supreme Soviet of the USSR elicited much comment in the United States.

Jimmy Carter, President of the United States of America, forwarded the following telegram to Brezhnev: "Dear Chairman Brezhnev, please accept my congratulations on your assumption of the office of Chairman of the Presidium of the Supreme Soviet of the USSR. I would like to express my hope for the continuation of the friendship which exists between our two peoples, and for progress in improving relations between our two countries."

Numerous distinguished political leaders and representatives of the United States business community commented on Brezhnev's election.

Averell Harriman, former United States ambassador to the Soviet Union, welcomed Brezhnev's election to the high office of Chairman of the Presidium of the Supreme Soviet of the USSR. He also voiced his confidence that Brezhnev would use his offices of leader of the Communist Party and President of the country to strengthen peace.

Harriman went on to say that Brezhnev is sincere in his peacekeeping and is doing much toward this end. Brezhnev's dedication to easing Soviet-American tensions, to the principles of cutting back and controlling nuclear weapons, is well known. There is no task of greater priority or worth than that of working to prevent a world conflagration.

Harriman expressed his trust that Brezhnev's election to the office of Chairman of the Presidium of the Supreme Soviet of the USSR would facilitate the normalization of relations between the Soviet Union and the United States and progress in the limitation of strategic armaments. He said there were serious technical difficulties impeding the strategic arms limitation talks, but agreement on these questions was essential for both countries, and a frank exchange between the Soviet and American representatives would further the process. He said it was a complex question and its solution required patience. Harriman said he was confident that Brezhnev and Carter would finally succeed in solving this problem of importance for mankind.

In conclusion, Harriman said he had met the Soviet leader on three occasions and referred with great warmth to his talks with Brezhnev.

Senator John Sparkman, chairman of the Senate Foreign Relations Committee, expressed confidence that the election of Brezhnev, General Secretary of the Central Committee of the Communist Party of the Soviet Union, to the office of

With his great-granddaughter Galia

At polling place with his wife

*Addressing the 25th Congress of the Communist Party
of the Soviet Union*

Meeting with the press

At the office

OVERLEAF
With his great-granddaughter Galia in the Crimea, August 1976

Time for relaxation

Chairman of the Presidium of the Supreme Soviet would help broaden the efforts for peace and détente.

He said that the most important task facing mankind was to safeguard and strengthen peace. In this, the Senator emphasized, the United States and the Soviet Union—the two great powers possessing colossal nuclear arsenals—bore a special responsibility.

The director of the American Institute of Public Opinion, George Gallup, stressed that the American nation was hopeful that Brezhnev's election as Chairman of the Presidium of the Supreme Soviet would facilitate the improvement of American-Soviet relations.

Donald Kendall, Pepsico's president and chairman of the board of directors, who is also the United States co-chairman of the board of the US-USSR Trade and Economic Council, said he was glad Brezhnev had been elected to the high office because he showed great interest in economic cooperation between the two countries and was sincerely seeking an improvement of relations between them.

Karl Pamer, president of Cleveland Crane and Engineering, said that Brezhnev had performed a great service by translating the concepts of détente into specific practices in Soviet-American relations. He said that Brezhnev's name was associated with the progress achieved in Soviet-American cooperation and that representatives of the business community particularly appreciated the interest shown by the Soviet leader in arranging trade and economic relations between the Soviet Union and the United States. He said that business relations between the two countries would get a fresh impulse after Brezhnev's election as Chairman.

Armand Hammer, president of the Occidental Petroleum Corporation and chairman of its board of directors, said that he was happy to learn that General Secretary of the Central Committee Brezhnev had become President. He also said that in his opinion the Soviet people were quite right to entrust the high office of Head of State to a man like Brezhnev.

He said further that Brezhnev in many ways reminded him of Lenin, the founder of the Soviet state. He said that he had met Lenin several times and had never forgotten those meetings and that Brezhnev, like Lenin, was a great leader.

General Secretary Brezhnev is very popular among Americans. When, four years ago, he spoke on American television, public opinion polls showed that some 70 million Americans had switched on their television sets specifically to listen to the Soviet leader. Americans liked Brezhnev's forceful speech, and many cheered him.

Hammer predicted that the election of Brezhnev, General Secretary of the Central Committee of the Communist Party of the Soviet Union, to the office of Chairman of the Presidium of the Supreme Soviet of the USSR would facilitate an improvement in Soviet-American relations. . . .

With his natural vigor and dynamism Brezhnev assumed the duties of his new office. The day following his election he chaired a meeting of the Presidium of the Supreme Soviet, which discussed in concrete terms the measures taken by the Supreme Soviets of the Ukrainian and Lithuanian Soviet Socialist Republics to promote the public discussion of the draft new Constitution of the Soviet Union.

In his program speech Brezhnev outlined the tasks of extending all the aspects of the work of the Supreme Soviet.

While paying unflagging attention to the development of legislation and examination of the plan and budget, he noted that the Supreme Soviet is turning its attention more and more frequently to the state of affairs in various spheres of the economy and culture, hearing government reports on these matters. The control exercised by the Supreme Soviet over organs of government is becoming ever more effective and systematic. As noted at Congresses of the Communist

Party of the Soviet Union, a conspicuous part in this is played by the thirty standing commissions consisting of more than two-thirds of the Supreme Soviet deputies.

Brezhnev emphasized that the adoption of a new Constitution would give the Supreme Soviet new opportunities since "the comprehensive powers of the Supreme Soviet will be still more clearly enshrined in the new Constitution. It can accept for examination and decide any question coming within the competence of the Union of Soviet Socialist Republics.

"The new Constitution," Brezhnev said, "will be the basis for a further expansion of our legislative work." The Constitution lists about ten laws to be adopted in the near future, including such legislative acts as the regulations of the Supreme Soviet, the Law on the Council of Ministers of the Soviet Union, and the Law on Elections.

Having dwelt in detail on many aspects of the work of the Supreme Soviet and its Presidium in the new conditions Brezhnev pointed out that "the Supreme Soviet of the USSR and its Presidium have always attached great importance to foreign policy."

The new Constitution offers a precise and clear formulation of the fundamental principles of Soviet foreign policy, said Brezhnev. The Supreme Soviet of the USSR, its Presidium, standing commissions, and deputies are called upon to make a substantial contribution to the implementation of these principles and to the promotion of contacts with other countries.

As Chairman of the Presidium of the Supreme Soviet, Brezhnev received the heads of diplomatic missions accredited in Moscow in the summer of 1977. Some of them he had known for a long time; others he was still to become acquainted with. The heads of diplomatic missions warmly congratulated Brezhnev on his election as Head of State.

The friendly atmosphere of this reception is reflected specifically in the speech of Robert A. D. Ford, the ambassador of Canada to the Soviet Union, dean of the diplomatic corps. Ford said, ". . . I have followed with considerable awe the skillful way in which, as General Secretary, you lent your personal touch to the determination of the domestic policy of your country and, of even greater interest to us, its foreign policy.

"It is with great satisfaction that we now see this completed by your assumption of the post of Head of State."

Ford pointed out that Brezhnev's name is identified with détente and expressed hope and confidence that this trend of Soviet foreign policy would continue.

In his reply, Brezhnev expressed his sincere gratitude to the heads of embassies for their congratulations. Stressing the important part ambassadors play in shaping an atmosphere of friendship, goodwill, and greater or lesser confidence in the relations of their respective countries with the Soviet Union, Brezhnev said:

"The international life of today is very dynamic. The opportunities to strengthen peace are growing steadily. But the threats to peace are growing as well. Evidently one of the prime objectives of a farsighted policy and diplomacy of reason is to expand in every way the range of opportunities and to reduce the magnitude of the threats. . . .

"I take this opportunity to ask you to convey the following message to your heads of state and leaders of your countries:

"There is no country or people in the world, in fact, with which the Soviet Union would not like to have good relations.

"There is no topical international problem to the solution of which the Soviet Union would not be willing to contribute.

"There is no seat of military danger in the removal of

which by peaceful means the Soviet Union would not be interested.

"There is no type of armaments and, first of all, of weapons of mass destruction which the Soviet Union would not be ready to limit, prohibit on a basis of reciprocity, in agreement with other states, and then remove from the arsenals.

"The Soviet Union will always be an active participant in any negotiations or any international action aimed at developing peaceful cooperation and strengthening the security of peoples.

"It is our belief, our firm belief, that realism in politics and the will to détente and progress will ultimately triumph, and mankind will step into the twenty-first century in the conditions of a peace more dependable than ever before. We shall do everything we can for this to come true."

The adoption in October 1977, a few weeks before the celebration of the 60th anniversary of the Great October Socialist Revolution, of a new Constitution, which had been drafted and prepared by the Constitution Commission under the direction of Leonid Brezhnev, was an outstanding event in the life of the country.

We have every reason to say that the new fundamental law of the Soviet Union and the further development of socialist democracy will go down in history as events intrinsically linked with the name of Leonid Brezhnev.

Brezhnev's election to the office of Chairman of the Presidium of the Supreme Soviet of the USSR opened a new chapter in the biography of this outstanding political leader and statesman of our time.

His entire life is witness to his great and exceptionally varied experience—experience of personal participation and leadership in virtually all the economic and political spheres of one of the greatest powers of the world, the Soviet Union.

His approach to all the problems of the present day is filled with lofty ideological content and a high degree of creativity; his profound knowledge of politics, economy, and social development is well known. His efficiency and integrity blend with profound modesty.

Brezhnev cannot think of himself apart from the country in which he was born and where he grew up, apart from the party in which he matured as a political leader of world stature.

Brezhnev cherishes the trust of the people. He often meets with working people and corresponds extensively with workers, collective farmers, scientists, workers in culture, and war veterans. He is always happy to congratulate those who have displayed constructive initiative or shown good results in their work. For many years Brezhnev has been the deputy of the Supreme Soviet of the USSR representing the people of the Bauman electoral district of Moscow, and he performs his duties of deputy with the utmost industry. Addressing his electors, he said, "I regard your trust as the highest honor and will do everything to justify it, for a Communist puts the interests of the people above all else, and there is no greater reward for him than the people's trust." Time and again he has justified this confidence in full measure.

The warm words addressed to him, the acts of confidence and recognition expressed by the people Brezhnev relates to the Communist Party, which sees its supreme purpose in serving the people and "teaches all of us," as Brezhnev put it, "to fulfill this sacred duty." "Communists have no privileges," Brezhnev emphasizes, "save the one privilege of giving more of themselves than others to the common cause and of fighting and working better than others for its triumph. Communists have no special rights, save the one right of always being in the forefront, of being where things are the hardest."

Brezhnev has often said that he would not have been able

to accomplish all the useful things he has done for the people in his life without the constant support of his comrades in work and struggle, who, like himself, devote all their energies to the common cause. "Facing the tremendous and complicated tasks that are still to be accomplished," Brezhnev said, "I am inspired by the knowledge that we in the Politburo, the Secretariat, the entire Central Committee and government work as a close-knit, friendly collective, relying on one another's assistance."

Today there is every reason to speak of a modern style in the work of the top echelon of the party and state, shaped under the immediate influence of Brezhnev's own style and qualities as man and leader.

Characteristic of the work of the Central Committee is a scientific approach, collective spirit, and efficiency in guiding Communist construction and conducting the home and foreign policy of the Soviet state.

The entire work of the Central Committee is based on scientific theory—*i.e.*, on the Marxist-Leninist world outlook and concept of socialist and Communist construction. Engels made this remarkable observation: the moment socialism became a science it had to be treated as a science. All the work done by the Central Committee of the Communist Party of the Soviet Union and its General Secretary is consonant with precisely this constructive, scientific attitude to questions of building socialism, based not on voluntaristic decisions but on a profound theoretical understanding of the phenomena and tendencies of life.

Members of the Politburo of the Central Committee of the Communist Party of the Soviet Union note that the working atmosphere in the Central Committee and Politburo is always efficient and constructive.

A. N. Kosygin, Chairman of the Council of Ministers of the Soviet Union, emphasizes that the outstanding progress made by the country has been "considerably predetermined by the climate of ideological unity, comradely confidence, high exactingness, and strict adherence to party principles which prevails in our party, in its Central Committee and Politburo led by Comrade Brezhnev, General Secretary of the Central Committee of the Communist Party of the Soviet Union."

M. A. Suslov, member of the Politburo of the Central Committee and Secretary of the Central Committee, said the following of Brezhnev's personal qualities: "Communist Brezhnev, in whom the party has shown the greatest confidence and who is shouldering a truly gigantic responsibility, is still a plain and modest person. . . . He is boundlessly dedicated to the interests of the people, loyal to his principles, considerate to people, and mindful of the opinion of his comrades. He shows truly Communist exactingness, intolerance of complacency, and a lively interest in everything that is new and progressive."

The many letters addressed to Brezhnev by Soviet citizens of all generations convey words of gratitude for the fact that the Soviet country has had peace for many years, sparing people the still-remembered partings on going to war, the heart-rending death notices, the terrible blackouts—the privations and suffering of war.

"There has been no war for more than thirty years. Many thanks to the party, to you, Leonid Ilyich, for the joy of working in peace and seeing the laughter of our children. Man is made not for war, but for work," wrote bricklayer A. Alekhin of Polevskoi in the Sverdlovsk region, in a letter to Brezhnev.

And the following lines are from a letter by Andrei Maidanov, a Riga schoolboy: "Of course, I have never been in a war, but I know that peace is happiness, and happiness has to be fought for. This is why our family will always stand by you, dear Leonid Ilyich, in your great mission—the struggle for peace."

Forward-looking and tireless, Brezhnev is always in the thick of life, with people, both at home and abroad. He always checks the considered conclusions of experts against other opinions and will draw no conclusions until he weighs them all. Once the conclusions are drawn, he works perseveringly to put them into effect.

For Brezhnev, leadership is, first of all, motion. Few people know our country in all its variety as well as he does. The Ukraine and the Soviet Far East, Byelorussia and Kazakhstan, the Baltic republics and Central Asia, the Caucasus and the northern part of Russia—all these areas of the Soviet Union he knows not from maps but from personal impressions and from working there.

For him, international affairs are not a summary of reports and surveys prepared by the foreign service. Having assumed general responsibility for the country's foreign policy, he takes direct part in conducting it. His many trips abroad were packed with activity. He left himself no time to rest— all of it was devoted to establishing state contacts and holding consultations and talks. He did not spare his energy wherever he went. At the same time his every visit abroad yielded personal experiences, abundant firsthand information, and opportunities for effective and competent decisions. And for Brezhnev that is what matters most.

But though his character is highly dynamic, Brezhnev, the leader, is remarkably poised and cautious. A popular proverb says, "Measure thy cloth thrice before cutting." To a certain extent this is true of Brezhnev, the political leader who shoulders a supreme responsibility. He does not tolerate trivial considerations when making a choice of principle. He makes his decisions on the basis of objective information and its proper evaluation. He deals with only those problems that are mature in real life, not just in the minds of imaginers. If they are not ripe, he is prepared to wait; he has patience.

Such is Leonid Brezhnev, the General Secretary of the Central Committee of the Communist Party of the Soviet Union and Chairman of the Presidium of the Supreme Soviet of the USSR, the President of the Soviet state.

On receiving the Order of Lenin and the second Gold Star medal of Hero of the Soviet Union in December 1976, Brezhnev said, "I take pride in the fact that no day in my life can be separated from the past and present causes of our Communist Party and of our Soviet land."

And then, on that auspicious occasion, he spoke these words addressed to the future, which sound as a pledge:

"I HAVE ALWAYS BEEN AND SHALL REMAIN THE PARTY'S LOYAL SOLDIER, A LOYAL FIGHTER FOR THE CAUSE OF THE WORKING PEOPLE, FOR THE HAPPINESS AND PROSPERITY OF OUR MOTHERLAND, FOR PEACE AND COMMUNISM."

The Great
October Revolution
and Human Progress

Report of Leonid I. Brezhnev,
    General Secretary of the Central Committee of
      the Communist Party of the Soviet Union
      and Chairman of the Presidium of the
      Supreme Soviet of the USSR,
at a joint jubilee session
    of the Central Committee of the Communist
      Party of the Soviet Union, the Supreme
      Soviet of the USSR, and the Supreme
      Soviet of the RSFSR
to mark the 60th anniversary of the Great
    October Socialist Revolution

November 2, 1977

Dear comrades; esteemed foreign guests:

The Soviet people, the Communists of all countries, and all progressive mankind are now marking a great anniversary. Sixty years ago, led by the party of Lenin, the workers and peasants of Russia overthrew the power of the capitalists and landowners. That was the first victorious socialist revolution in world history.

Those unforgettable October days stirred the entire planet. A new epoch, the epoch of the world's revolutionary renewal, the epoch of transition to socialism and communism, was ushered in. It opened the road along which hundreds of millions of people are moving today and along which the whole of mankind is destined to move.

We were the first. We did not have an easy time. We had to hold out in a hostile encirclement. We had to break out of age-old backwardness. We had to surmount the enormous force of historical inertia and learn to live by new laws, by the laws of collectivism.

Today, when we assess the main result of six decades of struggle and work, we can say with pride: We have held our ground; we have stood fast and won.

We won in the stormy, anxious years of the Civil War and armed intervention, when it was a question of the life and death of the Soviet power.

We won in the fast-moving, teeming years of the first five-year plans, when it was a question of whether the workers and peasants of our country would be able to lay the foundations of socialism and convert the Motherland into a great industrial power within the extremely short period allotted to them by history.

We won in the grim, flaming years of the Great Patriotic War, when it was a question of whether socialism would withstand the onslaught of world imperialism's shock forces and save mankind from fascist bondage.

We won in the difficult, tense postwar years. The ravaged economy was speedily restored, and the advanced lines of economic, scientific, and technical progress were reached, despite the cold war and nuclear blackmail.

The Soviet Union has been living in peace for more than thirty years. A developed socialist society, the result of the historic creative work of the masses, has been built, exists, and is being perfected.

Honor and glory to the Soviet people, to the victor people!

Honor and glory to all generations of the Soviet people, to the men and women, Communists and nonparty people, who spared neither strength nor energy nor, whenever necessary, their very lives and raised the Motherland to the summits of social progress!

We address the warmest, most sublime words of gratitude and affection to the veterans of the revolution. The numbers of those who stormed the old world under the banner of the Leninist party in October 1917 are dwindling. But the grandeur of their feat stands out with growing vividness. Honor and glory to the pioneers of the October Revolution!

During these jubilee days we speak with gratitude of the revolutionary solidarity that was unswervingly displayed for the Land of Soviets by our class brothers abroad. Their determined action time and again helped to disrupt imperialism's aggressive designs.

Long live proletarian internationalism, that mighty weapon of the working people of all countries!

I. THE SOVIET UNION IN THE VAN OF SOCIAL PROGRESS

Comrades, every time we celebrate the anniversary of the October Revolution we perceive anew its significance and the force of its impact on the course of history, on the destiny of the world.

The October Revolution has, of course, solved, above all, the problems of our country, the problems posed by its history, by the concrete conditions obtaining in it. Basically, however, these were not local but general problems posed before the whole of mankind by social development. The epochal significance of the October Revolution lies precisely in the fact that it opened the road to the solution of these problems and thereby to the creation of a new type of civilization on earth.

The October Revolution proved that a radical change of society's political foundations was possible. The proletariat of Russia gave the answer to the most pressing, the most burning question of politics—namely, whether the exploiters' monopoly of power was eternal or could and should be replaced by the power of the working people.

The six decades of socialist construction are the most eloquent demonstration of what can be achieved by working people who have taken the political leadership of society into their own hands and assumed responsibility for their country's destiny. These decades have proved that there neither has been nor can be a road to socialism without the power of the working people, without socialist statehood.

The victory of the October Revolution gave the working people their first opportunity of putting an end to exploitation and tearing out of bondage to economic anarchy. This key problem of social progress was resolved through the abolition of private property and its replacement with public property. Anarchy of production gave way to scientific, planned economic management.

Within a short period of time, in terms of history, a huge backward country was turned into a state with a highly developed industry and collectivized agriculture. It now takes only two and a half working days for our industry to produce as much as was produced in the whole of 1913. Today we produce more industrial goods than was produced by the whole world a quarter of a century ago. The gigantic economic growth of history's first socialist country is the result of emancipated labor, the result of the labor of people who are aware that they work for themselves, for the good of all.

The October Revolution and socialism have also enriched the history of mankind with experience of the spiritual emancipation of working people. One of the "secrets" of the rule of the oppressors has always been the reinforcement of direct physical oppression of the masses with spiritual oppression. The ruling classes did all they could to make access to education and culture difficult for the working people, to keep them captive to false ideas and concepts. That is why the cultural revolution was a natural continuation of the political revolution in our country.

Within the lifetime of a single generation the Soviet Union delivered itself entirely and for good from the onerous burden of illiteracy. The working people began to be active in cultural life, becoming the creators of cultural values. A new, socialist intelligentsia, which brought the country glory with outstanding achievements in science, technology, literature, and art, came from the midst of the people. A union that mankind's finest minds dreamed of, the historic union of labor and culture, has taken place. In the history of our country, in the history of world culture, this was a turn of immense significance.

Among the achievements of the October Revolution a noteworthy place is held by the settlement of the national question, one of the most painful and dramatic questions in the history of human society.

In urging a militant alliance of the working people of all nations and ethnic groups, the party and Lenin had always upheld the right of nations to self-determination, to complete and unconditional equality. The victory of the October Revolution was thus also a victory in the struggle for national liberation. The peoples of former tsarist Russia got their first-ever possibility of making a historical choice, the right to determine their own destiny.

They made their choice. They united voluntarily in a powerful federal state and, relying on disinterested assistance from the Russian people, resolutely embarked upon a new life.

The strength of unity and mutual assistance between nations gave unprecedented acceleration to the development of all the republics. Hostility and mistrust in the relations between nations gave way to friendship and mutual respect. Internationalism was firmly established where the mentality of national egotism had been implanted for ages. Mutually enriched national cultures, forming the integral Soviet socialist culture, shone forth with fresh, vivid colors.

The equality, fraternity, and unbreakable unity of the peoples of the Soviet Union became a fact. A new historical community, the Soviet people, took shape. The mounting process of the drawing together of nations permeates every sphere of life in our society. Such, comrades, is the remarkable result of the Leninist national policy; such is our experience, whose epochal significance is indisputable.

The assertion of the principles of social equality and justice is one of the greatest achievements of the October Revolution. We have every right to say that no other society in the world has done or could have done as much for the masses, for the working people, as has been done by socialism. Every Soviet citizen enjoys in full the rights and freedoms enabling him to participate actively in political life. Every Soviet citizen has the possibility of choosing a calling in life that conforms to his vocation and abilities and of being useful to his country and people.

The conditions under which the Soviet people live and work are steadily improving. Soviet citizens do not know the humiliating sense of uncertainty of the morrow, the fear of being left without work, without medical care and without a roof over their heads. Society safeguards their rights and interests and protects their civic and human dignity.

Conscientious work, a high sense of civic duty, and high ideological and moral standards are what determine a person's standing and prestige in our country. This is an inexhaustible fount of the individual's creative initiative and intellectual growth. This is the most convincing proof of social justice and social equality.

A new Constitution of the Soviet Union was adopted recently. It has reaffirmed that in our country the prime purpose of all transformations, of all changes, is to provide every person with the conditions enabling him to live like a human being. It has given further convincing testimony that the concepts of human freedoms and rights, democracy and social justice receive a tangible content only under socialism.

Comrades, the victory of the Great October Socialist Revolution has brought our country and our people to the van of social progress. Today, sixty years later, we hold a worthy place in its most advanced positions: we have been the first in the world to build a developed socialist society, and we are the first to have embarked upon the building of communism.

Never before has our country had such a huge economic, scientific, and technical potential. Never before has its defense capability been so sound and dependable. Never before have we had such favorable possibilities for carrying out the tasks for which, in the long run, the revolution was accomplished: for promoting the welfare of the masses, unfolding socialist democracy, and furthering the harmonious development of the individual.

The heroic spirit of our time lies, if you like, in making full use of the potentialities of developed socialism. This is what determines also the measure of the responsibility that history has now devolved upon us.

The party and its Central Committee are aware of this responsibility. The 24th and 25th congresses of the Communist Party of the Soviet Union charted the strategy and tactics of Communist construction at the present, extremely important stage of our history. In the economy the course has been steered toward an intensive growth of social production, toward enhancing the efficiency and quality of all economic activity.

On this course we have achieved considerable successes. From 1967, the 50th anniversary of the Soviet power, our country's economic potential has virtually doubled. But the qualitative changes are perhaps just as important. Scientific and technical progress is becoming an increasingly more effective factor of economic development. The most modern industries are developing at priority rates. Labor productivity is growing steadily.

In accordance with the party's policy, economic development is being increasingly oriented on the performance of the most diverse tasks directly linked with improving the conditions of the Soviet people's life and work.

To a large exent the fulfillment of these tasks is determined by the state of the agrarian sector of our economy. One can safely say that never before has so much been done in our country to promote agriculture. Within a short period the material and technical basis and economy of the countryside have been fundamentally restructured. Land improvement, comprehensive mechanization, and chemicalization have been started on an unparalleled scale.

We already see the results of these enormous efforts. It will be recalled that in 1967 we produced 148 million tons of grain, 11.5 million tons of meat, and about 6 million tons of cotton. In this year, which is far from being the best and not even average in terms of weather, we expect to produce 194 million tons of grain, nearly 15 million tons of meat, and 8.4 million tons of cotton. I believe these figures merit due appreciation, although we are aware that not all the problems of agriculture have been resolved. The party is making every effort to ensure that this branch fully satisfies the country's growing requirements.

There has been marked progress also in the solution of a difficult problem like housing, which requires huge outlays. One-third of the housing erected during the entire period since the establishment of the Soviet power has been built during the past decade. In that decade 110 million of our compatriots have experienced the joy of moving into new housing.

Large resources have been allocated for the expansion of consumer-goods production. During the past ten years this industry has virtually doubled its output and substantially renewed and improved it. The retail-trade turnover has also doubled. The Soviet people's demand for many durables that were only recently regarded as being in short supply is now being satisfied.

Economic growth has made it possible substantially to raise wages and increase social consumption funds. During the past ten years the real incomes of the Soviet people have grown 60 percent.

I should like to make special note of the fact that the living standard and the conditions of everyday life of the rural population have improved appreciably.

Every fact and every figure characterizing the rate of our development are convincing evidence of developed socialism's enormous possibilities. This has been seen with renewed force during the socialist emulation to mark the anniversary of the October Revolution. The Soviet people made higher commitments and have kept their word. They put forward their own plans, which they have not only fulfilled but also overfulfilled. The Motherland thanks the participants in the anniversary movement. It thanks all those who have marked the glorious anniversary of the great revolution with valorous labor.

Comrades, while noting our successes, we are fully aware that we still have many problems and that a vast field of activity lies ahead.

The main orientations of our party's work and the concrete tasks of the day have been determined by the recent party congresses and plenary meetings of the Central Committee. Their decisions are known to everybody. They make new, higher demands on the work of our cadres, on the work of all the working people. These demands spring from the fact that the course of social development poses increasingly more complex tasks in various spheres of life. The more complex the tasks and the more difficult the work, the greater becomes the importance of coordination, efficiency, and discipline, of everything that may be defined as a high level of organization.

Efficient organization at every level, in every link of party, state, and economic leadership, at every workplace, is an indispensable and mandatory precondition for the fulfillment of the tasks set by the 25th Congress.

At the same time this is a very important premise for solving the problems that we shall have to face in the future. At the dawn of Soviet power Lenin said that "our natural wealth, our manpower and the splendid impetus which the great revolution has given to the creative powers of the people are ample material" to make swift progress and build a truly mighty and abundant Russia (V. I. Lenin, *Collected Works*, Vol. 27, p. 161). To this has now been added our great economic, scientific, and technical might, as well

as our rich experience in building a new life. We do have everything that we need to advance confidently to our cherished goal—
communism—and to rise to ever new summits of progress.

But, comrades, these are indeed summits. And the path to them
may be steep and difficult. In order to traverse it at an optimal
regime, to use a technical term, we need to gear even our present
plans to fulfilling the tasks of the future. That is exactly what the
party has been doing.

Orientation not only on current needs but also on the future is a
distinctive feature of our agrarian policy in particular. We have
been working for a radical solution of the food problem and the
satisfaction of the country's growing needs, and doing this in conditions in which the population and its requirements are growing,
but the land area remains the same. That is why accelerated and
intensive development of every branch of agriculture is in our plans
for the future. That is why we have allocated and will continue to
allocate large investments for agriculture and to build up the facilities in the industries catering to the countryside.

An important role in these plans is assigned to the nonblack-soil
zone. This vast area in the very heart of the country must become
a zone of highly productive cropping and animal husbandry. It
will add considerably to our food resources.

Other comprehensive programs worked out in the past few years
are also oriented on the future. These are, above all, the programs
for developing western and eastern Siberia and for building the
Baikal–Amur Railway and industrial and timbering complexes in
the Far East. They are designed to meet the future requirements of
the economy in oil, gas, coal, ferrous and nonferrous metals, timber, and other raw materials. There is much social meaning, too, in
the implementation of these programs. This implies developing
many remote regions of the country, where dozens of new towns
are to be built and new cultural centers established. The very concept of "undeveloped outskirts" will disappear completely from
our usage.

The great construction projects of our day have most forcefully
brought out the steadfastness, creative élan, and ideological sea-
soning of the Soviet young people. Carrying on the fine traditions
of their fathers and grandfathers, the members of the Komsomol,
young men and women, have been advancing in the front ranks of

the builders of communism, gaining in stature in their labor effort, and learning to manage the economy and govern the affairs of society and the state. The country's future is in their hands. We are sure that it is in reliable hands.

When pondering the future, we attach much importance to science. It has to make a tremendous contribution to fulfilling the most important tasks of Communist construction, including the discovery of new sources of energy and substitutes for many types of natural resources, the technical reequipment of the economy to reduce manual and especially arduous labor to a minimum, the boosting of agriculture, the combating of disease, and the prolongation of the human life span.

The future of our economy lies in ever greater efficiency. There is no alternative to ensure the successful and dynamic development of the economy. That is why the party has pursued and will steadily continue to pursue a policy of accelerating scientific and technical progress, perfecting planning and management, enhancing organization and order at every workplace and at every management echelon.

When looking into the future, we have to draw yet another conclusion. The Soviet people's level of political consciousness, culture, and civic responsibility will have an ever greater part to play in every sphere of life and the development of our society. One of the primary tasks is to foster in our citizens the urge to attain high social goals, a high standard of ideological conviction, and a truly creative attitude toward work. This is where a very important front line runs in the struggle for communism, and the course of economic construction and the country's sociopolitical development will increasingly depend on our victories on this front.

You see that we have many problems ahead, and these are big problems. But the power of socialism lies precisely in the fact that the new social system makes it possible not only to anticipate such problems but also to plan their solution in advance.

Comrades, the Soviet people look confidently to the future. They are sure that life will steadily become better, finer, and richer. An earnest of this is the dedicated work of millions of men and women, inspired by the ideals of communism. An earnest of this is the Communist Party's Leninist scientifically grounded policy.

For each of us Leninist Communists, it is a source of the highest satisfaction that the Soviet people connect all their achievements and victories with the party. That is quite natural because the party is inseparable from the people. In its ranks are the finest representatives of the working class, the collective-farm peasantry, and the people's intelligentsia. It enjoys the people's boundless confidence.

But, comrades, the confidence of the people is exacting. That is why all the party's decisions, every step it takes, political or in organizational, ideological, and educational work, has to be such as to consolidate still further the unity of the party and the people and to keep the people's trust in the party unshakable in the future as well.

Our party has everything to live up to its historical responsibility. We are inspired by the noble goal of promoting the people's well-being. We have rich experience in building the new life over a period of many years. Our actions are guided by Marxism-Leninism, a science which has absorbed all the achievements of human genius. We are confident in our strength.

The great advance begun in October 1917 and the great struggle for communism continue. Lenin wrote that "since we are out to fight, we must desire victory and be able to point out the right road to it" (V. I. Lenin, *Collected Works*, Vol. 9, p. 57). We do desire victory. We do know the road to it. And we shall attain victory and reach communism!

II. THE OCTOBER REVOLUTION HAS CHANGED THE FACE OF THE WORLD

Comrades, no event in world history has had such a profound and lasting effect on mankind as the Great October Socialist Revolution. The flashes of the October storm illumined the way into the future for the peoples of many countries. History began to advance literally in seven-league strides.

The most important of the international consequences of the October Revolution which have shaped the face of the epoch have been the emergence and development of the world socialist system. At one time the bourgeoisie, terrified by the victory of the October

Revolution and its powerful influence on the minds of millions, sought to uncover "the hand of Moscow" in every revolutionary event in the world. Nowadays few people give credence to such fairy tales. Revolutions start and triumph by virtue of each country's internal development and of its people's will. The series of triumphant socialist revolutions in Europe, Asia, and America signified a continuation of the ideas and cause of the October Revolution.

As a result, the practice of world socialism has been extended and enriched. Each of the countries that have taken the socialist road has in some respects in its own specific way dealt with the problems of socialist statehood, the development of socialist industry, the drawing of the peasantry into cooperatives, and the ideological reeducation of the masses.

There is no doubt that the transition to socialism by other peoples and countries with different levels of development and national traditions will invest socialist construction with an even greater diversity of concrete forms. That is quite natural.

However, life provides confirmation that the general fundamental and inalienable features of the socialist revolution and socialist construction remain in force and apply everywhere. The sum total of experience in the development of world socialism provides convincing evidence, among other things, of the following:

Power continues to be the main issue in a revolution. It is either the power of the working class, acting in alliance with all the other working people, or the power of the bourgeoisie. There is no third possibility.

Transition to socialism is possible only if the working class and its allies, having gained real political power, use it to end the socioeconomic domination of the capitalist and other exploiters.

Socialism can win only if the working class and its vanguard, the Communists, are able to inspire and unite the masses of working people in the struggle to build the new society and transform the economy and all social relations on socialist lines.

Socialism can consolidate its positions only if the working people's power is capable of defending the revolution against any attacks by the class enemy (and such attacks, both internal and, most probably, external, are inevitable).

Those are only some of the lessons of the development of socialism today. They once again confirm the great international importance of the experience of the October Revolution, for all the specific conditions of our revolution. They once again confirm the great truth expressed by Lenin in these words: "It is the Russian model that reveals to *all* countries something—and something highly significant—of their near and inevitable future" (V. I. Lenin, *Collected Works,* Vol. 31, p. 22).

But world socialism also has experience of a different kind, which confirms that departures from the Marxist-Leninist course, departures from proletarian internationalism inevitably lead to setbacks and hard trials for the people.

It is well known what grave consequences have been brought about in China by attempts to ignore the economic laws of socialism, by the departure from friendship and solidarity with the socialist countries, and by alignment with the forces of reaction in the world arena. The Chinese people's socialist gains have been gravely endangered.

Some leaders in capitalist countries now obviously count on the present contradictions and estrangement between the People's Republic of China and the Soviet Union and other socialist countries continuing for a long time and even growing more acute in the future. We think that this is a shortsighted policy. Those who pursue it may well miscalculate.

There is no point in trying to guess how Soviet-Chinese relations will shape up in the future. I would merely like to say that our repeated proposals to normalize them still hold good.

Comrades, the new relations that have been established—thanks to the fraternal parties' internationalist policy—among the socialist countries, above all among the countries of the socialist community, are a great contribution to the life of the contemporary world by the world socialist system.

We can say with a clear conscience: Our alliance, our friendship, and our cooperation are the alliance, friendship, and cooperation of sovereign and equal states united by common purposes and interests and held together by bonds of comradely solidarity and mutual assistance. We have been advancing together, helping one another and pooling our efforts, knowledge, and resources to advance as rapidly as possible.

We have taken the line of jointly tackling the problems of raw materials, fuel and energy, food and transportation. We have been deepening our specialization and cooperation, especially in engineering, on the basis of the latest scientific and technical advances. We intend to solve these problems reliably, economically, and for a long term. We intend to solve them with due consideration for the interests and needs of each fraternal country and the community as a whole.

Comrades, in the distant days of the 1917 October Revolution, the workers and peasants of Russia came out alone against the old world, the world of greed, oppression, and violence. They built socialism in a country surrounded by the hostile forces of imperialism. They built and defended it successfully. Today we are not alone. Our country has become part of a great family of socialist states. Can we Soviet Communists and all the other Soviet people cherish anything more in the world around us than this socialist family? For its prosperity, for our common well-being we have been doing everything we possibly can!

It is hard to overestimate the tremendous influence that our October Revolution exerted on the development of the national liberation movement.

It was the victory of the October Revolution that truly awakened the political consciousness of the colonial peoples and helped them to score tremendous successes in fighting for liberation from oppression by imperialism. As early as 1919 Lenin wrote that "the emancipation of the peoples of the East is now quite practicable" (V. I. Lenin, *Collected Works,* Vol. 30, pp. 153–54).

Since the Second World War, since our victory over fascism, more than 2 billion people have thrown off the yoke of the colonialists and have risen to independent statehood. The colonial system of imperialism in its classical forms can, on the whole, be regarded as having been dismantled. That, comrades, is an epoch-making development.

It is of exceptional importance that many of the countries that have achieved liberation reject the capitalist road of development and have set themselves the goal of building a society free from exploitation and have adopted a socialist orientation.

The socialist countries are staunch and reliable friends of these countries and are prepared to give them utmost assistance and support in their development along the progressive path. This means not only moral and political but also economic and organizational support, including assistance in strengthening their defenses.

The fighters for freedom have no easy way before them. They have to work hard to lay the foundations of the public economy required for socialism. Fierce battles with the exploiter elements and their foreign patrons are inevitable. Now and again these result in zigzags in the policies of the young states and sometimes even lead to retreats. But the overall trend of development is incontestable. The will of millions of working people who have become aware of their goals and their place in life is a sure guarantee that national independence will be strengthened and that the social system free from exploitation and oppression will ultimately be victorious.

None of this means, of course, that imperialism has reconciled itself with such a course of development. No, indeed, for its positions in the former colonies are at times still quite strong, and the imperialists are doing everything to try to retain these and to deepen and extend them wherever possible.

It is no longer a simple matter for them to decide on direct armed intervention in the affairs of the countries that have freed themselves. The latest major act of this kind—the U.S. war against the people of Vietnam—ended in a defeat that was too crushing and ignominious to encourage a repetition of such gambles.

There is growing resistance to the attempts to involve the young states in imperialist military blocs, and the nonalignment movement is one piece of evidence of this.

It is likewise doubtful whether imperialism will be helped by the efforts to use the reactionary regimes it has set up or suborned in former colonies. After all, these regimes cannot offer the people anything but new forms of dependence on the same old imperialism.

When the first waves of the people's struggle for national liberation were mounting in the countries of the East, Lenin wrote: ". . . no power on earth can restore the old serfdom in Asia or wipe out the heroic democracy of the masses in the Asiatic and semi-Asiatic countries" (V. I. Lenin, *Collected Works,* Vol. 18, p. 584). Today we can state confidently: No power on earth can wipe out the results of the heroic liberation struggle of the millions upon millions of people in the former colonies and semicolonies of imperialism. The cause of the people's liberation is indomitable; the future belongs to it. The light kindled by the October Revolution shall not fail at this front of world history either.

Comrades, the victory of the October Revolution ushered in a new stage in the struggle of the international working-class movement.

The building of socialism in the USSR and then in other countries helped to foster the political maturity of the proletariat in the capitalist countries. Its ranks became more organized. There arose a force destined to play a great role in history—the international Communist movement. The front of the proletariat's allies in the struggle against monopoly domination, for democracy and socialism grew broader.

Meanwhile, capitalism is ever more clearly showing that it is a society without a future. Its economy is afflicted by chronic fever. Technological progress is pushing masses of workers out of the factories on a scale that threatens to shake the entire sociopolitical system. Prices are rising continually, and inflation remains the cardinal problem. Shocking exposures of unsavory political manipulations, corruption, abuse of power, and flagrant transgressions of the law by leaders at the highest level explode like bombshells first in one country and then in another, demonstrating the degradation of the ruling class. A record crime rate completes the picture. All this signifies that the objective economic and sociopolitical preconditions for the transition to socialism have attained a high degree of maturity. The desire of the masses in the capitalist countries for radical changes is mounting.

Of course, the bourgeoisie is an experienced adversary. It changes its tactics, and it maneuvers. It has recourse to partial reforms in an effort to bolster up its positions and blunt the gravitation of the masses toward socialism.

In this situation the Communist parties are working to perfect the strategy and tactics of their revolutionary struggle. They are striving to rally all the democratic forces against domination by the monopolies. Their theoretical guidelines in this context contain interesting points, although probably not everything can be regarded as finalized and incontrovertible. This is understandable; a quest is a quest. What is important is that it should proceed in the right direction.

Whatever routes may be chosen, the ultimate mission of the Communists is to lead the masses to the principal goal, to socialism. The experience of the struggle for the victory of the October Revolution has shown that changes of tactics, compromises in order to win new allies are quite possible in revolutionary practice.

But we have also become convinced of something else: under no circumstances may principles be sacrificed for the sake of a tactical advantage. Otherwise, as they say, you'll keep your hair but lose your head.

The greater the influence of the Communist parties, the more vigorously imperialism tries to divert the Communists from the correct path. This is done both crudely—by pressure and threats—and subtly. At times the Communists in bourgeois countries are now promised that their "right to a place in society" will be "recognized." A mere "trifle" is demanded in exchange: that they give up fighting the power of capital, for socialism, and abandon international class solidarity. But the Communists won a place for themselves in society long ago. They won it precisely by their revolutionary struggle. Their role in society is recognized by the people, and no one can deprive them of it!

The imperialists would very much like to undermine the solidarity of the Communist ranks. That is why, for example, the falsehood is persistently being spread that the Communist parties in the socialist countries—and especially the Communist Party of the Soviet Union—are imposing upon the Communists in the West their prescriptions for the socialist transformation of society. But this is an obvious fabrication.

Our party, like all the other Marxist-Leninist parties, firmly adheres to the principles generally accepted in the Communist movement: equality, independence, noninterference in internal affairs, solidarity, and mutual support among the Communists of different countries.

Today, as we mark the 60th anniversary of our revolution, we Communists of the Soviet Union declare once again that we will always be loyal to the great brotherhood of the Communists of the world! We warmly wish the Communist and workers' parties and their allies, fighting against the dictatorship of capital, for freedom, peace, and social progress, every success. You can always rely on our friendship, solidarity, and support!

Comrades, the Soviet government was born under the sign of Lenin's Decree on Peace, and ever since then our country's foreign policy has been one of peace. Objective historical conditions have dictated its concrete content: peaceful coexistence of states with different social systems.

In our day the principles of peaceful coexistence have taken fairly firm root in international affairs as the only realistic and reasonable principles. This is a result of the changed correlation of forces in the world—above all, of the increased might and international prestige of the Soviet Union and the entire socialist community. It is also a result of the successes of the international working-class movement and the forces of national liberation. It is, finally, a result of the acceptance of the new realities by a definite segment of the ruling circles in the capitalist world.

At the same time it is a result of the tremendous work done in recent years by the Soviet Union and the other countries of the socialist community to reorient international relations toward peace.

The salutary changes in the world, which have become especially appreciable in the 1970s, have been called international détente. These changes are tangible and concrete. They consist in recognizing and enacting in international documents a kind of code of rules for honest and fair relations among countries, which erects a legal and moral-political barrier to those given to military gambles. They consist in achieving the first—if only modest, for the present—understandings blocking some of the channels of the arms race. They consist of a ramified network of agreements covering many areas of peaceful cooperation among states with different social systems.

The changes for the better are most conspicuous in Europe, where good-neighborly relations, mutual understanding, and the mutual interest of the nations and their respect for one another are gaining in strength. We highly appreciate this achievement and consider it our duty to safeguard and consolidate it in every way. Therefore, we attach great significance to cooperation with such countries as France, the Federal Republic of Germany, Britain, and Italy—with all the European states, big and small, belonging to a different social system.

It is natural, too, that we attach great significance to relations with the United States. There is much that divides our countries— from the socioeconomic system to ideology. Not everyone in the United States likes our way of doing things, and we too could say a great deal about what is going on in America. But if differences are accentuated, if attempts are made to lecture each other, the result will be only a buildup of distrust and hostility, useless to our two countries and dangerous to the world as a whole. At the very inception of the Soviet state Lenin made it clear to the American leaders of the time that "whether they like it or not, Soviet Russia is a great power" and "America has nothing to gain from the Wilsonian policy of piously refusing to deal with us on the grounds that our government is distasteful to them" (*Lenin Miscellany*, Vol. XXXVII, p. 254, in Russian). This was true half a century ago. It is all the more true today.

Life itself requires that considerations of a long-term character, prompted by a concern for peace, be decisive in Soviet-American relations. This is the course we follow, and this is what we expect in return. There is no lack of will on our part to continue developing relations with the USA on the basis of equality and mutual respect.

International relations are now at a crossroads, as it were, which could lead either to a growth of trust and cooperation or to a growth of mutual fears, suspicion, and arms stockpiles, a crossroads leading, ultimately, either to lasting peace or, at best, to balancing on the brink of war. Détente offers the opportunity of choosing the road of peace. To miss this opportunity would be a crime. The most important, the most pressing task now is to halt the arms race, which has engulfed the world.

Regrettably the arms buildup continues and acquires ever more dangerous forms. New modifications and types of weapons of mass destruction are being developed, and it is well known on whose initiative this is being done. But every new type is an equation with several unknown quantities in terms of political as well as military-technical or strategic consequences. Rushing from one type of arms to another—on the strength, evidently, of the naive hope of retaining a monopoly of them—tends only to step up the arms race, deepen mutual distrust, and hamper disarmament measures.

In this connection I would like to reiterate, most forcefully, something I said earlier. The Soviet Union is effectively looking after its defense capability, but it does not and will not seek military superiority over the other side. We do not want to upset the approximate equilibrium of military strength existing at present, say, between East and West in Central Europe or between the USSR and the USA. But in exchange we insist that no one else should seek to upset it in his favor.

Needless to say, maintaining the existing equilibrium is not an end in itself. We are in favor of starting a downward turn in the curve of the arms race and gradually scaling down the level of the military confrontation. We want to reduce substantially and then to eliminate the menace of nuclear war, the most formidable of dangers for humanity. That is the objective of the well-known proposals of the Soviet Union and other socialist countries.

Today we are proposing a radical step: *that agreement be reached on a simultaneous halt in the production of nuclear weapons by all states.* All such weapons—whether atomic, hydrogen, or neutron bombs or missiles. At the same time the nuclear powers could undertake to start the gradual reduction of existing stockpiles of such weapons and move toward their complete, total destruction. The energy of the atom for peaceful purposes exclusively— that is the call the Soviet state is making in the year of its 60th anniversary to the governments and peoples.

There is another important problem that has a direct bearing on the task of reducing the danger of nuclear war—namely, that of seeing through to the end the work of banning nuclear weapon tests, so that no such tests are conducted underground as well as in the atmosphere, in outer space, and underwater. We want to achieve progress in the negotiations on this matter and bring them to a successful conclusion. Therefore, we state that we are prepared *to reach agreement on a moratorium covering nuclear explosions for peaceful purposes along with a ban on all nuclear weapon tests for a definite period.* We trust that this important step on the part of the USSR is properly appreciated by our partners at the negotiations and that the road will thus be cleared to concluding a treaty long awaited by the peoples.

The Soviet Union is confidently following the road of peace. It is our active and consistent stand that the contest between socialism and capitalism should be decided not on the field of battle, not on the munitions conveyors, but in the sphere of peaceful work. We want the frontiers dividing these two worlds to be crossed not by missiles with nuclear warheads, but by the threads of broad and diversified cooperation for the good of all mankind. By steadfastly pursuing this policy, we are carrying out one of the main slogans of the October Revolution and the behests of Lenin: Peace to the peoples!

If it should prove possible to solve the major problem—that of preventing another world war and establishing durable peace—new vistas would open for the inhabitants of the earth. The preconditions would appear for solving many other vitally important problems, which are arising before mankind as a whole in our day.

What are these problems?

One such problem, for example, is that of providing enormous masses of people with food, raw materials, and energy sources. It will be borne in mind that, according to available estimates, the population of the earth will have increased from 4 billion to 6 billion by the end of the century. Another problem is that of ending the economic backwardness left by colonialism in Asian, African, and Latin American countries. This is necessary for the normal future development of the relations among states and in general for the progress of humanity as a whole. Last but not least is the problem of protecting man from the many dangers with which further uncontrolled technological development threatens him—in other words, the preservation of nature for man.

These are very real and serious problems. With every new decade they will become more acute, unless a rational collective solution is found for them through systematic international cooperation.

In our day the world is socially heterogeneous—it is made up of states with different social systems. This is an objective fact. By its inner development and by its approach to international relations the socialist part of the world is setting a good example of the lines along which the major problems arising before mankind can best be solved. But needless to say, it cannot solve them for the whole of humanity. What is needed here are purposeful efforts by the people of every country, broad and constructive cooperation by all countries, all peoples. The Soviet Union is wholeheartedly for such cooperation. In this—if one looks deeper—lies the essence of the foreign-policy course that we call the course of peaceful coexistence.

Comrades and friends, the achievements of the October Revolution and the potentialities of socialism are today the surest guarantee of mankind's further progress. The October Revolution is the banner of great changes raised aloft over the twentieth century by the will and hands of the working masses.

We are advancing toward the epoch when, in one specific, historically determined form or another, socialism will be the prevailing social system on earth, bringing with it peace, freedom, equality, and well-being to the whole of working mankind.

This is no utopia, no beautiful dream. This is a real prospect. It is brought nearer daily by our work and struggles, comrades. It is brought nearer by the work and struggles of millions of our contemporaries. This is the continuation of the cause begun by the October Revolution.

Let us always be loyal to the banner of the Great October Revolution, to the crimson banner of the revolution!

May the light of the immortal Marxist-Leninist ideals shine ever more brightly over the world!

Long live the great Soviet people!

Long live our great party, the party of Lenin!

Onward, to the victory of communism!